The Presidency:
The Power And Glory

VIEWPOINTS: The Presidency:
The Power
And Glory

Edited by **MARY KLEIN**

WINSTON PRESS 25 Groveland Terrace, Minneapolis Minnesota 55403

WINSTON PRESS

PUBLISHER: Thomas C. Wright
EXECUTIVE EDITOR: Clifford L. Snyder
MANAGING EDITOR: Robert deVilleneuve
PHOTO EDITOR: Donna Dennis
DESIGNER: Guy Smalley—Ruth Riley

ACKNOWLEDGMENTS

A note of thanks is also due to Sherry DeMatteo, Ellen Small, Dolores Snyder, Dean Ragland, and Dr. Kenneth L. Culver. Each has made a contribution of time and talent toward the publication of this volume.

Copyright 1973 by Winston Press
All Rights Reserved
Library of Congress Catalog Number: 73-78149
SBN: 0-03-006551-8
Printed In the United States of America
9 8 7 6 5 4 3 2 1

Preface

The American Presidency is a unique institution. Planned by the Founding Fathers to be equal in responsibility and authority with Congress and the Supreme Court, it has become—in the words of John F. Kennedy—"the vital center of action in our whole scheme of government."

It was not always so. Throughout much of the nineteenth century, for example, what was done on Capitol Hill had as much or more impact on the country than policies emanating from the White House. The political giants of the age were not Taylor, Tyler, or Harrison—but Clay, Webster, and Calhoun. And it was Congress, not the President, who maneuvered the nation into the Spanish-American War. Nevertheless, even under congressional government, the potential was always there for the Presidency to be "the vital center" should the President choose to make it so. One need only think of Jefferson and the Louisiana Purchase, Jackson destroying the Second Bank of the United States, Lincoln guiding the nation through the trauma of the Civil War, Cleveland breaking the Pullman strike, to recognize the power of the Presidency for good or ill when it is brought to bear on any issue or crisis, foreign or domestic. And since the twentieth century has been an almost constant period of crisis and rapid change for the United States, it is not surprising to find that Presidential power has increased proportionately. Whether it will continue to do so is not certain. Recent events—particularly the American involvement in Vietnam—have caused some antiwar critics to feel that Presidential leadership has gone beyond constitutional bounds, and they have called upon Congress and the courts to redress the balance. Only time will tell if—in this complex society—there are viable alternatives to an all-encompassing, all-powerful Presidency.

This volume of VIEWPOINTS explores the office of the President from several angles. It starts with the past—the office as it was conceived by the framers of the Constitution. And it ends with the future—the office as two historians believe it should become if it—and the government—are to survive. In between are essays on how the office developed and how we choose those who sit in the Presidential chair. There is a section that outlines in great detail the awesome, hidden powers of the Presidency today. These essays are controversial and provocative. But they are also important and timely, dealing as they do with a crucial constitutional and political issue. And finally, there are the words of the Presidents themselves—thoughts of the men who have worked at the job. It is a perspective that, surprisingly, is not often presented but should be. For a President's actions, no matter how much modified by experience, are undoubtedly influenced by his personal concept of the office.

These essays have been written by people of varying backgrounds—historians, political scientists, philosophers, journalists, working politicians. It is our belief that their words, along with the numerous photos in the book, will bring home to the reader the importance of the office on the lives of every citizen in this nation and the world.

As an institution of government, the Presidency is constantly changing to meet new needs and new pressures. But only if we fully understand what it has been in the past and what it is today can we hope to make it an effective instrument for the future.

March 1, 1973

Mary Klein
Winston Press

Contents

Preface v

PART 1 INTRODUCTION 1

1 The Presidency In The Constitution 3

PART 2 THE PRESIDENCY—AN OVERVIEW 9

2 The Historical Roots
    Clinton Rossiter *The Presidency In History* 11

3 The Office Is What They Make It
    Emmet John Hughes *Presidential Style* 17

4 Too Powerful—Or Not Powerful Enough?
    Marcus Cunliffe *A Defective Institution?* 24

5 The Twilight Of The Presidency
    George F. Reedy *The American Monarchy* 30

Photo Essay—*The First Ladies* 37

PART 3 THE GROWTH OF THE OFFICE 55

6 Setting the Precedents
    Richard L. Tobin *King George The First Of The U.S.A.* 57

7 Politician And President
    Dumas Malone *Presidential Leadership And National Unity: The Jeffersonian Example* 60

8	**Democratizing The Presidency**	
	Wilfred E. Binkley *The Jacksonian Revolution*	68
9	**The Presidency And National Crisis: The Civil War**	
	James G. Randall *Abraham Lincoln: The Constitution Stretched*	75
10	**The Presidency And National Crisis: The Depression**	
	Emmet John Hughes *FDR: The Happiest Warrior*	80
11	**President vs Congress**	
	Time *The Crack In The Constitution*	83
	Photo Essay—*The Also-Rans*	91

PART 4   FILLING THE OFFICE   109

12	**The First Step—The Presidential Primary**	
	Wilfrid Sheed *Memoir Of A Campaign Drop-In*	111
13	**Choosing The Candidate**	
	Paul O'Neil *Conventions: Nomination By Rain Dance*	117
14	**A Vanishing Phenomenon—The Whistle-Stop Tour**	
	Irwin Ross *The Long Campaign Trail*	124
15	**The Campaign Train Doesn't Stop Here Anymore**	
	National Journal *Campaign '72: Surrogates And TV*	130
16	**The Electoral College: An Imperfect Institution**	
	Louis C. Kleber *The Presidential Election of 1876*	136
17	**The Office Filled**	
	Gary M. Maranell *Rating The Presidents*	142
18	**Thoughts Of A Professional President-Watcher**	
	Richard H. Rovere *Eisenhower Revisited*	146

PART 5   THE PRESIDENCY TODAY—WHAT IS THE POWER?   155

19	**Commander In Chief**	
	Eric Goldman *The President, The People, And The Power To Make War*	157

20	**Chief Diplomat**	
	Saul K. Padover *Virtually A Dictator In International Affairs*	168
21	**Controlling The Budget**	
	Louis Fischer *Hiding Billions From Congress*	174
22	**Keeping Tabs On The Public**	
	Carl Cohen *The Poisonous Tree*	179
23	**Telling It Like He Says It Is**	
	Hedrick Smith *When The President Meets The Press*	182
24	**The President and The Media**	
	Nat Hentoff *A Deepening Chill*	187
25	**Executive Privilege**	
	Sam J. Ervin, Jr. *Secrecy In A Free Society*	191
26	**Making Military Policy**	
	Stuart Symington *The Secret War In Laos*	196
27	**Appointing The Judges**	
	Elizabeth Drew *The Nixon Court*	200
28	**An Awe-Inspiring Lifestyle**	
	U.S. News And World Report *The President's Pay Is Many Things*	206
	Photo Essay—*The Power And The Glory*	209
PART 6	**PRESIDENTS ON THE PRESIDENCY**	227
29	**The Stewardship Theory**	
	Theodore Roosevelt *I Did Greatly Broaden The Use Of Executive Power*	229
30	**The Progressive Tradition**	
	Woodrow Wilson *The Office Will Be As Big As The Man Who Occupies It*	231
31	**Pragmatism Raised To An Art**	
	Franklin Delano Roosevelt *This Nation Asks For Action And Action Now*	233
32	**An Office Of International Importance**	
	Harry S. Truman *Upon Its Functioning Depends The Survival Of The Free World*	235

33 Organization In The Presidency

Dwight D. Eisenhower *Executive Ability Is A Vital Attribute Of The Presidency* — 238

34 The Vital Center

John F. Kennedy *The People Demand A Vigorous Proponent Of The National Interest* — 241

35 Vehicle For Reform

Lyndon B. Johnson *The Presidency Belongs To All The People* — 244

36 In The Activist Tradition

Richard M. Nixon *The Days Of A Passive Presidency Belong To A Simpler Past* — 247

37 A Dissenting View

William Howard Taft *The Executive Power Is Limited* — 249

PART 7 THE PRESIDENCY—WHAT OF THE FUTURE? 253

38 Striking A Balance

Arthur Schlesinger, Jr. *The Limits And Excesses Of Presidential Power* — 255

39 To Make The Office More Creative

James MacGregor Burns *The Shadow Presidency* — 262

To Hildegarde and Fred—who have seen many changes in the Presidency, and to Jennifer, Jon, and Sara—who undoubtedly will see many more

Part 1
Introduction

1
The Presidency In The Constitution

Excerpts from the Constitution of the United States

ARTICLE II

Section 1. (1) The executive shall be vested in a President of the United States of America. He shall hold his office during the term of four years, and, together with the Vice President, chosen for the same term, be elected, as follows:

(2). Each State shall appoint, in such manner as the legislature thereof may direct, a number of electors, equal to the whole number of Senators and Representatives to which the Senate may be entitled in the Congress: but no Senator or Representative, or person holding an office of trust or profit under the United States, shall be appointed an elector.

The electors shall meet in their respective States, and vote by ballot for two persons, of whom one at least shall not be an inhabitant of the same State with themselves. And they shall make a list of all the persons voted for, and of the number of votes for each; which list they shall sign and certify, and transmit sealed to the seat of the government of the United States, directed to the president of the Senate. The president of the Senate shall, in the presence of the Senate and House of Representatives, open all the certificates, and the votes shall then be counted. The person having the greatest number of votes shall be the President, if such number be a majority of the whole number of electors appointed; and if there be more than one who have such majority, and have an equal number of votes, then the House of Representatives shall immediately choose by ballot one of them for President; and if no person have a majority, then from the five highest on the list the said House shall in like manner choose the President. But in choosing the President, the votes shall be taken by States, the representation from each State having one vote; a quorum for this purpose shall consist of a member or members from two thirds of the States, and a majority of all the States shall be necessary to a choice. In every case, after the choice of the President, the person having the greatest number of votes of the electors shall be the Vice President. But if there should remain two or more who have equal votes, the Senate shall choose from them by ballot the Vice President.

(3). The Congress may determine the time of choosing the electors, and the day on which they shall give their votes; which day shall be the same throughout the United States.

(4). No person except a natural born citizen, or a citizen of the United States, at the time of the adoption of this Constitution, shall be eligible to the office of President; neither shall any person be eligible to that office who shall not have attained to the age of thirty five years, and been fourteen years a resident within the United States.

(5). In case of the removal of the President from office, or of his death, resignation, or inability to discharge the powers and duties of the said office, the same shall devolve on the Vice President, and the Congress may by law provide for the case of removal, death, resignation or inability, both of the President and Vice President, and such officer shall act accordingly, until the disability be removed, or a President shall be elected.

(6). The President shall, at stated times, receive for his services, a compensation, which shall neither be increased nor diminished during the period for which he shall have been elected, and he shall not receive within that period any other emolument from the United States, or any of them.

(7). Before he enter on the execution of his office, he shall take the following oath or affirmation:—"I do solemnly swear (or affirm) that I will faithfully execute the office of President of the United States, and will to the best of my ability, preserve, protect and defend the Constitution of the United States."

Section 2. (1). The President shall be commander in chief of the army and navy of the United States, and of the militia of the several States, when called into the actual service of the United States; he may require the opinion, in writing, of the principal officer in each of the executive departments, upon any subject relating to the duties of their respective offices, and he shall have power to grant reprieves and pardons for offenses against the United States, except in cases of impeachment.

(2). He shall have power, by and with the advice and consent of the Senate, to make treaties, provided two third of the Senators present concur; and he shall nominate, and by and with the advice and consent of the Senate, shall appoint ambassadors, other public ministers and consuls, judges of the Supreme Court, and all other officers of the United States, whose appointments are not herein otherwise provided for, and which shall be established by law: but the Congress may by law vest the appointment of such inferior officers, as they think proper, in the President alone, in the courts of law, or in the heads of departments.

(3). The President shall have the power to fill up all vacancies that may happen during the recess of the Senate, by granting commissions which shall expire at the end of their next session.

Section 3. He shall from time to time give to the Congress information of the state of the Union, and recommend to their consideration such measures as he shall judge necessary and expedient; he may, on extraordinary occasions, convene both Houses, or either of them, and in case of disagreement between them, with respect to the time of adjournment, he may adjourn them to such time as he shall think proper; he shall receive ambassadors and other public ministers; he shall take care that the laws be faithfully executed, and shall commission all the officers of the United States.

Section 4. The President, Vice President and all civil officers of the United States, shall be removed from office on impeachment for, and conviction of, treason, bribery, or other high crimes and misdemeanors.

ARTICLE I

Section 7.   (2). Every bill which shall have passed the House of Representatives and the Senate, shall, before it become a law, be presented to the President of the United States; if he approve he shall sign it, but if not he shall return it with his objections to that house in which it shall have originated, who shall enter the objections at large on their journal, and proceed to reconsider it. If after such reconsideration two-thirds of that house shall agree to pass the bill, it shall be sent, together with the objections, to the other house, by which it shall likewise be reconsidered, and, if approved by two-thirds of that house, it shall become a law. But in all such cases the votes of both houses shall be determined by yeas and nays, and the names of the persons voting for and against the bill shall be centered on the journal of each house respectively. If any bill shall not be returned by the President within ten days (Sundays excepted) after it shall have been presented to him, the same shall be a law, in like manner as if he had signed it, unless the Congress by their adjournment prevent its return, in which case it shall not be a law.

(3). Every order, resolution, or vote to which the concurrence of the Senate and House of Representatives may be necessary (except on a question of adjournment) shall be presented to the President of the United States; and before the same shall take effect, shall be approved by him, or being disapproved by him, shall be repassed by two thirds of the Senate and House of Representatives, according to the rules and limitations prescribed in the case of a bill.

XII AMENDMENT (1804)

The electors shall meet in their respective States and vote by ballot for President and Vice President, one of whom, at least, shall not be an inhabitant of the same State with themselves; they shall name in their ballots the person voted for as President, and in distinct ballots the person voted for as Vice President, and they shall make distinct lists of all persons voted for as President, and of all persons voted for as Vice President, and of the number of votes for each, which lists they shall sign and certify, and transmit sealed to the seat of the government of the United States, directed to the president of the Senate;—The president of the Senate shall, in the presence of the Senate and House of Representatives, open all the certificates and the votes shall then be counted;—The person having the greatest number of votes for President, shall be the President, if such number be a majority of the whole number of electors appointed; and if no person have such majority, then from the persons having the highest numbers not exceeding three on the list of those voted for as President, the House of Representatives shall choose immediately, by ballot, the President. But in choosing the President, the votes shall be taken by States, the representation from each State having one vote; a quorum for this purpose shall consist of a member or members from two-thirds of the States, and a majority of all the States shall be necessary to a choice. And if the House of Representatives shall not choose a President whenever the right of choice shall devolve upon them, before the fourth day of March next following, then the Vice President shall act as President, as in the case of the death or other constitutional disability of the President.—The person having the greatest number of votes as Vice President, shall be the Vice President, if such number be a majority of the whole number of electors appointed, and if no person have a majority, then from the two highest members on the list, the Senate shall choose the Vice President; a quorum for the purpose shall consist of two-thirds of the whole number of Senators, and a majority of the whole number shall be necessary to a choice. But no person constitutionally ineligible to the office of President shall be eligible to that of Vice President of the United States.

XX AMENDMENT (1933)

Section 1. The terms of the President and Vice President shall end at noon on the 20th day of January, and the terms of Senators and Representatives at noon on the 3d day of January, of the years in which such terms would have ended if this article had not been ratified; and the terms of their successors shall then begin.

Section 3. If, at the time fixed for the beginning of the term of the President, the President-elect shall have died, the Vice President-elect shall become President. If a President shall not have been chosen before the time fixed for the beginning of his term, or if the President-elect shall have failed to qualify, then the Vice President-elect shall act as President until a President shall have qualified; and the Congress may by law provide for the case wherein neither a President-elect nor a Vice President-elect shall have qualified, declaring who shall then act at President, or the manner in which one who is to act shall be selected and such person shall act accordingly until a President or Vice President shall have qualified.

Section 4. The Congress may by law provide for the case of the death of any of the persons from whom the House of Representatives may choose a President whenever the right of choice shall have developed upon them, and for the case of the death of any of the persons from whom the Senate may choose a Vice President whenever the right of choice shall have devolved upon them.

XXII AMENDMENT (1951)

Section 1. No person shall be elected to the office of the President more than twice, and no person who has held the office of President, or acted as President, for more than two years of a term to which some other person was elected President shall be elected to the office of the President more than once. But this Article shall not apply to any person holding the office of President when this Article was proposed by the Congress, and shall not prevent any person who may be holding the office of President, or acting as President, during the term within which this Article becomes operative from holding the office of President or acting as President during the remainder of such term.

XXIII AMENDMENT (1961)

Section 1. The District constituting the seat of Government of the United States shall appoint in such manner as the Congress may direct:

A number of electors of President and Vice President equal to the whole number of Senators and Representatives in Congress to which the District would be entitled if it were a State, but in no event more than the least populous State; they shall be in addition to those appointed by the States, but they shall be considered, for the purposes of the election of President and Vice President, to be electors appointed by a State; and they shall meet in the District and perform such duties as provided by the twelfth article of amendment.

XXIV AMENDMENT (1964)

Section 1. The right of citizens of the United States to vote in any primary or other election for President or Vice President, for electors for President or Vice President, or for Senator or Representative in Congress, shall not be denied or abridged by the United States or any State by reason of failure to pay any poll tax or other tax.

XXV AMENDMENT (1967)

Section 1. In case of the removal of the President from office or of his death or resignation, the Vice President shall become President.

Section 2. Whenever there is a vacancy in the office of the Vice President, the President shall nominate a Vice President who shall take office upon confirmation by a majority vote of both Houses of Congress.

Section 3. Whenever the President transmits to the president pro tempore of the Senate and the Speaker of the House of Representatives his written declaration that he is unable to discharge the powers and duties of his office, and until he transmits to them a written declaration to the contrary, such powers and duties shall be discharged by the Vice President as Acting President.

Section 4. Whenever the Vice President and a majority of either the principal officers of the executive departments or of such body as Congress may by law provide, transmit to the president pro tempore of the Senate and the Speaker of the House of Representatives their written declaration that the President is unable to discharge the powers and duties of his office, the Vice President shall immediately assume the powers and duties of the office as Acting President.

Thereafter, when the President transmits to the president pro tempore of the Senate and Speaker of the House of Representatives his written declaration that no inability exists, he shall resume the powers and duties of his office unless the Vice President and a majority of either the principal officers of the executive department or of such other body as Congress may by law provide, transmit within four days to the president pro tempore of the Senate and the Speaker of the House of Representatives their written declaration that the President is unable to discharge the powers and duties of his office. Thereupon Congress shall decide the issue, assembling within forty-eight hours for that purpose if not in session. If the Congress, within twenty-one days after receipt of the latter written declaration, or, if Congress is not in session, within twenty-one days after Congress is required to assemble, determines by two-thirds vote of both Houses that the President is unable to discharge the powers and duties of his office, the Vice President shall continue to discharge the same as Acting President; otherwise, the President shall resume the powers and duties of his office.

Part 2
The Presidency – An Overview

2
The Historical Roots

Clinton Rossiter **THE PRESIDENCY IN HISTORY**

From *The American Presidency*, © 1956, 1960, by Clinton Rossiter. Reprinted by permission of Harcourt Brace Jovanovich, Inc.

The roots of the American Presidency run deep into history. In a world in which model constitutions with their model executives have come and gone in profusion over the past 150 years, this office stands forth as a truly venerable institution. We cannot take its full measure unless we know something of its history, and its history, in any case, is worth studying for its own exciting sake....

To understand the kind of executive created in Article II of the Constitution, we must know something of the men who wrote it, the purposes they had in mind, the materials with which they worked, and the experience that was their "final guide."

The men most influential in shaping the Presidency were James Wilson, who campaigned tirelessly for an executive that could operate with "energy, dispatch, and responsibility"; James Madison, who swung around slowly, but in the end decisively, to Wilson's advanced yet sensible views; and Gouverneur Morris, who led the battle for an energetic executive on the floor of the Convention and then sealed the victory by writing the final draft of the Constitution. Hamilton and Washington, too, each in his own way, deserve some credit for the original Presidency.

The purposes of all these men were the purposes of the whole Convention: to rescue the new republic from the turbulent aftermath of revolution by establishing a government with sufficient energy to insure domestic tranquillity, secure the blessings of ordered liberty, protect private property, create conditions favorable to commercial prosperity, gain respect for itself and fair treatment for its citizens abroad, unite the states in pursuit of common ends, and return the reins of power to the "enlightened gentry." Men like Wilson and Morris understood more clearly than men like Roger Sherman and Edmund Randolph that a strong and independent executive was an essential element of any such government.

The materials with which they worked were the colonial governorships and thus, more remotely, the British monarchy, the various solutions to the problem of executive power in the first state constitutions, the administrative departments that had developed under the Articles of Confederation, and the writings of such exponents of balanced government as Locke and Montesquieu. The experience, both happy and unhappy, of the leaders of the Convention finally dictated the choice of the New York Constitution of 1777 and the Massachusetts Constitution of 1780 as the chief materials. The contrast between these two states, where independent executives served the cause of stability and order, and states like North Carolina and Rhode Island, where unchecked legislatures engaged in all sorts of unseemly activities, did not escape the attention of the delegates at Philadelphia. They had had their fill of governments, both state and national, in which "everything has been drawn within the legislative vortex." Between 1776 and 1787 there had been a noticeable shift in the constitutional theory of the moderate Whigs, from whose ranks came the framers of the Constitution—a shift away from innate confidence in popular assemblies and toward the suspicion that, as Jefferson wrote in his *Notes on Virginia*, "173 despots would surely be as oppressive as one." The sharp decline in the prestige of Congress and the state assemblies among conservatives throughout the new republic was a major factor in the decision to adopt a form of government in which the legislature would be balanced by a strong executive, not mismatched with a "mere Cipher." Even George Mason went on record as opposing "decidedly the making the executive the mere creature of the legislature as a violation of the fundamental principle of good government."

The progress of the Convention toward this decision was labored and uncertain, however, and it often seemed that the hard lessons of the previous decade would be wasted on a majority of the delegates. Persistent voices were raised against almost every arrangement that eventually appeared in Article II, and Wilson and his colleagues were able to score their final success only after a series of debates, decisions, reconsiderations, references to committees, and private maneuvers that still leave the historian befuddled. I have followed the tortuous progress of the incipient Presidency through Madison's *Notes* several times, and I am still not sure how the champions of the strong executive won their smashing victory. It can be said for certain, however, that at least eight decisions on the structure and powers of the executive were taken at different stages of the proceedings, and that out of these arose the Presidency. Every one of these decisions, with one partial exception that history was shortly to remedy, was taken in favor of a strong executive. The consequences for the Presidency, indeed for our whole system of government, would have been enormous had any one of them been taken differently—as it could easily have been. Let me list these decisions briefly, first giving notice that this list lends a deceptive appearance of order to a highly disordered train of events:

1. An executive would be established separate from the legislature. Although this was surely the easiest of all eight decisions to adopt, there were those like Sherman who continued to wonder aloud if it would not be wiser to leave the legislature free to create and appoint such executives "as experience might dictate." To most delegates it was clear from the outset that the executive should be created in the Constitution itself. This had not been done in the first American constitution, and most hardheaded patriots considered this one of the serious defects in the Articles of Confederation.

2. The executive would consist of one man, a President of the United States. This fateful decision was taken only after considerable debate, and only after Wilson had used his position as chairman of the Committee on Detail to spike the plans of those like Randolph who feared the one-man executive as a "foetus of monarchy." Had Randolph and his friends had their way, the Presidency, or whatever it might have been

called, would probably have been shared among three men.

3. The President would have a source of election outside the legislature. To no problem of the executive did the framers devote more time, talk, and votes. Most of the delegates originally shared Sherman's view that the executive "ought to be appointed by and accountable to the legislature only, which was the depository of the supreme will of the Society." Both the Virginia and the New Jersey plans provided for election of the executive by the legislature, and five times in the course of the Convention the delegates voted for this method. Not until the very end were enough of them swayed by the eloquence and diplomacy of Morris to adopt the electoral system outlined in Article II, Section 1, which was borrowed from the method for electing state senators in the Maryland Constitution of 1776. Morris and Wilson, an ill-assorted pair of prophets, were the only delegates to raise their voices clearly for election by the people. Another forty to fifty years would pass before the onward sweep of American democracy would carry the election of the President the rest of the way to the people, but the key decision in behalf of his independence was taken at Philadelphia: the removal of the regular machinery for choosing him to a location outside the legislature and beyond its control.

4. The President would have a fixed term of office, which could be terminated only by the extraordinary method of conviction on impeachment for a high crime or misdemeanor. Hamilton devoted an entire number of *The Federalist* to arguing the vast merits of this decision, which, he insisted, would guarantee the "personal firmness" of the President and the "stability" of his administration. Yet neither he nor any of his associates recognized the real implication of the fixed term: that it would render impossible the rise of a parliamentary form of government. They can hardly be blamed for not recognizing it, since the sharpest minds in England had not yet noticed how far their constitution had moved in the direction of responsible cabinet government.

5. The President would be eligible for re-election to an indefinite number of terms. Had this decision been taken differently, had no President been permitted even to seek a second term, the office would surely be a less splendid and powerful one than it is today. The second terms of Washington, Jackson, Wilson, the two Roosevelts, and Truman, landmarks in the evolution of the Presidency, would never have taken place at all; and their first terms, no mean landmarks themselves, would have been severely hampered had not friend and foe alike expected them to go for a second. And as Hamilton wrote in *The Federalist:*

> Would it promote the peace of the community, or the stability of the government to have half a dozen men who had had credit enough to be raised to the seat of the supreme magistracy, wandering among the people like discontented ghosts, and sighing for a place which they were destined never more to possess?

6. The President would be granted his own powers by the Constitution. It is a matter of great moment that he has prerogatives of his own, that all his authority does not come to him in the form of grants from Congress. What would he be without the constitutional right to command, nominate, pardon, negotiate treaties, supervise the execution of the laws, convene Congress, and, above all, defend himself with the qualified veto? . . . "The executive power shall be vested in a President of the United States of America"; could an apologist for the strong Presidency ask for anything more?

7. The President would not be encumbered with a council to which he would have to go for approval of his nominations or vetoes or other acts. In every state government of the time the

executive was restrained in the use of one or more of his powers by a "council of revision," and the disappointed advocates of a plural executive insisted strenuously that the unity of the Presidency be qualified at least to this extent. "The Grand Signor himself," Mason grumbled, "had his Divan," but he grumbled in vain. The last of a persistent series of efforts to saddle the President with a council was beaten off at the end of the Convention. The unity of the executive had been preserved against all assaults.

8. A clause was inserted in Article I that would forbid any "person holding any office under the United States" to be a "member of either house during his continuance in office." The concern of the delegates over "corruption and the low arts of intrigue" was responsible for this copy of the ill-fated Place Bill of 1692; its real significance, which naturally escaped their notice, lay in the roadblock it still throws up against the evolution of any system of cabinet responsibility to Congress. A motion to strike this clause from the Constitution in preparation was frustrated by a tie vote. There is no telling what a President like James Monroe or Franklin Pierce, or even Thomas Jefferson, might have made of the absence of this prohibition against a backstairs union of executive and legislature.

It is not hard to think of decisions the Convention might have taken to strengthen the Presidency even further. It could have fixed a longer term, granted the President an item veto over appropriations, named four or five departments and made them clearly responsible to him, and required only a majority of the Senate to confirm treaties. But we can well be satisfied with Article II. When we realize that just two weeks from the end of the Convention the proposed Senate held exclusive authority to make treaties and appoint ambassadors and justices, we must marvel at the way in which the story came to a happy ending for Wilson and Morris.

The framers were fully aware, as they read over their finished work, that the Presidency would come under severe attack from those who had opposed the whole idea of the Convention from the beginning and were now about to learn that some of their worst fears had been realized. The case against the Presidency was well summed up in Patrick Henry's warning that this new executive office was an "awful squint toward monarchy." Hamilton, to be sure, proved equal to the task of refuting the charge. One can almost hear him sigh under the burden as he begins the eleven numbers of *The Federalist* devoted to the Presidency with the remark:

> There is hardly any part of the system which could have been attended with greater difficulty in the arrangement of it than this; and there is, perhaps, none which has been inveighed against with less candor or criticized with less judgment.

The big if silent gun in the arsenal of those who insisted upon the essential republicanism of the proposed Presidency was the universal assumption that George Washington, the Cincinnatus of the West, would be chosen as first occupant of the office, and chosen and chosen again until claimed by the grave. This assumption surely had something to do with the fact that all arguments over the executive at Philadelphia were resolved in favor of power and independence. As Pierce Butler wrote to a relative in England about the powers of the executive, "Entre nous, I do [not] believe they would have been so great, had not many of the members cast their eyes toward General Washington as President; and shaped their ideas of the Powers to be given a President, by their opinions of his Virtue." And it made things a good deal easier for those who carried the brunt of the debate in 1788.

Let me now review briefly the outlines of the Presidency as it left the hands of the framers. Considering the temper of the times, it was an office of remarkable vigor and independence. Hamilton pointed out in *The Federalist* that it combined energy, unity, duration, competent powers, and "an adequate provision for its support" with "a due dependence on the people" and "a due responsibility." The President had a source of election divorced from the legislature, a fixed term, indefinite re-eligibility, immunity from conciliar advice that he had not sought, and broad constitutional powers of his own. It was his first task to run the government: to be its administrative chief, to appoint and supervise the bureaucrats, and to "take care that the laws be faithfully executed." He was to be ceremonial head of the nation, a republican king with the prerogative of mercy, and he was to lead the government in its foreign relations, whether peaceful or hostile. Despite the principle of the separation of powers, he was not to be completely isolated from the houses of Congress. To them he could tender occasional advice, and over their labors he held a qualified but effective veto. The President was to be a strong, dignified, nonpolitical chief of state and government. In two words, he was to be George Washington. . . .

The Presidency today has the same general outlines as that of 1789, but the whole picture is a hundred times magnified. The President is all the things he was intended to be, and he is several other things as well.

First, [the office] is distinctly more powerful. It cuts deeply into the powers of Congress; in fact, it has quite reversed the expectations of the framers by becoming itself a vortex into which these powers have been drawn in massive amounts. It cuts deeply into the lives of the people; in fact, it commands authority over their comings and goings that Hamilton himself might tremble to behold.

Next, the President is more heavily involved in making national policy. It was, to be sure, the nineteenth-century Whigs who insisted most arrogantly that his sole task was to carry out the policies determin by an all-wise Congress, but even Washington cannot be said to have taken much of a hand in making policy except in the fields of foreign and military relations. Although Hamilton, his Secretary of the Treasury, exercised imaginative leadership and independent judgment in the areas he occupied by right or had invaded by stealth, his was considered a virtuoso performance that would probably not be repeated. Yet it has been repeated and much improved upon by every President worth his salt. Whether as legislator, opinion-maker, commander, or administrator, the President molds lasting policy in every sector of American life.

To a large extent this is true because he is now so highly political a figure, and over this development the framers would have shaken their heads in wonder and sorrow. The plunge of the Presidency into party politics, which Jefferson took for himself and all his successors, may seem to have been unavoidable. The framers, however, would not have seen it that way. They believed sincerely in the idea of a patriot President, one who would rise coolly above the "heats of faction"; they would have considered it a mockery of all their pains to create a republican king if the king, like George III, were to turn his energies to party intrigue.

Another development would probably have shocked the framers, although one or two of them seem to have suspected that it was in the offing: the conversion of the Presidency into a democratic office. The extent to which he has become the "tribune of the people" is never so apparent as in an election year. When we contrast the decentralized, nonpolitical, dignified election of Washington with the "heats and ferments" of the presidential canvass as it has existed at least since 1840, we begin to sense how far the American people have gone to make the Presidency their peculiar possession.

Finally, the office has a kind of prestige that it did not know under Washington and lacked as late as the turn of this century. Washington, after all, lent his prestige to the Presidency, but today quite the reverse process takes place when a man becomes President. He becomes the great figure in our system because the office is the great institution. We forget too easily that Congress—with sometimes the House on top and at other times the Senate—was the focus of the people's interest in their government through most of the first century under the Constitution. The Presidency carried with it very little of the magic that is now so notable an element in its strength.

All this evidence leads me to assert that the outstanding feature of American constitutional development has been the growth of the power and prestige of the Presidency. This growth has not been steady, but subject to sharp ebbs as well as massive flows. Strong Presidents have been followed by weak ones; in the aftermath of every "dictator," Congress has exulted in the "restoration of the balance wisely ordained by the fathers." Yet the ebbs have been more apparent than real, and each new strong President has picked up where the last strong one left off. Lincoln took off from Jackson and Polk, not from Pierce and Buchanan. Franklin Roosevelt looked back to Wilson over the barely visible heads of the three Presidents who came between them. As to the fate of the Presidency under the assaults of Thaddeus Stevens, Ben Wade, Schuyler Colfax, and their friends and heirs, I call Henry Jones Ford to witness: "Although once executive power, in the hands of an accidental President, was bent and held down by the weight of a huge congressional majority, its springs were unbroken, and it sprang up unhurt when the abnormal pressure was removed." In the face of history, it seems hard to deny the inevitability of the upward course of the Presidency—discontinuous, to be sure, but also irreversible....

3

The Office Is What They Make It

Emmet John Hughes   **PRESIDENTIAL STYLE**

From *Smithsonian*, Vol. 2, No. 12 (March 1972), 28–36. Copyright © Smithsonian Institution, 1972.

"The Presidency is the most peculiar office in the history of the world." Harry S Truman, 1959

The nation's 33rd President had a gift for stating complex truths in a simple way. He had read his history and lived his Presidency more than casually; and obviously, he discerned this Chief Magistracy as something historically unique. Less obviously, he meant another sort of distinction: the singular quality not only of *the* Presidency but also of *any* Presidency.

As the political commoner from Kansas City who had succeeded the patrician squire from Hyde Park, Truman must have reflected how he himself provided the latest proof of the idiosyncrasy of Presidential succession and the variety of Presidential behavior. And with this perception of the "peculiar" marks of every Presidency, Harry Truman was crisply defining life in the White House as a matter of Presidential style.

Of all myths and fancies about the Presidency, there may be none more untrue than the notion that Presidential *style* has become a transcendant issue only in this age of manipulative politics, attesting the Merlin-like power of national television. But Franklin Delano Roosevelt, with his mastery of radio, roused national opinion— 30 years ago—far more ingeniously than any of his successors. Still another 30 years earlier, Theodore Roosevelt had set up a press office in the White House and become "the darling of the working newspaperman." The stunning successes of both Roosevelts loom like studies in contrast to the fate (or the style) of two Presidents who served since television became the supreme medium in politics.

Lyndon Johnson [for example] found Presidential use of television so far from being a device for the "sale" of his policies that he became the first modern President to give up his office in the face of a chilling display of popular disbelief.

All this hints at one critical paradox of the Presidency: The effective style of any administration has depended less on the newest techniques of Madison Avenue than on political truths as old as the age of James Madison—and on the Constitutional Convention and the struggle to define the Presidency by written law. On no other matter were the Founding Fathers so anguished as by their colliding fears of an Executive so weak as to allow anarchy or so strong as to threaten tyranny. During the fight over ratification of the Constitution, Patrick Henry decried its grant of Executive power as an "awful squint toward monarchy." A majority of the 55 Convention delegates had planned, till near the end, to give the Senate alone full authority over making treaties, designating ambassadors, and appointing Supreme Court justices —while also voting, before a final reconsideration, to have all Presidents elected by Congress. There finally prevailed the call for a Presidency "with sufficient vigor to pervade every part of it."

The *way* in which this argument was won, however, foretold a great deal about the way in which Presidents "with sufficient vigor" would act. A small group of delegates commissioned to "revise" and "arrange" the Constitution's articles was called the Committee of Style. From them came the hazy—and hence sweeping—declaration: "The executive power shall be vested in a President of the United States of America." It continues to outline powers at once far broader and far vaguer than the basic definitions of legislative or judicial powers. This Constitutional grant acknowledged that the nature of Presidential power could not be penned on parchment or chiseled in stone, but that the impact of each President would forever stay a matter of style—his own "peculiar" style. From this original determination, a straight line ran to Wilson's assessment of any man in the White House: "His office is anything he has the sagacity and force to make it. . . . The President is at liberty, both in law and conscience, to be as big a man as he can."

What the political jargon of the 20th century would call the "image" of George Washington was actually what brought, in more than one way, the American Presidency to life. To begin with, the Founding Fathers heard no argument for risking executive power nearly so persuasive as the simple, quiet presence of the general presiding over their debates.

Great President, great actor

Almost from the moment of his unanimous election, Washington showed how effectively the style of a President could fill the void left by the substance of the Constitution. His eight-day journey by carriage and horse from his home in Mount Vernon to his inauguration in New York was celebrated with a regal pageantry—booming guns and tolling bells and cheering mobs— fit for a returning Roman conqueror. As Chief Executive, with his extraordinary mixture of prudence and persistence, he set precedent after precedent to fill in the blank spaces of Presidential authority. All the while he freely showed his taste for public pomp, as he moved about in a fine coach drawn by six horses or on a white steed with leopard-skin housing. As ever since the Revolution, the larger towns elaborately commemorated his birthday, driving one critical journal to cry out: "Even Cincinnatus received no adulations of this kind."

All such criticisms now sound at once inevitable and irrelevant. When Washington went to Congress to give his first report on the state of the nation, he was publicly chastised for a "Speech from the Throne"—but the precedent survived. When he traveled through New England and the South, so that people might see how a President looked, he was assailed for monarchic manners—but the Presidency profited.

Years after his death, his successor, John Adams, himself no master of the flourishes and theatrics of "the Washington court," looked back and wrote, with an insight sharpened by envy: "If he was not the greatest President he was the best Actor of the Presidency we ever had."

The first President was, in short, precisely what the Founding Fathers expected him to be: an artist in political style.

There appeared in the first transfer of Presidential power a warning of the eccentric rhythm that would mark so many almost incongruous transitions in the White House, A Martin Van Buren following an Andrew Jackson, an Andrew Johnson following an Abraham Lincoln, a William Howard Taft following a Theodore Roosevelt, a Warren Harding following a Woodrow Wilson, a Dwight Eisenhower following a Harry Truman: Each of these, in his "peculiar" way, reflected something of the alternative styles of Presidential leadership first foreshadowed by a John Adams, called to take the place of a George Washington. But the distance between the martial hero and the portly intellectual may be judged by Vice President Adams' explosion to Benjamin Rush in 1790: "The history of our Revolution will be one continued lie. . . . The essence of the whole will be that Dr. Franklin's electrical rod smote the earth and out sprang George Washington."

As such querulousness might suggest, the Presidential life of John Adams amounted to what has been called "a full agenda of woe." Succeeding to office by the margin of three electoral votes, he suffered the taunt of being a "three-vote President" from the start; and, at the end of his one term, his bitterness over Thomas Jefferson's victory drove him to shun his successor's inauguration. He displayed admirable qualities of intelligence and tenacity, above all in keeping the young nation from involvement in the conflict between England and France. A man of singular talent and insight, he would be judged by Vernon Parrington to be possibly "the most notable thinker . . . among American statesmen." But he was other things too: arrogant, cranky, aloof, vain, and secretive enough to alienate both Jeffersonians and Hamiltonians. This confident and cerebral Chief Executive lacked, in short, all decisive sense of Presidential style.

T.R.: "able to face anything"

The same Presidential drama, essentially, was reenacted a little more than a century later. The protagonists this time were Theodore Roosevelt and William Howard Taft. In this instance, Taft came to the White House as T.R.'s insistently chosen successor. But this only brought a memorable irony to the conflict between each man's ideas of *how* a President should act and lead.

In the headlong process of staking his claim to being the first modern President, Theodore Roosevelt played his role with the zest of a crusader and the glee of a boy. After Ohio's Republican boss Mark Hanna lamented on "that damned cowboy" gaining the White House, Roosevelt happily took the sneer as a cue and proceeded to give the Presidency what one scholar later called "the breathless drama of a Western movie."

The act was no affectation. Back in 1884, Roosevelt had written a friend that, once he put on his special cowboy suit, complete with revolver and rifle, "I feel able to face anything." Or as a relative, fully aware of his love of center stage, once commented: "When Theodore attends a wedding, he wants to be the bride, and when he attends a funeral he wants to be the corpse." The tireless display of such enthusiasm drove another observer to see him as "an interesting combination of St. Vitus and St. Paul." More importantly, his use of drama was no mere indulgence. In the words of Archie Butt, his military aide: "One never gets away from Mr. Roosevelt's personality . . . when he comes into a room and stands as he always does for one second before doing something characteristic, he electrifies the company."

The process of "electrification" relied upon a

rare skill with words and gestures to convey his message. With seeming ease, he coined phrases and slogans—from "muckraker" and "lunatic fringe" to "square deal" and (most characteristically of all) "my hat is in the ring." Traveling with as much studied purpose as he talked, he became the first President to travel beyond the nation's borders when he went down to take a proprietary view of the site of the Panama Canal.

Disdain for Cabinet and Congress

For all his aggressive reforms on the national scene, the style of T.R.'s leadership became most vivid in foreign affairs—whether he was negotiating for the Panama Canal Zone, which earned the Republic the distrust of Latin America for decades, or mediating the Russo-Japanese conflict, which earned him the Nobel Peace Prize. In major decisions he acted with a kind of impartially divided disdain for both his Cabinet and Congress. He once confided his Presidential dream to his cousin, young Franklin Roosevelt: "Oh, if I could only be President and Congress too for just ten minutes!"

The most dramatic as well as effective Rooseveltian thrust in world affairs was his dispatch of the battle fleet—16 battleships and 12,000 men—on the 1907-1909 world cruise to impress all nations. By all judgments, the impact of the fleet upon the great powers was as electrifying as this President's entry into a drawing room. But the manner in which he delivered it had to be almost as significant as its results. The plan provoked immediate opposition from Congress, finally focusing on the threat to refuse funds for the grandiose operation. Unruffled, Roosevelt replied that he already had funds enough to move the fleet from its Atlantic bases to the Pacific, and if Congress chose to leave the battleships there, the decision to strip the East's defenses would be theirs. How could a mere Senator combat a Rough Rider?

Whatever the failings of this Roosevelt, probably no President has proved so surely the greater importance of style than of statute. He had ample reason to write to a friend, "While President I have been President, emphatically."

The William Howard Taft who followed him proved to be the retort incarnate. If Roosevelt was the frustrated general, almost lusting for combat, Taft clearly was the frustrated judge, longing for quiet. The two ended by being as much at odds as their dreams. While Taft's Presidency was not without victories, he once told Archie Butt: "I have made up my mind. . . . I cannot be spectacular." . . .

The contrast in styles, between Taft and Roosevelt, led to the anguishing conflict of the two Presidents in 1912. Roosevelt had known Taft intimately for years when he had told Taft *directly* in 1908: "I have always said you would be the greatest President, bar only Washington and Lincoln. . . ." T.R. had foreseen everything but the essential: how a Taft would *act* as President. When the final break became public and bitter, Taft openly wept and exclaimed, with pained disbelief: "Roosevelt was my closest friend." And when the division became formal with Roosevelt's rebellious Progressive candidacy, the Republican leader, Chauncey M. Depew, promptly spoke the political obituary of both men: "The only question now is which corpse gets the most flowers."

The political postscript for Taft—at once happy and revealing—came with his service as Chief Justice from 1921 to 1930. He had once written his brother of his love for the bench: "Perhaps it is the confort and dignity and power without worry I like." No President could ever have enjoyed power so serene. As a fretful President prone to sleeping too much and eating too much, Taft had betrayed the size of his worry in the size of his waist, but as a confident Chief Justice he worked hard and controlled his weight. After four reassuring years on the

Supreme Court he wrote: "The truth is that in my present life I don't remember that I ever was President."

While William Howard Taft was distinguishing and enjoying himself on the highest bench, the 29th and 30th Presidents, Warren Gamaliel Harding and Calvin Coolidge, gave an eight-year lesson on one much-neglected aspect of Presidential style. These two Chief Executives could hardly have appeared more different: Harding congenitally warm and gregarious and trusting, Coolidge calculatedly cool, reserved, and shrewd. Both men shared, nonetheless, a notion that the office should be dignified and detached, uncombative and unpolemical. So believing, each man, by the very slackness of his grasp on power, behaved in the White House quite as the nation liked and expected. And so behaving, they served to remind that the style of any President could not be prescribed by formula, nor was it "peculiar" merely to each President. It also had to be judged by the peculiar mood or the people at a particular time.

With Harding, the Presidency took on exactly the tone wanted by the nation—after eight years of Wilson. It was typical of Wilson's bitterness, after his vain fight for his Treaty and his League, to sneer at Harding as "the bungalow mind"; and it is true that a bourgeois quality seemed to fit the times. The popular longing of 1920 was for a return to the lazy peace of a small town Main Street. A relaxed, kindly, and tolerant Harding offered near-perfect relief to the rigid, doctrinaire, and abrasive Wilson. When Harding suddenly died after but two and a half years in office, the procession-by-train bearing his body back to Washington was wept over by mourners across the land—a general grief that *The New York Times* called "the most remarkable demonstration in American history and affection, respect, and reverence for the dead." A perhaps more surprising eulogy came from the most keen-eyed European student of the President, Harold J. Laski, in his voluminous correspondence with Oliver Wendell Holmes: "I was very moved by Harding's death... I thought him mediocre in ability but with a real and generous goodwill to his fellowmen, a quality I am still sentimental enough to think important."

With Coolidge, the White House took on exactly the air needed by the nation—after its years with Harding. The temper of the times echoed in the Holmes-Laski correspondence, now with the American Justice writing his English friend, ". . . while I don't expect anything very astonishing from [Coolidge], I don't *want* anything very astonishing." The President obliged. In the memory of the permanent White House staff, as one of them wrote, "no other President in my time ever slept so much." He raised passivity to nearly the level of strategy.

There was another, more positive way that Coolidge suited his time. The scandals of the Harding regime—Teapot Dome, the Veterans' Bureau and the Department of Justice—did not erupt until after Harding's death, bringing on what Will Rogers called the "great morality panic of 1924." But with Coolidge in the White House—a model of personal rectitude who could be dubbed a "Puritan in Babylon"—the Presidency itself was spared public scandal and popular distrust. And thus a Republican administration that, in a different time and with different luck, would have been hounded from office actually suffered not at all: A Coolidge at once so clean and cool easily won election in his own right, when a trusting and shrugging electorate (less than half the eligible voters bothered to go to the polls) gave him almost twice as many votes as his Democratic challenger.

The Harding-Coolidge era is looked back upon as a strange, almost lifeless prelude to the most harrowing modern test of Presidential leadership. The Great Depression was an ordeal matched in all the nation's history by the Civil War alone. For a nation as for a man, the time of searing crisis can become the time of enlightening self-discovery. So it was now. The meeting and surviving of the Great Depression revealed and dramatized, as never before or since, the fateful meaning of the style of two Presidents who successively faced the same test with memorably contrary political ways and manners—Herbert Hoover and Franklin Delano Roosevelt.

The fate of Hoover amounted to a study in irony almost too extreme to be credible. Few Presidents stayed so loyal to their convictions, beyond all reach of contradicting circumstance or tempting expedience. Few would thereby force themselves, as well as their country, to pay so harsh a price for their fidelity. When he entered the White House in 1929, Hoover had long been hailed as the masterful technician of 20th-century economy and technology; and by the time he made his farewell Presidential drive down Pennsylvania Avenue in 1933, he had been denounced as a kind of co-conspirator in the worst economic debacle in American history.

But the ironies had deeper roots in his past. The man whom the angry jobless bitterly honored by christening their shacks and slums Hoovervilles, had been the hero of relief and reconstruction during and after World War I, who had moved thankful Europeans to name many a *Hooverstrasse*. From World War I, he had emerged—rather like General Dwight Eisenhower after World War II—as a figure above ordinary politics, without known partisanship. In 1920, an Assistant Secretary of the Navy had written excitedly to a friend about Hoover: "He certainly is a wonder, and I wish we could make him President of the United States. There could not be a better one." The Democrat, with this ardent hope, was Franklin Delano Roosevelt.

There was a pathos to go with the folly after 1928. Much of it was to be found in prophecies and promises of Hoover so far from reality as to suggest the utterances less of an economist than of an exorcist. He celebrated his Presidential nomination in 1928 with the assurance that the Republic stood "nearer to the final triumph over poverty than in any land." The decade soon to begin would mark, instead, the first time since 1789 when a greater number of people chose to leave the Republic than to enter it. By the end of 1931, the folk-humorist Will Rogers could only laugh a little nervously over repeated Presidential forecasts of imminent prosperity: "We are the first nation in the history of the world to go to the poorhouse in an automobile." And to all of this, Hoover would later add in his *Memoirs* the earnest and still uncomprehending commentary: "I was convinced that efficient, honest administration of the vast machine of the Federal government would appeal to all citizens. I have since learned that efficient government does not interest the people so much as dramatics."

Such stubborn sincerity set the tone and foretold the end of the 1932 campaign as decisively as Roosevelt's often florid and forgettable rhetoric. In this campaign the statistics of life were vastly more persuasive than the speeches of candidates. The nation's industrial production had fallen to barely one-half its 1929 level, and 12 million citizens were without jobs. To begin his campaign, Hoover had gone back to his native Iowa, there to be greeted by a couple of thousand farmers marching through the streets of Des Moines under banners of derision: "In Hoover We Trusted—Now We Are Busted." To end his campaign, Hoover faced the placards of crowds in St. Paul protesting his dispersal of the thousands of war veterans who had marched on Washington, the summer past, as the Bonus Expeditionary Force seeking financial help.

How had this "guardian of the people" worked and responded, looked and sounded, through his four years in the White House? Hoover struggled through 18-hour days until "so tired that every bone in my body aches." After the pain of such work, the public or partisan outcries against a "do-nothing" President could provoke only an unspeakable bitter resentment.

Hoover's dogmatic orthodoxy had little patience, and no answer, for questions about individual need and federal aid. He could offer two prescriptions for the proper national response to the drought of 1930: He approved a Congressional appropriation of $45 million to save the livestock of Arkansas; and he opposed an outright grant of $25 million to aid the farmers and families affected, since such governmental relief "would have injured the spiritual responses of the American people." Under such a definition of the "spiritual" needs of citizens, all who hoped for federal help only could envy the happier lot of those incorruptible cattle.

Hoover never laughed

This 31st President moved with tragic lack of humor, warmth or confidence—except in his own rightness. Back in 1919, at the Versailles conference, economist John Maynard Keynes had much admired Hoover, but made note of "his habitual air of weary Titan." And precisely this became the "air" of his Presidential leadership. A veteran of the administrative staff in the White House, who had seen many Presidents pass through, later remembered of Hoover that he "never laughed aloud" but "always had a frown on his face." In communications with his staff, he observed chill courtesy, avoiding either rebuke or debate, since "A man should not become embroiled with his inferior." In communications with the press, he nervously kept his distance, and he was angered or confounded by almost any criticism. In communications with the people as a whole, he could display neither flexibility nor force: He found the struggle with words difficult and dismaying, as he labored over his own texts in longhand, and the hazy homilies finally spoken left him without one victory in prose.

He once bluntly said, "I have never liked the clamor of crowds.... The crowd is credulous, it destroys, it hates and it dreams—but it never builds." It appears never to have crossed his mind to wonder how a President could govern the "crowd" of the American Republic if they stayed *in*credulous toward him. Obviously, he had never heard the first President described as "the best Actor" in the role. Nor could he have remembered the pointed sense of Washington's own aphorism: "The truth is the people must *feel* before they will *see*."

4

Too Powerful-Or Not Powerful Enough?

Marcus Cunliffe **A DEFECTIVE INSTITUTION?**

From *Commentary*, Vol. 45, No. 2 (February 1968), 27–33. Reprinted from *Commentary*, by permission; Copyright © by the American Jewish Committee.

The American Presidency is an office of such power, prestige, and historical dignity that most of us are content to accept it as one of the prime given facts of the political universe. There would seem to be no more point in questioning its basic shape than in questioning the shape of the Matterhorn....

What may be called the received view of the Presidency . . . is that the office has exhibited a vast though intermittent growth in authority and responsibility; that the growth, though disputed, has been beneficial, in providing firm, personal, and humane leadership for the government and the people of the United States.

Many commentators, including such chief executives as Theodore Roosevelt and John F. Kennedy, see a division between "strong" (i.e. active, desirable) Presidents of the Jackson-Lincoln persuasion and "weak" (i.e., passive, undesirable) Presidents of the "Whig" or Buchanan-Grant variety. The early Presidents are usually regarded as strong, and for the 19th century their strength (or stubbornness) has brought Polk and Cleveland into the ranks of the approved. In the 20th century, T. R., Wilson, F.D.R., Truman, and perhaps Kennedy are admitted to the company, while Taft, Harding, Coolidge, Hoover, and Eisenhower are frequently written off as weak....

In this received formulation, the growth of Presidential power is historically associated with the assertion of federal as against state sovereignty, and of executive over legislative initiative: a collective triumph of liberalism over conservatism, welfare-state concern over laissez-faire indifference, energy over lethargy, national unity over parochial squabbling, internationalism over isolationism. On the whole, it has also come to be associated with the role of the Democratic party. Jackson and F.D.R. alike can be portrayed as "People's Presidents," exercising their executive power on behalf of the lowly citizen as well as in the cause of national integrty.

In the last few years this kind of interpretation, seemingly so self-evident to men of good will, has been jarred by events. The assassination of Kennedy in 1963 has produced a strange subterranean uneasiness, not only over the disputed data of the crime itself, but over larger, vaguer conundrums involving Presidents and the general public. The subsequent conduct of Lyndon Johnson heightened the uneasiness. Democratic liberals have begun to talk like some of the Republicans who thirty years ago were accusing Franklin Roosevelt of dictatorship.

In other words, Americans who were once sure that strong leadership was necessarily wholesome leadership no longer take the belief as axiomatic. What if strength is brutally misused? Or misused with the best intentions? What is the margin for error when the chief executive may commit the nation, and the whole world, to catastrophe? In these disturbed, confused circumstances there are signs of an attempt to rethink the received view of the Presidency.

The effort is easier talked about than made. In the first place, there is much historical truth in the conventionally respectful view of the office. It would demand a remarkable display of forensic skill, which no one has yet tried, to contend that Buchanan was a better man for the job than Lincoln, or Taft than Teddy Roosevelt. Taking the whole picture, the stability of the office and the caliber of its occupants would define the Presidency as an exceptionally successful governmental device. In general, it is hard to deny that the strong Presidents *have* been good Presidents: good as specimens of humanity, good as leaders, good for their country.

Other factors would appear to reinforce the familiar estimates. The almost permanent crisis situation of the past quarter-century shows little sign of easing. In foreign affairs, both tradition and necessity seem to locate authority in the hands of the executive. External problems, while not the sole ones, have dominated the American government since 1940. The spread of executive power has therefore, it would seem, been inevitable. Its further spread, or at least its continuance, would seem equally inevitable.

Similarly, the trend toward centralized governmental authority has been conspicuous and seems an unavoidable movement, observable in many other countries. It does not follow that the powers of the President *as an individual* have outranged or even kept pace with the trend. Some observers point to the appearance of a huge federal bureaucracy as a phenomenon apt to muffle and weaken rather than heighten Presidential power. Nevertheless, the swing toward executive, appointive government instead of legislative, elective government might be taken to determine the Presidential sphere of activity beyond the possibility of significant alteration.

Again, historically the legislative branch has been dazzlingly impressive. If the alternative to executive dominance were legislative dominance, few Americans would welcome the prospect. In past decades when such was the case, notably in the last third of the 19th century, congressional performance was generally sluggish, obstructionist, and obsessed with devious bargaining for pelf and privilege. In face of the inveterate congressional habit of resisting executive requests, one is tempted to argue that in this area at any rate the trouble with the Presidency is not that it enjoys too much power but that it suffers from too little; for power, properly defined, must be the power to achieve results. If this is an unjust assessment of Congress, it is a commonly held one. . . .

We seem to be left where we started: namely either with the cheerful belief that the Presidency comes as near perfection as can be achieved in an imperfect world, or with the pragmatic belief that it is unwise to tinker with long-established mechanisms. The State of the Union, we may conclude after tracking through a hundred and seventy years of Presidential utterances, was and is as good as may be expected.

But such testimony leaves much unsaid. The historical record is in actuality less clear and less unanimous. Thus, it is worth stressing that over most of America's past the White House has been occupied not by "strong" but by "weak" Presidents. Some no doubt were truly weak: inept, timorous, petty. Others however were "weak" not out of temperamental inability but out of conviction: men who did not think it right for the federal government to encroach upon the states, or else for the executive to encroach upon the legislature. Some have insisted that the prime duty of the President is to act as head of state, rather than as head of government or as head of a political party.

Pursuing this line, we might more revealingly divide Presidents not into "strong" and "weak" groups, but into the "aggrandizers" and the "moderates." It then becomes possible to see the undesirable consequences of executive "strength." One of the worst effects has been on Congress.... Through being robbed of initiative, or being treated as a bunch of boobies and crooks, Congress has been made to appear negative and irresponsible. It has responded, like the cast of a play whose principal performer constantly hogs the limelight, by unworthy but perfectly understandable sulks and threats of sabotage. The price paid for an enlarged and glorified Presidency has been a diminished, neurotically self-important legislative branch.

Moderate Presidents have themselves had to pay a price for the performances of aggrandizing predecessors. Every bold Presidential administration has induced a violent reaction. Congress has kicked back.... The victims have been the unoffending new occupants of the White House. Van Buren was punished for the vehemence of his predecessor, Andrew Jackson. The repercussions of Jacksonianism led to a run of "weak" Presidents interrupted briefly by the Mexican War and then resumed through the 1850's. Andrew Johnson bore the brunt of the aggrandizements of Abraham Lincoln; again the consequence was a run of one-term, "weak" Presidents terminated only by another war—that of 1898. William Howard Taft's tribulations were heightened by the previous executive forays of Theodore Roosevelt. Strong executives may think of themselves as dominant characters; they rarely realize that they strike resentful contemporaries as domineering. After the large claims of Woodrow Wilson came the deliberate "abdication" or moderateness of Harding and Coolidge. Harry Truman, faced with the hostilities accumulated during Franklin Roosevelt's Presidential tenure, would probably have met with less resistance if F.D.R. had not held on to office so long. Truman's own assertions of executive authority did nothing to dissipate the nation's stored-up antagonism to Presidential overlordship. In the wake of a double dose of Roosevelt-Truman "strength," the nation was ready for a milder and more congressionally-oriented regime....

Such an analysis gains in credibility when we note that several of the so-called "weak" Presidents have had quite clear conceptions of their role. Andrew Jackson's successors shared a coherent "Whig" view of the Presidential office. The duty of the chief executive, they agreed, was to symbolize the nation's aspirations, to symbolize the party of which he was the titular and temporary head, and to confine his tenure to a single term—as Jackson himself had initially recommended. For all his personal inadequacy, President Grant was in tune with the tradition of executive moderateness when he said of the Depression of 1873, "It is the duty of Congress to devise the method of correcting the evils which are acknowledged to exist, and not mine." Taft was not simply trying to rationalize his own failure, or to be revenged on Teddy Rooesvelt, when he wrote *Our Chief Magistrate and His Powers* (1916). Irritated that Roosevelt had likened himself to Lincoln, and Taft to Buchanan, the ex-President retorted that this was crude egotism and that T.R.'s doctrine was dangerous. Taft adhered to the numerous company of objectors to those Presidents who "played their parts upon the political stage with histrionic genius and commanded the people almost as if they were an army and the President their Commander-in-Chief." Fortunately, Taft added, "there have always been men in this free and intelligent people of ours, who apparently courting political . . . disaster have registered protest against this undue Executive domination. . . ." In the same way, Warren G. Harding's declaration of Presidential moderation, in his first annual message to Congress of December 1921, was not necessarily indicative of crass indolence, but of a widely held viewpoint:

> During the anxieties of war, when necessity seemed compelling, there were excessive grants of authority and an extraordinary concentration of powers in the Chief Executive. The repeal of wartime legislation and the automatic expirations which attended the peace proclamations have put an end to these emergency excesses, but I . . . wish to go further than that. . . .

Coolidge, Hoover, and Eisenhower abided by the same convictions. None seems likely to be celebrated by posterity as a great and wise upholder of the American political creed. The charge against the non-aggrandizing Presidents of the 20th century, however, is not that they failed to take personal charge over every facet of national life. It is that they failed to imbue the nation with a sense of Presidential greatness. . . .

The President does not of course wield absolute power; on most domestic issues his freedom of maneuver is severely restricted. The problem is that the President is *thought* to be a superman. Americans yearn to be convinced that Presidential candidates are men of magical attainments. With each quadrennial contest the voters, once they have decided that one particular candidate will be the most popular, immediately hypnotize themselves into the notion that his popularity is proof of transcendent abilty. It is expected that with each new incumbent the office will undergo a transfiguration. The victorious candidate invariably enjoys a brief early spell of ecstatic acclaim. The limitations of his role are temporarily forgotten. The immense federal structure is dramatized and personalized as if it consisted of only one man, remotely attended by colorless underlings and challenged only by a horde of bloody-minded Congressmen. The President is counted upon to eradicate all the nation's ills. Far too much is expected of him. Soon the reaction sets in; having failed to usher in the millennium, he becomes a target for criticism as exaggerated as the previous adulation. Both attitudes are unhealthy. Both spring from the excessive claims made by and for the office in the 20th century. Partisan emotion and residual millenial expectations encourage the incumbent's supporters to back him for a second term. The second time round, his reputation almost always slumps disastrously, even among his followers. . . .

Nor is the opening chorus of praise which greets incoming Presidents unanimous. As many observers have remarked, there is something unwholesome in an arrangement that establishes the leader of a political party as the head of state. The head of state has a ceremonial, symbolic function; he must represent *all* the people. But in American Presidential elections the successful candidate is frequently elected by very little more than 50 per cent of the popular vote. Indeed, in no less than fifteen elections, the winner has failed to secure a popular majority. Political analysts tend on the whole to congratulate the United States on the stability that accrues from so evenly balanced a two-party system. But there are harmful aspects. Roughly half the population, sometimes more, have to accept a man they did not want, a candidate against whom they voted, as the "elective monarch" of their country. Still more galling, in 20th-century circumstances, they will almost certainly have to put up with him for a second term: eight years in all.

Assassination attempts are an index of the frustrations created by the American Presidency. The first known attempt, significantly, was made on Andrew Jackson, in 1835. The would-be assassin was insane: he believed that he was the rightful heir to the throne of America, and that "King Andrew" was a usurper. Yet his crazed logic was not much at variance with the political discourse of the day. Jackson, after announcing that he favored a single-term Presidency, ran a second time and was elected. Jackson's enemies, including Senators Clay and Calhoun, were in earnest in denouncing him as a tyrant. Jackson claimed he had received five hundred letters from people who threatened to kill him. He himself believed the assassin had been hired by Whig adversaries. There followed a macabre episode in American political history: John C. Calhoun, a former vice-president and a member of the Senate, felt obliged to rise from his seat and deny that he had plotted to kill the President.

The second attempt on the life of a President, against Lincoln in 1865, was likewise directed against a chief executive who had been heatedly accused of tyranny, and who had also been re-elected for a second term. Though not temperamentally an aggrandizing President, McKinley acquired sudden prominence and authority as the result of the Spanish-American War; he too, at the moment of his assassination in 1901, had recently been reelected. Theodore Roosevelt was much criticized for attempting to return to power —and in effect to a third term—by campaigning as a Progressive candidate in 1912. In a hostile cartoon of that year he is shown brandishing a scroll inscribed "THEODORE ROOSEVELT FOR EVER AND EVER"; in another he pins up a proclamation signed "TR REX" which announces: "*I* am the will of the people. . . . *I* chose myself to be leader. . . . *I* will have as many terms in office as *I* desire." He received a bullet wound in the chest; the shot was fired in the midst of a campaign address by a self-styled patriot who cried out "No Third Term!"

John F. Kenendy was still in his first term when he was murdered in November 1963, and the circumstances are still shrouded in mystery. But there was no doubt that he would seek reelection, and was almost certain to win. If we accept that Lee Harvey Oswald was *an* assassin, he may stand as a type of the kind of person who, in a virulent context, cannot bear the contrast between his own obscurity and the dazzling yet not properly "legitimate" figure presented to him as the nation's head. Strong Presidents are "usurpers," dictators. The Buchanans are safe: it is the Lincolns who are shot at, though not until the supreme crisis of their particular administration is over: in periods of national emergency, especially wars, notions of usurpation are perhaps held in abeyance. (The other moment of high danger, to judge from the attacks made on Garfield in 1881 and President-elect Roosevelt in 1933, comes when a chief executive is still new to office, and has therefore not demonstrated any impressive claim to legitimacy.)

"Strong" Presidents, in other words, store up trouble for themselves and for their successors. . . . But what genuine alternatives *are* there? Why seek to revive the ancient "Whig" or the anachronistic "Republican" conceptions of the Presidency?

The answer is that some of these old conceptions still possess vitality: in fact, have acquired new vitality. Like the states'-rights view of governmental functions, they are a good deal better than some of the men who have professed them. The Presidency works badly. Among other things it embraces a paradox. The President has at once too much prestige and—in domestic affairs—not enough real executive leeway. His frustrations match those of his countrymen. In the sphere of foreign policy he and the executive branch possess too much capacity to commit the nation to disaster. Liberal advocates of an aggrandizing Presidency now sense uneasily that they have created a Frankenstein: an executive which, in the name of leadership and patriotism, may respond to the demand for spectacular Presidential direction by acting in the only untrammeled way open to it—belligerently.

Perhaps something is to be learned after all from the misgivings of the 19th-century. . . . There are many straws in the wind, signs of a possible profound realignment. There could well now be a retreat from the prevailing assumption that the United States has a universal, messianic involvement in every corner of the globe. The retreat might turn into a new wave of sour isolationism. With guidance it might be diverted into a wholly desirable drawing-in of horns, resulting in a more modest, more legislatively responsible executive demeanor. . . .

The United States too might be a better place if the federal government with its overpublicized White House functioned with more decentralization. Perhaps the need is to take away the still-valid arguments from the Southern states-righters and the reactionaries, and refurbish them as weapons in the liberal arsenal.

The effort is as difficult as it is urgent. The federal government is bound to remain rich, multifarious, and powerful; and . . . the President will still be an equivocal figure, so long as he remains both head of state and head of government. To avoid this disquieting duality it would be necessary to separate the respective roles and entrust them to *two* men. In his early book *Congressional Government*, Woodrow Wilson implied that the governmental function was already more or less in the hands of the Speaker of the House of Representatives. Given the general caliber of 20th-century Speakers, that is not a prospect to enthuse over.

But the difficulties are not insuperable. The federal government can attempt a greater degree of devolution by making (or withholding) financial grants to the individual states. Any reform which links the President more organically with his cabinet and with Congress is a move in the right direction. There is no suggestion that the nation can afford candidates who are morally and intellectually "weak." On the contrary, there is a greater need than ever for candidates of exceptional quality.

If the President were genuinely *primus inter pares*, instead of being elevated to an impossible regality, the nation would have a richer, wider range of possible incumbents from which to choose. The slogan for liberals—by which I mean the several million responsible, articulate Americans who want a decent future for their countrymen and for mankind—should be that politics are too important to leave to the politicians. But there are liberal no less than reactionary clichés; and at the moment some of the apparent reactionaries may be saying the right things, if for the wrong reasons.

5

The Twilight Of The Presidency

George E. Reedy   **THE AMERICAN MONARCHY**

From *The Twilight of the Presidency* by George E. Reedy. Copyright © 1970 by George E. Reedy. Reprinted by arrangement with The New American Library, Inc., New York, New York.

A President cannot have problems which are personal to him alone. His troubles are the troubles of the nation and if they become disastrous, the nation is in peril. It is vital, consequently, to identify those aspects of his position which are most likely to bring him to grief. And the most important, and least examined, problem of the Presidency is that of maintaining contact with reality. Unless a President starts giving thought to this question—and on the available evidence, very few do—immediately following the fine flush of his election victory celebration, he is headed inevitably for trouble.

There are very few warnings to the President-elect that this problem will be encountered. . . . No one comes rushing to him with somber warnings and Dutch-uncle talk. The state of euphoria induced by political success is upon him at the very moment that caution, introspection, and humility are most needed. The process of erosion by which reality gradually fades begins the moment someone says, "Congratulations, Mr. President."

There is built into the Presidency a series of devices that tend to remove the occupant of the Oval Room from all of the forces which require most men to rub up against the hard facts of life on a daily basis. The life of the White House is the life of a court. It is a structure designed for one purpose and one purpose only—to serve the material needs and the desires of a single man. It is felt that this man is grappling with problems of such tremendous consequence that every effort must be made to relieve him of the irritations that vex the average citizen. His mind, it is held, must be absolutely free of petty annoyances so that he can concentrate his faculties upon the "great issues" of the day.

To achieve this end, every conceivable facility is made available, from the very latest and most luxurious jet aircraft to a masseur constantly in attendance to soothe raw presidential nerves. Even more important, however, he is treated with all of the reverence due a monarch. No one interrupts Presidential contemplation for anything less than a major catastrophe somewhere on the globe. No one speaks to him unless spoken to first. No one ever invites him to "go soak your head" when his demands become petulant and unreasonable.

In theory, privilege is accorded to, and accepted by, a man in accordance with his responsibilities. It is a supposed compensation for heavier burdens than those carried by lesser mortals. In practice, privilege is a status that feeds upon itself—with every new perquisite automatically becoming a normal condition of life. Any President upon entering office is startled—and a little abashed—at the privileges that are available to him. But it is only a matter of months until they become part of an environment which he necessarily regards as his just and due entitlement—not because of the office but because of his mere existence.

It is doubtful whether even Harry S Truman —the most democratic of contemporary Presidents—wore the same size hat when he left the White House as he did the day he entered.

This status was built into the American government by the Constitution itself. The founding fathers had rejected the concept of the divine right of monarchy. But when they sat down to write a constitution that would assure freedom, they were incapable of thinking of government in any terms other than monarchy. Someone, they reasoned, must reign and rule. Someone must give orders that could not be questioned. Someone must have ultimate and final authority. Thereafter, their conclusion, although not stated in these terms, was a solution which placed in office a monarch but limited the scope of the monarch's activities.

In the context of the late eighteenth century, the solution was an excellent one. First, the founding fathers analyzed the functions of the government and divided them into three basic categories—the determination of policy, the execution of policy, and the adjudication of disputes arising out of the determination and the execution. The determination of policy was granted to Congress and the adjudication of disputes to the judiciary. The execution of policy they lodged in the hands of the President and within that area they gave him, for all practical purposes, total authority, not so much by affirmation but by failing to set many boundaries on what he could do. They felt that by dividing functions they had created competing power centers within the government and that the competition would prevent any one center from assuming a complete monopoly of power. As an additional safeguard, they limited the term of the President to four years (with an option for renewal if mutually agreeable between the President and the electorate) and gave Congress the authority to remove the President from office, although only on the basis of cumbersome machinery.

The accent was on stability and the firebrands of the Revolution—Tom Paine, Patrick Henry, James Otis—were given short shrift, the traditional fate of revolutionaries when men meet to put the pieces together after the crockery has been smashed. But the founding fathers were neither reactionary nor timorous. They provided —whether consciously, intuitively, or by sheer luck—ample room for the constitutional institutions to react in new ways to new circumstances, as long as the institutions themselves did not change in any fundamental respect. Generally, this objective was achieved by indirection.

The President, for example, was forbidden to legislate or adjudicate, but there was remarkably little definition of his executive powers. As a result, the size of the President in office at any given time determined the extent of what he regarded as his mandate. It was inevitable that strong men such as Jackson, Lincoln, and the two Roosevelts would interpret the absence of specific prohibitions as the presence of specific authority and act accordingly. Harry S Truman even invoked the doctrine of "inherent" Presidential powers to seize the nation's steel mills despite the lack of any legislative authorization —an effort that did not succeed because his popular following at the time was far short of his own supply of willpower.

Of equal importance was the failure to provide a method of determining whether acts of Congress transgressed the permissible boundaries of the Constitution. It was inevitable that such questions would arise and would be regarded differently by men whose function was to represent the popular will and men whose function was to administer a theoretically impersonal body of law. Had the doctrine of judicial review of legislative acts not been established by John Marshall, it is virtually certain that one of his successors would have done so. This particular gap was so huge that it had to be plugged somehow. But it is only a matter of time until a body which has succeeded in acquiring the power to forbid (which is essentially the power of the Supreme Court over Congress and the executive) also takes over the power to direct. This is the process that has made the judiciary a major agency for social change in the past two decades.

The framers of the Constitution had no way of foreseeing the effects of their most important decision—to give the Presidency the functions of both chief of state and chief of government. It is doubtful whether they were aware at the time that the functions could exist separately. They knew that there had to be someone who spoke for all the government. They also knew that there had to be someone to manage the affairs of the country. The concept that these two functions could be separated was alien to their experience, even though the origins of separation were already apparent in the relationship between the king of England and the English prime minister.

They lived in a universe dominated by the concept of ownership and in which management independent of ownership was unknown. The parallel to government seemed obvious in their minds. Furthermore, they were confronted with an immediate and apparent problem which far overshadowed what could then only be abstract ideas of the distinction between reigning and ruling. They had a nation which was being pulled apart by the centrifugal forces of state pride. Their task was to devise some method by which thirteen quite independent political units could be merged into a collective whole. Their problem was to find some counterweight that would balance forces of disunity and induce Americans to think of themselves as citizens of the United States rather than as citizens of Connecticut, New York, Virginia, or Georgia.

The most practical method of unifying people is to give them a symbol with which all can identify. If the symbol is human, its efficacy is enhanced enormously. The obvious symbol was the President—the man who held the role of commander-in-chief of the armed forces; the man to whom all could pay respects as the first citizen. In short, the founding fathers established the Presidency as a position of reverence and, as they were truly wise and sophisticated men, their efforts were as effective as human wisdom could make them.

The consequences of this decision were ultimately inescapable although not immediately discernible. In the simple society of the eighteenth-century United States, it was not easy to conceive of the Federal government in terms of grandeur. An Abigail Adams could hang her washing in the East Room; a Dolley Madison could act as a porter, running to safety with important works of art in advance of British occupation; an Andrew Jackson could invite all his frontier friends into the White House for a rollicking party where they could trample the official furniture with muddy boots and pass out dead drunk on the plush carpets of the Oval Room. But even in a nation as close to the realities of the frontier as the United States, a position established to inspire awe and reverence would inevitably pick up the trappings of reverence. And the trappings could not fail to have an effect upon the man whom they served as a buffer against the rest of the world....

By the twentieth century, the Presidency had taken on all the regalia of monarchy except ermine robes, a scepter, and a crown. The President was not to be jostled by a crowd—unless he elected to subject himself to do so during those moments when he shed his role as chief of state and mounted the hustings as a candidate for re-election. The ritual of shaking hands with the President took on more and more the coloration of the medieval "king's touch" as a specific for scrofula. The President was not to be called to account by any other body (after the doctrine of executive privilege was established). In time, another kingly habit began to appear and Presidents referred to themselves more and more as "we"—the ultimate hallmark of imperial majesty.

These are the conditions under which a President-elect enters office in the modern era. In fact, the aura of majesty begins to envelop him the moment it becomes apparent that the electorate has decided upon its next president. Trusted assistants who have been calling him by his first name for many years switch immediately to the deferential "Mr. President." The Secret Service agents who have been protecting him during the campaign are suddenly joined by their chiefs who, up to that point, have stayed away from him and the other candidates in order to emphasize their neutrality. Members of the Army Signal Corps almost silently appear with communications equipment such as he has never seen before. All these developments take place as he bathes in the universal congratulations that always come to the successful candidate, even from his bitterest opponents. The agents that corrupt the democratic soul creep into his life in the guise of enthusiastic supporters, tactful policemen, self-effacing telephone linemen, and well-trained house servants. Even the members of the press, for a few months at least, regard him with some awe. The apotheosis has begun.

During the early days of a President's incumbency, the atmosphere of reverence which surrounds him acquires validity in his own eyes because of the ease with which he can get results. Congress is eager to approve his nominees and pass his bills. Business is anxious to provide him with "friends" and assistants. Labor is ready to oblige him with a climate of industrial peace. Foreign ambassadors scurry to locate suitable approaches.

It is a wonderful and heady feeling to be a President—at least for the first few months.

The environment of deference, approaching sycophancy, helps to foster another insidious factor. It is a belief that the President and a few of his most trusted advisers are possessed of a special knowledge which must be closely held within a small group lest the plans and the designs of the United States be anticipated and frustrated by enemies. It is a knowledge which is thought to be endangered in geometrical proportion to the number of other men to whom it is passed. Therefore, the most vital national projects can be worked out only within a select coterie, or there will be a "leak" which will disadvantage the country's security.

Obviously, there *is* information which a nation must keep to itself if it is to survive in the present world climate. This means that the number of minds which can be brought to bear on any given problem is often in inverse proportion to the importance of the problem.

The steps that led to the bombing of North Vietnam were all discussed by a small group of men. They were intelligent men—men of keen perception and finely honed judgment. It is doubtful whether any higher degree of intelligence could have been brought to bear on the problem. But no matter how fine the intelligence or how thoroughgoing the information available, the fact remained that none of these men was put to the test of defending his position in public debate. And it is amazing what even the best of minds will discover when forced to answer critical questions. Unfortunately, in this as in many other instances, the need to comment publicly came after, and not before, irreversible commitment.

Of course, within these councils there was always at least one "devil's advocate." But an official dissenter always starts with half his battle lost. It is assumed that he is bringing up arguments solely because arguing is his official role. It is well understood that he is not going to press his points harshly or stridently. Therefore, his objections and cautions are discounted before they are delivered. They are actually welcomed because they prove for the record that decision was preceded by controversy.

As a general rule, the quality of judgment usually varies directly with the number of minds that are brought to bear upon an issue. No man is so wise as to play his own "devil's advocate," and workable wisdom is the distillation of many different viewpoints which have clashed heatedly and directly in an exchange of opinion. To maintain the necessary balance between assurances of security and assurances that enough factors have been taken into consideration is perhaps the most pressing problem of statecraft. The atmosphere of the White House, in which the President is treated constantly as an infallible and reverential object, is not the best in which to resolve this problem. . . .

The real question every President must ask himself is what he can do to resist the temptations of a process compounded of idolatry and lofty patriotic respect for a national symbol. By all the standards of past performance, he should be well equipped to face it. As a general rule, he has fought his way up through the political ranks. He has flattered and been flattered—and the mere fact that he has survived to the threshold of the White House should indicate a psychological capacity to keep flattery in perspective. He has dealt with rich people, poor people, wise men, fools, patriots, knaves, scoundrels, and wardheelers. Had he not maintained his perspective on human beings generally, it is doubtfult that he would ever have received his party's nomination.

But the atmosphere of the White House is a heady one. It is designed to bring to its occupant privileges that are commensurate in scope with the responsibilities that he must bear. A privilege is, by definition, a boon not accorded to other people. And to the extent that a man exercises his privileges, he removes himself from the company of lesser breeds who must stand in line and wait their turn on a share-and-share-alike basis for the comforts of life. To a President, all other humans are "lesser breeds."

Furthermore, a President would have to be a dull clod indeed to regard himself without a feeling of awe. The atmosphere of the White House is calculated to instill in any man a sense of destiny. He literally walks in the footsteps of hallowed figures—of Jefferson, of Jackson, of Lincoln. The almost sanctified relics of a distant, semimythical past surround him as ordinary household objects to be used by his family. From the moment he enters the halls he is made aware that he has become enshrined in a pantheon of semidivine mortals who have shaken the world, and that he has taken from their hands the heritage of American dreams and aspirations.

Unfortunately for him, divinity is a better basis for inspiration than it is for government. The world can be shaken from Mount Olympus but the gods were notoriously inefficient when it came to directing the affairs of mankind. The Greeks were wise about such matters. In their remarkable body of lore, human tragedy usually originated with divine intervention and their invocations to the deities were usually prayers of propitiation—by all that is holy, leave us alone!

A semidivinity is also a personification of a people, and Presidents cannot escape the process. The trouble with personification is that it depends upon abstraction and, in the course of the exercise, individual living people somehow get lost. The President becomes the nation and when he is insulted, the nation is insulted; when he has a dream, the nation has a dream; when he has an antagonist, the nation has an antagonist. . . . It is increasingly evident that the tasks of the Presidency are more and more demanding. It is also increasingly evident that Presidents spend more of their time swimming in boiling political waters. . . .

As a general rule, efforts to remedy the deficiencies of the Presidency center on proposals to bring a greater administrative efficiency to the White House itself. It is held that the problems would become manageable if the President had better tools at his command. In my mind there is a strong suspicion that the problems are no more unmanageable today than they have been in the past. They are, of course, bigger in terms of consequence. But they are still decision rather than management problems. Perhaps a more fruitful path lies in an exploration of the extent to which the atmosphere of the White House degrades a man's political instincts and abilities. Our thoughts should be centered not on electronic brains but on the forces that would foster the oldest, the noblest, and the most vital of all human arts—the art of politics.

First Ladies

Abigail Smith Adams

Abigail Smith Adams, the wife of John Adams, second President of the United States, was a brilliant woman famed for her insightful letters to relatives and friends. Scantily educated herself, she was an outspoken advocate of equal education for women. She is represented here in a steel engraving after a Gilbert Stuart painting.

Mary (Mamie) Geneva Doud Eisenhower

Mary (Mamie) Geneva Doud was long an Army wife before becoming first lady. She married Dwight David Eisenhower on July 1, 1916, the day he became a first lieutenant. Their eight years in the White House was the longest time their busy and mobile military lives had permitted them to live in one place. Mamie was a typical Army wife, following her husband through every step of his career. She performed her hostess role in a variety of places—during the war in soldiers and sailors canteens, and after the war, when her husband became head of Columbia University, as the wife of a university President.

In her own way, Mamie was a style setter during her White House years. The color of her pink inaugural gown was soon to be known as Mamie pink, and her bangs and pillbox hats were copied by millions of America's women.

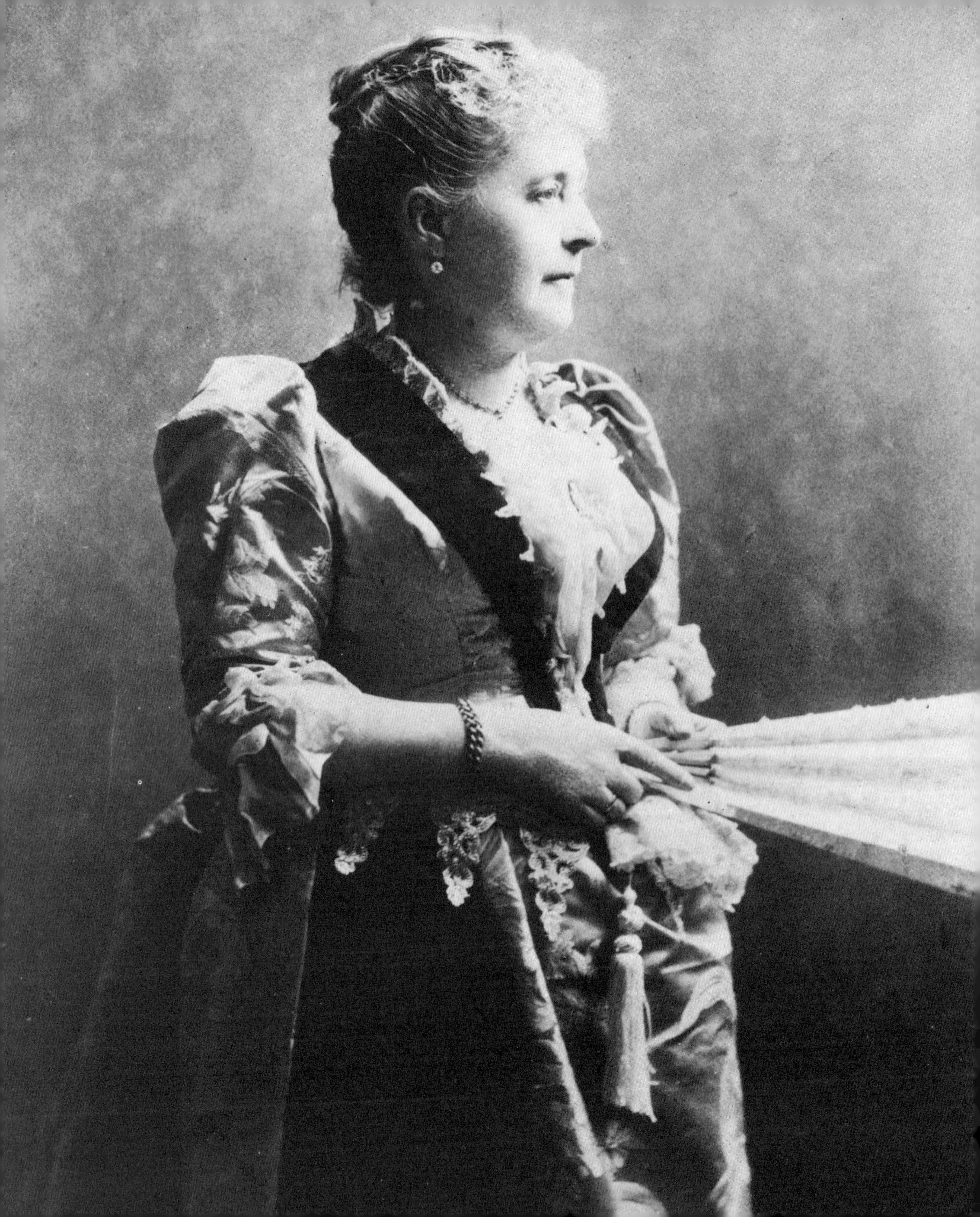

Caroline Livinia Scott Harrison

Caroline Livinia Scott, whose father was president of a small women's college in Ohio, met her future husband, Benjamin Harrison, while he was a student at nearby Farmer's College. They were married in 1853 and had two children, Russell and Mary. Although she suffered from poor health, Mrs. Harrison was an active First Lady. She died two weeks before her husband was defeated for re-election in 1892.

Florence Kling De Wolfe Harding

Florence Kling De Wolfe Harding of Warren, Ohio, was a divorcee, five years Warren Harding's senior. Nicknamed the Duchess, she had a dominating personality and great ambition for her husband. She helped him build the Marion (Ohio) Star into an important newspaper, and was equally persuasive in encouraging him to seek the Presidency.

Florence Harding shared her husband's affections, according to reasonably well-documented gossip, with two other women, Carrie Phillips and Nan Britton, but her marriage survived the boudoir adventures and high-level wheeling and dealing of her husband.

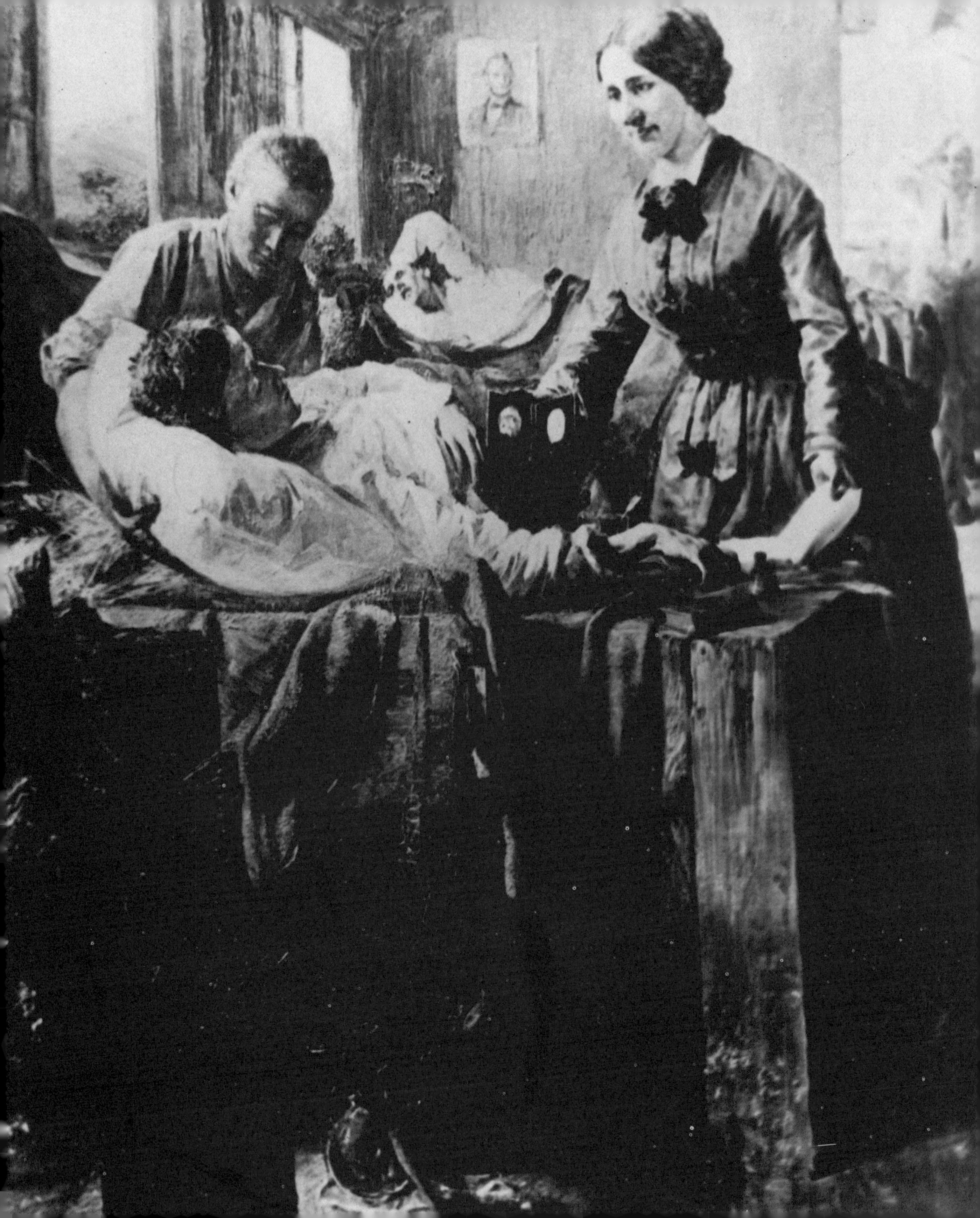

Lucy Webb Hayes

Lucy Webb Hayes, wife of Rutherford B. Hayes, was the first First Lady to have graduated from college. The daughter of a physician, she was a graduate of Ohio Wesleyan. This painting done by C. T. Webber of Cincinnati in 1877, shows Mrs. Hayes in a field hospital at Middletown, Maryland after the Antietam Campaign of September 1862. Her husband, who was a Lt. Colonel in the Union Army at the time, was wounded in the left arm later that same month at the Battle of South Mountain.

Claudia (Lady Bird) Taylor Johnson

Claudia (Lady Bird) Taylor Johnson, wife of President Lyndon Baines Johnson, got her unusual nickname, as legend has it, when a nurse exclaimed of the newborn infant, "Why, she's as pretty as a little lady bird!"

Lady Bird Johnson became a millionaire businesswoman through wisely investing a portion of her inheritance in an Austin, Texas radio station. This was a considerable change from her early small town life in Karnak and Fern, but journalism had been her academic major at the University of Texas, so radio had a natural appeal. Growth and self-improvement were characteristic of her. Lyndon Johnson wanted a "certain" kind of wife; he was not seeking a career woman. She strove to please him by dressing stylishly, taking courses in make-up and fashion, and generally becoming a polished wife of a promising politician.

As First Lady, Mrs. Johnson was a notable success. Her entertaining was informal and friendly and her work on behalf of the beautification programs was substantial.

Mary Todd Lincoln

Mary Todd Lincoln, a banker's daughter from Lexington, Kentucky was born December 13, 1818. An ambitious, nagging, and emotionally troubled First Lady, she suffered from great unpopularity and was even accused of disloyalty to the Union. The life she lived in the White House was a tragic disappointment compounded by the frustrations of having a younger brother, three half-brothers and two brothers-in-law serving in the Confederate Army. Her three half-brothers were killed in Civil War battles fighting against her husband's cause.

Mary Todd, a radiantly pretty child with a winsome smile, was accustomed to getting everything she wanted from her well-to-do parents. In her adult life she rarely got what she wanted—and this proved the greater part of her undoing. When John Wilkes Booth shot Lincoln at Ford's Theatre, the blood of the President spilled on her party gown. She followed as his body was carried across the street to a boarding house, trying frantically but futilely to rouse him from his coma. Tragedy was heaped upon tragedy for her. Tad, her son, contracted typhoid and died; she was pronounced insane after she tried unsuccessfully to kill herself. Mary Todd Lincoln died July 16, 1882, a broken, bitter, and sad woman. She had earlier remarked, "I have no tears left."

Jacqueline Lee Bouvier Kennedy

Jacqueline Lee Bouvier, the daughter of a wealthy Wall Street broker, attended Vassar College and the Sorbonne. Later, while working as an inquiring photographer for the Washington Times-Herald, she met then-Senator John Fitzgerald Kennedy. They were married in 1953. Mrs. Kennedy brought a new style and grace to the Executive Mansion. Her interest in the arts and culture created a sense of drama and excitement on the Washington scene, often referred to as "Camelot," that was in sharp contrast to the blandness of the Eisenhower years. In the photograph shown here, Mrs. Kennedy, the epitome of elegance, is being escorted up the steps of Versailles Palace by President Charles de Gaulle of France.

Dolley Payne Todd Madison

Dolley Payne Todd Madison was a delightful and distinguished First Lady for sixteen years. She fulfilled the role for the widowed Thomas Jefferson during his two administrations as well as for her husband.

The daughter of Quaker parents, she was born in Guilford, North Carolina in 1768 and spent her childhood in Scotchtown, Virginia, where she was noted for her charm and tact. Dolley Madison is best remembered for her legendary exploits in saving White House papers and a portrait of George Washington from the flames when the British burned the Executive Mansion in 1814.

Dolley survived her husband and after his death in 1836, she returned to Washington from their retirement home, Montpelier, the family estate in Orange County, Virginia.

Thelma Catherine (Pat) Ryan Nixon

Thelma Catherine (Pat) Ryan was born March 16, 1913 in a miner's cabin in Ely, Nevada. She grew up on a truck farm in Artesia, California where she "didn't know what it was not to work . . ." Her mother died when Pat was thirteen and she became the surrogate mother for her brothers, kept house and fed farm hands, and helped out in the fields.

At eighteen—with both parents dead and her brothers on their own—Pat began her own education at Fullerton Jr. College. She swept floors and worked as a teller in a bank to earn her way. After assorted odd jobs and much effort, she graduated with honors from the University of Southern California—a teacher of commercial subjects. Her first teaching job led her to Whittier, California and a meeting with a young Quaker lawyer named Richard Nixon.

A woman of uncommon drive and courage, she was at her best in Caracas, Venezuela, when a jeering mob hurled stones and spat at her. Grimly she walked through the confrontation, offered her hand to one of the mob, then proceeded to the protection of bayonet-drawn Venezuelan guards.

It was perhaps appropriate that her inaugural ball gown outglittered any previously worn by a President's wife. This wife of an ambitious though not always victorious politician had earned the right to be resplendent in a dress that required two hundred and sixty hours of labor to embroider.

Anna Eleanor Roosevelt

Anna Eleanor Roosevelt, wife of President Franklin Roosevelt, was a distinguished American in her own right. Renowned as a humanitarian, she was a longtime champion of civil rights for American blacks and worked tirelessly for the young and underprivileged of all races.

A niece of President Theodore Roosevelt, she married her distant cousin Franklin in 1905. After he was crippled by polio in 1921, she became increasingly active on his behalf—making many fact-finding trips for him while he was

Governor of New York and, later, President. After her husband's death, she continued to lead an active and productive life. From 1945 to 1951, she was a delegate to the United Nations General Assembly and became chairman of the United Nations Human Rights Commission. She wrote a syndicated daily newspaper column entitled My Day and was the author of a number of books, including Tomorrow Is Now (1963), published after her death. By the time she died in 1962, Eleanor Roosevelt was acknowledged to be "The First Lady of the World."

Elizabeth (Bess) Virginia Wallace Truman

Elizabeth (Bess) Virginia Wallace was born in Independence, Missouri on February 13, 1885. The daughter of a farmer, she retained the image of a modest, self-effacing housewife even after entering the White House.
Bess Truman married her childhood sweetheart, Harry Truman, in 1919. They had met in Sunday School, when he was seven and she was six. She accompanied the President on his famous whistle-stop tour during the 1948 Presidential campaign, where her husband always introduced her to the crowd as "The Boss."

Angelica Singleton Van Buren

Angelica Singleton Van Buren presided as First Lady for her father-in-law, Martin Van Buren, who was a widower when he entered the White House. The daughter of a South Carolina planter, she had been introduced to Abraham Van Buren by her cousin, Dolly Madison. The two were married in 1838 and lived in the White House for the remainder of Van Buren's term in office.
As this portrait by Inman shows, Angelica Van Buren was a rare beauty. In later years, she was to continue as a trend-setter in New York society.

Martha Dandridge Custis Washington

Martha Dandridge Custis was a young widow of 27 with four children when she married George Washington on January 6, 1759. Their combined property made them, for the times, a very rich couple. She brought to the marriage 17,000 acres and $100,000 in cash.

Mrs. Washington was reputed to have been a good hostess in their Mt. Vernon estate home. She was also a devoted wife who traveled long distances to share her husband's hardships at Valley Forge and Morristown. She organized a women's sewing circle and mended clothes for the troops.

When Washington became President, his wife who he called by her childhood nickname, Patsy, had never traveled beyond Virginia before their marriage, became America's first First Lady. It was a role she did not enjoy, complaining that she felt herself a state prisoner. She died in 1802 and was buried near her husband at Mt. Vernon.

Edith Bolling Galt Wilson

Pictured here at the 1915 World Series are a smiling President Woodrow Wilson and Mrs. Edith Bolling Galt, soon to become his second wife. The President's first wife, Ellen Louise Axson Wilson, died on August 6, 1914, after being First Lady for only seventeen months.

The second Mrs. Wilson came from a distinguished Virginia family and was the widow of Norman Galt, a Washington, D.C. jeweler. A woman of great strength, she was accused by many of assuming power and becoming "acting president" when Wilson's illness prevented him from handling his duties toward the end of his second term. It was she who decided what mail should be brought to the President's attention, read it aloud to him, and dictated the responses she felt he would have made. Some documents were signed with her name. It was apparent that she was a person of considerable executive ability.

Mrs. Wilson died on December 28, 1961, at the age of 89, outliving her husband by twenty-four years.

Part 3
The Growth Of The Office

6
Setting The Precedents

Richard L. Tobin   **KING GEORGE THE FIRST OF THE U.S.A.**

From *Mankind Magazine*, Vol. 3, No. 2 (August 1971), 45–46. Copyright © 1971 by Mankind Publishing Company. All rights reserved.

One-man rule, by whatever name, is as old as mankind. Most primitive societies have had it at one time or another; many still do and so do a few not so primitive. Monarchy is, of course, only one of many forms of one-man rule and there are many kinds of monarchy that run the gamut from absolute control over the life and death of every inhabitant to limited, enlightened monarchy usually tied in with a people's constitution and legislature. Hitler's Germany typified one of the former; the British system the latter.

By whatever name, though, one-man rule has more often been hereditary than elective, a single family being in firm control one generation after another. In most cases of hereditary government the titular head has been called king, and some of the kings of earth have claimed to hold their power through divine right. A few, such as the Japanese emperor prior to World War II, have actually been deified by their subjects.

Monarchy was, by all odds, the rule rather than the exception at the time of the American Revolution. Indeed, the idea of absolutism was so common by the end of the eighteenth century that when the average American colonist spoke of breaking away from his British government he had little idea and great trepidation of government by the people, for the people. In spite of the brave words of the Declaration and of the Constitution Convention that followed it a decade later, almost everyone in North America thought as most Europeans thought in terms of politics. And that meant monarchy supported by a constitutional legislature or more commonly by no truly constitutional procedures at all.

It is not strange then, that in this context, the idea of a king of the United States should gain such momentum in the new nation just unshackled from Europe. Though there was plenty of popular support for a democratic way of government among the leaders and intellectuals of the new United States of America, a vast majority of the landholders and tradesmen, the great middle class, couldn't see democracy for dust. To them it was the most natural thing in the world to turn to a constitutional monarchy with a king.

Those who believe it absurd that George Washington could have been King George I of the

United States know little or nothing about our early history. Six years after the Declaration of Independence, Gouverneur Morris, one of the signators of that document and a patriot whose family name had long been devoted to the cause of the common man, wrote to General Nathaniel Greene of Carolina: "I have no hope that our Union can subsist except in the form of an absolute monarchy." Even John Adams questioned the stability of the democratic way of life and for a long time leaned in the direction of a strong chief executive. John Jay is known to have supported the idea of an American royal family and monarchy. The common people of America, for whom the Revolution was to have been most beneficial, were, as usual, the first to be disillusioned by self-governing democracy, and it was among them, particularly, that cries for a return to monarchy early arose, especially at Washington's headquarters at Newburgh, just up the Hudson River from New York. The forgotten, unpaid, miserable Continental Army felt that only a man of Washington's incandescence would be able to pull the country together—the hoop for the barrel, as a popular song of the time put it. . . .

Even in the newly formed Congress, bills were presented to make Washington, King George I, and others often reflected monarchial sentiments. The Senate, early in its career, actually voted to refer to George Washington as "His Highness, the President of the United States." But though this measure won in the upper chamber, the House voted it down. The thing wasn't settled finally and forever until Washington himself wrote an historic letter once and for all repudiating the idea of an American monarchy.

The campaign to make Washington King George of America probably was ignited in the spring of 1782, when news of the birth of a Dauphin in France created at unprecedented rejoicing in an America grateful for French support during the Revolution. The Continental Army at Newburgh also had a lot to do with the formal petition to make Washington king, for the worn-out heroes of the Revolutionary War were finding it difficult to keep body and soul together, and the use of paper money didn't help matters much. The country was at such a low ebb that its credit was virtually nonexistent, and the pay certificates issued to officers and men alike were, in a phrase that has come down to our time, "not worth a Continental."

In this context, a distinguished Philadelphian and army officer of excellent standing and renown, Colonel Lewis Nicola, wrote a carefully argued letter to General Washington. First, he recited the injustices and disasters that had befallen Washington's heroic troops since Yorktown, dwelling at length on the worthlessness of American currency. Coloney Nicola knew better than most how impotent were the Continental Congress and the Articles of Confederation and, after a series of carefully made points indicating the crying need for a strong head of government, rammed home his vital point to the man who had been first in war but was now hesitant to lead the country politically: "The same abilities which have led us, through difficulties apparently insurmountable by human power, to victory and glory, these qualities that have merited and obtained the universal esteem and veneration of an army would be most likely to conduct and direct us in the smoother paths of peace. Some people have so connected the ideas of tyranny and monarchy as to find it very difficult to separate them; it may therefore be requisite to give the head of such a constitution as I propose some title apparently more moderate, but if all things are once adjusted I believe strong arguments might be produced for admitting the title of King." . . .

From army headquarters at Newburgh, on May 22, 1782, eight weeks after the new British Cabinet had recognized American independence, General Washington replied to Colonel Nicola, and his answer quickly burst the bubble of American one-man rule forever. Here is his letter to Nicola in full: "Sir,—With a mixture of great surprise and astonishment, I have read with attention the sentiments you have submitted to my perusal. Be assured, sir, no occurrence in the course of the war has given me more painful sensations, than your information of there being such ideas existing in the Army, as you have expressed, and I must view with abhorrence and reprehend with severity. For the present the communication of them will rest in my bosom, unless some further agitation of the matter shall make a disclosure necessary. I am much at a loss to conceive what part of my conduct could have given encouragement to an address, which to me seems big with the greatest mischiefs, than can befall my country. If I am not deceived in the knowledge of myself, you could not have found a person to whom your schemes are more disagreeable. At the same time, in justice to my own feelings, I must add, that no man possesses a more sincere wish to see ample justice done to the Army than I do; and, as far as my powers and influence, in a constitutional way, extend, they shall be employed to the utmost of my abilities to effect it, should there by any occasion. Let me conjure you, then, if you have any regard for your country, concern for yourself or posterity, or respect for me, to banish these thoughts from your mind, and never communicate, as from yourself or anyone else, a sentiment of the like nature. I am, sir, your most obedient servant G. Washington."

Less than nine months before the Constitutional Convention of 1787, the issue of monarchy was still raising its head in spite of Washington's letter to Nicola, and though the father of the American republic never again felt it necessary to write a letter like the one to the Philadelphia colonel, he did admit in writing to John Jay just before the Consitutional Convention: "What astonishing changes a few years are capable of producing! I am told that even respectable characters speak of a Monarchial form of government without horror. From thinking proceeds speaking; thence to acting is often but a single step. But how irrevocable and tremendous! What a triumph for the advocates of despotism to find that we are incapable of governing ourselves, and that systems founded on the basis of equal liberty are merely ideal and fallacious! Would to God that wise measures may be taken in time to avert the consequences we have but too much reason to apprehend."

Wise measures were soon taken, and in time. Within two years a nearly perfect union had been established, legalized, and ratified. Its keystone, the Federal Constitution, provided for a President, not a king, and that President was to be elected—and replaceable. A great British prime minister once called the Constitution "the most wonderful work ever struck off at a given time by the brain and purpose of men." Though the average American had been slow to see it that way, that was the direction the new nation would grow. And to the six foot three inch red-headed aristocrat, who had led hungry troops with bleeding feet through to victory and freedom at Yorktown, goes most of the credit. For there is little doubt that George Washington could have been king had he so wished, and his greatest gift to his grateful country is not that he was first in war, but that he deeply understood why the war was fought. He turned the nation that came out of that war onto the irrevocable paths of democracy, not monarchy.

7
Politician And President

Dumas Malone   **PRESIDENTIAL LEADERSHIP AND NATIONAL UNITY: THE JEFFERSONIAN EXAMPLE**

The Journal of Southern History, Vol. 35, No. 1 (February 1969), 3–17. Copyright February 1969 by the Southern Historical Association. Reprinted by permission of the Managing Editor. Footnotes omitted.

[Thomas Jefferson's] exercise of the Presidential office . . . [would] seem to have relevance today. To be sure, the similarity between his situation and that of a President in our time may appear less noteworthy than the contrast. At his first inauguration he walked from his lodgings to the one section of the Capitol that was completed. At his second he rode down Pennsylvania Avenue, accompanied only by his secretary and a groom. He spoke of the "splendid misery" of the Presidential office, but it was not marked by much spendor in his day. As the country is more powerful now, so is the President; and his problems have become so enormous and so complex as to beggar description. No early President assumed such an awesome task. But Jefferson had important functions and problems in common with all his successors. He had to deal with Congress and with foreign governments, while retaining the support of his partisans he had to establish rapport with his constituents, the people of the United States; and at all times he had to maintain the security and essential unity of the country . . .

In his day and for a century thereafter the President was inaugurated on March 4. Unless he should call Congress in special session it would not meet until fall. Jefferson had nine months before first encountering that loquacious body. He designated the period between congressional sessions as a "blessed interim" and spoke with dread of his annual "winter campaign.". . .

Any and every President in dealing with the legislative branch is faced with difficulties imposed by the constitutional separation of powers. . . . Hardly anybody questioned the desirability of the separation of powers at the time of Jefferson's accession. Members of his own party had emphasized it during their years in opposition. That party came into being in reaction against the policies of the leader most conspicuously identified with the consolidation of governmental power, Alexander Hamilton, who was also the only leader of the first rank in this period who clearly favored positive government. Jefferson, whose early public career had centered on resistance to tyranny, could not have been expected to doubt the wisdom of the division of powers; and the circumstances of the delivery of his first presidential message could have been interpreted as a clear sign that he would encroach in no way on the independence of Congress. Indeed, Hamiltonians feared that the era of legislative dominance of the federal structure had returned.

Instead of delivering his message in person, the third President sent it by his secretary, Captain Meriwether Lewis. There were practical reasons for this procedure. He wrote much better than he spoke, and he said he was consulting the convenience of the legislators, as no doubt he was, along with his own. He was well aware, however, that his followers would welcome this abandonment of a ceremony that derived from colonial practices and smacked of royalty. He was making an antimonarchical gesture and disarming potential critics of Presidential authority within his own party in advance.

He himself was convinced that concentration of authority was extremely dangerous. . . . But his experience as war governor of his state, when he had little power, had been traumatic, and he by no means shared the extreme fear of the executive that was written into the early state constitutions. In fact he was as opposed to legislative omnipotence as John Adams and sought to attain balance in government as in personal life. . . .

One of his major functions was in fact legislative. The President has the power to veto acts of Congress, thus exercising a negative influence on legislation. But, while President Washington disapproved two bills, Jefferson, like John Adams, vetoed none. (Franklin D. Roosevelt vetoed 631.) On the positive side, the President was enjoined not only to inform Congress of the state of the Union but also to recommend legislation. The practical question was whether or not he should content himself with doing so in a formal message, and Jefferson concluded that he could not. Summing things up after five years of experience, he said that if he thus limited himself the result would be "a government of chance & not of design." . . .

He stressed the importance of having in the House of Representatives a man "in the confidence & views of the administration" who would see that measures recommended by the President should get a hearing. That such a person should have been at the same time the recognized leader of a legislative body jealous of its prerogatives was certainly not inevitable; it might even have been regarded by constitutional purists as contradictory. After he had ceased to play this dual role John Randolph referred indignantly to "backstairs counsellors," and the President had to be constantly on guard lest he be charged with encroachment on the prerogatives of Congress. Actually, the majority in the House and Senate did not formally elect a floor leader as yet, and Jefferson did not limit his representations to a single person in either case; as a rule he and his cabinet members explained things to the chairmen of the committees to which particular recommendations would be referred. . . .

The business of the House was controlled by the chairmen of committees, who were appointed at this time by the Speaker, Nathaniel Macon. He had named his intimate friend John Randolph chairman of the Ways and Means Committee and thus opened the door of influence to that brilliant and erratic congressman.

Randolph remained as chairman of this key committee after he had ceased to enjoy the confidence and share the views of the administration. Jefferson was confronted with a congressional Establishment that he had no recognized power to control, just as any President is today.

Operating in this constitutional framework and doctrinal atmosphere, he conveyed information to Congress by informal as well as formal means but sought to avoid the impression of bringing pressure to bear on that self-conscious body. Under these circumstances this unusually tactful man could hardly have escaped the charge of being devious.

Despite the difficulties which are inherent in our divided government and which were accentuated by continuing fears of executive power, he was one of the most successful of Presidents in his relation with Congress. Except for James K. Polk, who had a more positive program and was not subjected to the ordeal of a second term, perhaps no other President prior to Woodrow Wilson was equally successful in getting through Congress the measures he favored. His grip weakened toward the end of his administration, and his relations with the legislators were never as harmonious as he would have liked, but he gained from them a remarkable degree of cooperation. . . .

Apparently he did not need to engage in arm-twisting—an operation at which, in fact, he was not adept. As a rule, a clear understanding of his wishes was enough for his supporters. On some highly controversial questions he appears to have deliberately refrained from putting his prestige on the line. The question of the Yazoo claims, on which his own mind may have been divided as the minds of his followers undoubtedly were, is a case in point. On certain other matters he was noncommittal, and he may be criticized for not risking enough. But, as he said privately before his first Congress met, there was wisdom in Solon's remark that "no more good must be attempted than the nation can bear . . ."; and his highly sensitized political antennae warned him against asking too much of a legislative majority which was even more economy-minded that he was. This was not a time when many people expected the federal government to do much. With respect to unmistakable measures of the administration, his legislative record was exceedingly high.

He was no party boss, even on the national level. His political enemies saw his hand in everything, to be sure, but, while he made a special point of keeping himself informed and was always available as a confidant and encourager, he was chiefly concerned to maintain party unity and, besides trying to keep out of party squabbles, he left management to others. On several occasions he suggested to particular men that they run for Congress, but, by and large, he followed a policy of laissez faire. His trust of his followers was too uncritical at times, but it was rewarded by their extraordinary loyalty.

At the outset, and again toward the end of his administration, a pressing problem was that of maintaining essential national unity. His concern over this is abundantly reflected in his first inaugural, in which he said: "We are all republicans: we are all federalists." He had good reason to be troubled by the intransigence of his foes, especially the politicos of New England who had refused to concede his election. He had long been aware of separatist tendencies in the West, and throughout his administration he sought to remove the causes of discontent in that region. This problem did not arise from political differences, for the trans-Appalachian region was predominantly Jeffersonian; and in attempting to solve it he was at no disadvantage because he was the chieftain of a party that had consistently identified itself with Western interests.

The situation with respect to New England was very different. There at the beginning of his administration his followers constituted a weak minority, despised and bitterly resented by the Establishment. He himself cherished no illusion that he could come to terms with this Establishment, which to his mind represented the union of church and state, but he would unquestionably have denied that he was indifferent to the interests of the region and its people as a whole. From the beginning of his Presidency he sought to gain support for his government in New England; and, stimulated and encouraged by him, his party grew greatly in that previously disaffected region until, at the time of the Embargo, it appeared that his policies were injurious to it. He had never been able to crack the Connecticut nutmeg, however, and the bitterness of the Federalist irreconcilables had shown little sign of diminution.

I am not convinced that the dilemma which this situation presented was clearly perceived by Jefferson. The recalcitrance of the hard-line Federalists was a real danger to the Union, but to have destroyed the opposition altogether would have been to create a one-party system. His implacable foes in the land of steady habits and elsewhere among "the wise, the rich, and the good" (as the New England Federalists regarded themselves) viewed him as the head of a party to which they were bitterly opposed rather than as the President of a united country who deserved a degree of loyalty by virtue of his official position....

There is a certain incompatibility between the roles of chief of state and party chieftain; and under our system this basic contradiction can never be fully resolved. George Washington, as he began to be identified with a party toward the end of his administration, became the object of partisan attack instead of the universal praise to which he was accustomed. But, while Washington detested parties and remained above the conflict between them as long as he could, Jefferson was unquestionably a party man and a rarity among Presidents in the degree of his party leadership. I do not believe that he ever lost sight of the national interest, and I am sure that he exercised a moderating influence on his own partisans; but some of the extremists among them pressed him from the left while Federalist die-hards belabored him from the right, and he did not always succeed in maintaining his equilibrium. Opinions may be expected to differ respecting his Presidential performance, but in my judgment he was notably successful during at least three-fourths of it in attaining and maintaining the balance he sought.

Throughout Jefferson's Presidency foreign policy was a sharply divisive issue. In looking back on this period one is impressed with the absence of bipartisanship. It is true that Federalist Senator John Quincy Adams, had favored the Louisiana Purchase, even supported the Embargo, but he was disowned by his own party as a consequence. The opposition of Federalist senators to the foreign policy of "that man" in the President's House was virtually automatic, and foreign diplomats did not hesitate to exploit this division to the advantage of their own countries.

Also, there was some conflict regarding the respective functions and responsibilities of the executive and legislative branches in foreign affairs. Jefferson never doubted that, under the Constitution, the conduct of external affairs was an executive function, and he had had too much experience in the Continental Congress to believe they could be effectively directed by a legislative body or even by one of its committees. As an experienced diplomat, he recognized that premature publicity could easily wreck crucial negotiations. He expected to be granted wide discretion, believing that in no other way could the diplomacy of the country be conducted. When negotiations had been completed, however, or had reached a stage when it seemed safe to report them, he promptly communicated full information to the legislators. One is impressed by the quickness with which important diplomatic documents were revealed. Even when they were communicated in confidence, their tenor soon became widely known. The secrets of the government were often shared with the British minister by Federalist senators, and legislators have been noted for their silence. It would seem that effective diplomacy and participatory democracy are incompatible.

While it appears that the *conduct* of foreign affairs cannot be safely democratized and that delicate diplomatic negotiations cannot be successfully carried on in the white light of publicity, there can be no possible doubt that in a self-governing society, foreign *policy* has to be generally acceptable to the sovereign people. It does not have to be acceptable day by day, and one wonders if the samplings of immediate reactions to particular events as reported on television screens and elsewhere in our publicity-ridden society have any real significance or value. In the long run, however, foreign policy has to be approved. No President ever realized this more fully than Jefferson, to whom popular sovereignty was the distinctive principle of our government. . . .

His foreign policy was brilliantly successful in his first term, when, because of good luck as well as wise foresight, he acquired the province of Louisiana. But his effort to cause the boundaries of this imperial domain to be defined by peaceful negotiation and to acquire West Florida in the process were dismally unsuccessful. And his recourse to economic reprisals in defense of American maritime rights led many of his countrymen to conclude that the cure was worse than the disease. It may be that his inveterate optimism and patriotic zeal caused him in both instances to seek more than he should have expected to gain by formal agreement, and he undoubtedly made tactical mistakes in both cases, but the fact remains that in each of them the course he pursued was an alternative to war. In neither case was his policy thoroughly satisfactory to his constituents; nor has it been generally applauded by scholars who have examined it since his time. . . . But at least we should recognize that at times a President must choose between alternatives no one of which is intrinsically desirable. The only choice may be between a greater and a lesser evil.

Jefferson faced such a situation more than once on the southern border, but the presidential dilemma can be more clearly seen in the better-known circumstances that occasioned the ill-fated Embargo. The grave infringements on American rights in the course of the titanic duel between Great Britain and France would have warranted war against either power, but the Mistress of the Seas was inevitably the greater offender. Perhaps our government asked too much of a country involved in what is regarded as a death struggle, but we may doubt if the American public would have been content with lesser demands. At any rate, diplomacy failed and Jefferson then faced a dilemma. He himself was not entirely averse to war, and at times he seems to have expected it. But there was some question about which country we ought to fight; and, while it would have been logical to fight the British, a war against them would have been bitterly opposed in New England—except possibly in the days immediately following the outrage committed on the *Chesapeake* by the *Leopard*. All the rest of the time war might have been expected to divide the country. We may well doubt if any policy could have met the demands of this situation. A neutral country caught in the cross fire of contending major powers is in a most unenviable situation. Some historians have regarded the Embargo as a noble experiment that failed. As an economic substitute for war it may be described as forward-looking, but it also looked backward to the nonimportation and nonexportation agreements of the American Revolution. It can best be regarded as a choice between alternatives, all of which were unpalatable; and its fate leads one to wonder if human beings are really willing to pay the high price of peace.

An American President today can lead from strength which was only potential in those days, but, like Jefferson, he may be forced to choose between alternatives no one of which is desirable in itself. Accordingly, he may expect to be damned if he does and damned if he doesn't. In an age when wars are waged without being declared and speed is often of the essence, he may have to act without waiting to feel the pulse of public opinion. By so doing he may stay the march of totalitarianism or even save mankind from nuclear destruction; but, on the other hand, he may dangerously commit us. Thus he and our self-governing society with him face a continuing dilemma. He bears a burden of responsibility far greater than that of Jefferson, but his power to control the actions of other countries is sharply limited. We have to view his actions with a keenly critical eye, but in fairness we should be aware of his difficulties. As the architect of foreign policy in a revolutionary age, his lot is not a happy one.

It is now obvious that no President can do much in either the foreign or the domestic field without popular support. Jefferson perceived this more clearly than either of his predecessors had done.... During at least three-fourths of his Presidency he had this to a notable degree. The voices of his political enemies were strident and their tones bitter, but the preponderant majority of his countrymen stood behind him. No doubt this was chiefly because of their approval of policies which were designed to lighten the burdens of ordinary mortals and widen their opportunities, though they did not offer positive benefits of the modern sort. But there can be no question of his enormous popularity; and one cannot help wondering how this could have been attained by this intellectual who loathed crowds, cherished privacy, and built his house upon a mountain. There are numerous references to his amiability, and throughout life he made a fine art of friendship. With rare exception those who knew him well liked him, but few people actually knew him. Besides his two inaugurals and his addresses to Indian delegations, he made virtually no speeches while President; he made no good-will tours, as Washington and Monroe did; and very few of his countrymen, relatively, ever saw him. In our day a President is subjected to indecent exposure, but this one was almost invisible. Employing the language of our own generation we may ask: What was his image, and how was it projected?

In the first place it should be noted that, while no military hero, he was recognized as a distinguished patriot of the American Revolution. He was very fond of referring to the "spirit of 1776," and the jealousy with which he and his friends guarded his patriotic image is shown by the pains they took to meet the charges arising from his conduct and misfortunes as war governor of his commonwealth.

By the "spirit of 1776," however, he meant more than national patriotism, just as he regarded the Declaration of Independence as more than a national manifesto. His contemporaries probably did not identify that document with him personally to the same degree that we do; but I think it safe to say that he was regarded by his followers and many others as the foremost champion of the principles and ideals that are set forth in it.... At times his enemies tried to cast him in the role of autocrat; but only during the Embargo, when the curtailment of economic freedom by governmental action was indisputable, do they appear to have had much success. The role of autocrat did not fit him, and he had none of the manner of a tyrant.

It should not be supposed that his past services to human liberty were forgotten during his Presidency, but the designation that suggests the prevailing view of him was that of "The Man of the People." Actually, the term "democrat" was rarely on his own lips at this time or any other; he called himself a republican—that is, an antimonarchist and a believer in self-government. He called his party "Republican," not Democratic-Republican, as historians have so generally come to do in order to distinguish it from the Republican party of our day. He unquestionably belonged to the intellectual elite of his time, and his manner of life accorded with the practices and traditions of the landed gentry of Virginia to which he belonged by birth and education. The revolt against gentility had not gone as far as it went later, but the fact that a person of his tastes and status should have been hailed as the man of the people does seem surprising.

His enemies had an explanation. They claimed that, besides ignobly catering to the multitude in his policies and public procedure, he affected for political purposes a plainness, even a boorishness, which was unnatural to him personally and unbecoming in a President. These critics had little ground for complaint about the dinners in the President's House. At his generous table senators and congressmen consumed food prepared by a French chef and served by liveried retainers and drank in vast quantity wines that their host had imported. . . .

Unlike his predecessors, he was accessible to visitors at any time—that is, until he set out on his daily horseback ride, unattended by a groom; this was just before his three-o'clock dinner. What was most remarked upon was that he received his visitors, including foreign ministers, in any sort of dress. Why should a cultivated gentleman, occupying the highest post in the country, do such things? . . .

Jefferson's contemporary critics saw demagoguery in it. But these seeming vagaries can be largely explained in more human terms. Elderly widowers, deprived of feminine supervision, often become indifferent to dress; and, except on formal occasions, members of the Virginia gentry showed little concern about their external appearance. (The same has often been said of the Proper Bostonians.) This particular widower, who hated the cold and lived in a big barn of a house, dressed for warmth and comfort during his working hours, and his visitors, including occasional diplomats, had to take him as they found him. He seems to have been well dressed for dinner unless this was merely a family affair. As President, Jefferson was disposed to conduct himself just as he would have at Monticello. Since he was following his own custom, he was not assuming a false front. His dislike of ceremonies of all sorts and of the artificial distinctions that he had observed in royal courts was genuine, but he was well aware of the past objections of his own followers to Presidential formality, and in dispensing with it to the extent he did he may have been putting on something of an act.

No doubt it was fortunate for him that his physical image could not be projected on the television screen. The modern microphone could have made his voice more audible than it was at his last two inaugurals, but his gift was not for speaking. It was for writing, and he projected his personality to his countrymen effectively in his huge personal correspondence. People constantly wrote to him—all sorts and conditions of men—and to an amazing number of them he responded with his own pen. He wrote any number of off-the-record letters to political supporters in all parts of the country who voluntarily sent him information and shared their problems with him. He also discussed vaccination with Dr. Benjamin Waterhouse and gardening with nurserymen and horticulturists, exchanging plants as well as ideas. He was constantly consulted by men of learning and frequently by students, and it would also seem that anybody who had observed something of interest in the natural world or the realm of knowledge of who had invented something he hoped might be useful felt free to communicate with the President of the United States. As one person said, they believed that "the mild and philanthropic *Jefferson*" might be addressed "with the freedom and familiarity of a *fellow citizen & friend*." He did not really have time for what Charles Willson Peale called "the minutiae of the public good," and he received fantastic and ludicrous suggestions, but his countrymen had sensed that he was interested in anything and everything that bore on human happiness and well-being. Certain clerical foes of his in New England called him the "man of sin," but he received many letters and resolutions of thanks from those who had benefited from the religious freedom he had done so much to further. The hundreds of recipients of private letters from his hand had good reason to regard him as not merely a friend to mankind in general but to individual human beings. This was not mass appeal, and communication was painfully slow in those days, but reports of his invariable friendliness got around.

A major reason for his personal appeal, in my opinion, was his genuine respect for human personality. He treated his major associates, especially Madison and Gallatin, not as subordinates but as his peers, rightly believing that they would never take advantage of him. The same cannot be said of the attitude and conduct of General James Wilkinson, and Jefferson was never at his best in dealing with aggressive self-seekers. He could be tough when he thought it necessary, but he may not have thought that often enough. Very many of his correspondents were far from being his peers, except in their human rights, but it would be difficult to find anything condescending or patronizing in his letters to the humblest of them. Though certainly not unaware of the dark side of human nature, he never lost faith in human beings. That faith endeared him to his fellow citizens and constitutes one of the most precious parts of his rich legacy to posterity....

Obviously, the problems of our next President will be magnified many times because of the enormous increase in the size and complexity of everything in the last century and a half. Jefferson lived in what we used to call *the* age of revolution, but our age is far more revolutionary. To study his conduct of the Presidency is to enjoy a richly rewarding and highly educational experience, but no one can rightly expect to find in his record detailed guidance for a President today. Far more memorable than his specific acts, policies, and methods is the spirit in which he conducted his high office. Recognizing the danger of power, he exercised it with notable restraint and was not corrupted by it; and he strove to be to all men, and in the fullest sense, humane. He deserves emulation on other grounds, but in these respects, above all, he offers a shining example to his successors in our generation or any other.

8

Democratizing The Presidency

Wilfred E. Binkley   **THE JACKSONIAN REVOLUTION**

From *President and Congress*, Third Edition, Revised, by Wilfred E. Binkley. Copyright 1937, 1947, © 1962 by Wilfred E. Binkley. Reprinted by permission of Alfred A. Knopf, Inc.

Jackson became the first President since Washington to be chosen in a manner involving Congress neither for nominating the candidate by the congressional caucus nor outright election by the House of Representatives as in the cases of Jefferson in 1801 and John Quincy Adams in 1825. Jackson's election was also practically coincident with the cessation of the choice of presidential electors by state legislatures and with the prevalence of popular election of them. Consequently he may be said to have been the first popularly elected President of the United States and his career in the executive office is strongly colored by his firm conviction that he bore a mandate fresh from the hands of the "sovereign" people. . . .

The place of the President in the American constitutional system may be said to have been the outstanding constitutional question raised by Jackson's eight years in the Presidential office. The Jeffersonian method of achieving mastery through secret influence with Congress had proved transient. Since the Presidency of Jefferson, the American political background had been transformed through the growth of the trans-Allegheny population and the diffusion throughout the older states of the doctrine of popular sovereignty with its practical manifestation in universal, white manhood suffrage. Here was a factor of enormous potency just as certain to leave its impress upon the character of the Presidential office as had the congressional caucus. Nothing had more to do with the rescuing of the Presidency from the hegemony of the congressional caucus and making it peculiarly the people's office, a rallying point of the agrarian and laboring masses. . . .

This transformation of the Presidency from a congressional to a popular agency was not to take place without a gigantic struggle, which came to a head in Jackson's veto of the bill to recharter the second Bank of the United States four years before the expiration of its charter. . . . In the 1820's this bank became extraordinarily unpopular in the rural West through its wholesale foreclosures of mortgaged farm land as a consequence of the severe depression of the early 1820's. Strangely unaware of this animosity, Senator Henry Clay sought to make political capital and perhaps advance his Presidential candidacy by confronting Jackson with a measure rechartering the bank in 1832, four years before the expiration of the charter. If Jackson should decide to veto the bill, Clay believed it would ruin him politically, strengthen the National Republicans, as the anti-Jackson party was now called, and perhaps make Clay the next President.

Jackson decided against the Bank Bill and his veto message is a landmark in the evolution of the Presidency. For the first time in American history, a veto message was used as an instrument of party warfare. Through it the Democratic party, as the Jacksonians were now denominated, dealt a telling blow to their opponents, the National Republicans. Though addressed to Congress, the veto message was an appeal to the nation. Not a single opportunity to discredit the old ruling class was missed. It utilized the bitterness of the state banks against the monster bank, the poor man's envy of the rich, and the nativist prejudice against the foreigners who owned considerable stock in the Bank. So adroitly was it phrased that the common man saw in it the apt expression of his own sentiments. It became a Democratic campaign document and even the National Republicans with the fatuity of reactionaries printed and distributed widely the veto message in the confidence that it would end the political career of President Jackson. Instead it contributed powerfully to his overwhelming re-election.

Half a dozen years before the veto message Marshall, giving the opinion of the Supreme Court, in *McCulloch vs. Maryland*, had declared that Congress had the power to establish the Bank of the United States. With such a precedent the National Republicans were dumfounded by Jackson's arguments in the veto message that the Bank was unconstitutional. . . .

This veto of the Bank Bill . . . contained the famous passage setting forth Jackson's opinion that the three great departments possessed coordinate power to determine questions of constitutionality. It had been contended by the proponents of the bank that since the Supreme Court, in the opinion given in the case of *McCulloch vs. Maryland,* had decided that Congress could constitutionally charter a bank then the opponents ought no longer to raise the question of constitutionality on any bank bill. Webster had said, "One *bank* is as constitutional as another *bank*." That question, it was claimed, should be regarded as settled and no longer debatable. In endeavoring to dispose of this point, the President had declared, "'If the opinion of the Supreme Court covered the whole ground of this act, it [still] ought not to control the coordinate authorities of the Government. The Congress, the Executive and the Court must each for itself be guided by its own opinion of the Constitution. Each public officer swears that he will support it as he understands it, and not as it is understood by others. It is as much the duty of the House of Representatives, of the Senate, and of the President to decide upon the constitutionality of any bill or resolution which may be presented to them for passage or approval as it is for the supreme judges when it may be brought before them for judicial decision. The opinion of the judges has no more authority over Congress than the opinion of Congress over the judges, and on that point the President is independent of both. The authority of the Supreme Court must not, therefore, be permitted to control Congress or the Executive when acting in their legislative capacities, but to have only such influence as the force of their reasoning may deserve."

Such constitutional doctrine drew from the National Republican lawyers of the Senate opposition a prompt and emphatic denial. Webster, alarmed at the threatened specter of tyranny stalking through the land, struck back with the consummate skill of the great advocate.

"According to the doctrines put forth by the President," he declared on the floor of the Senate, "although Congress may have passed a law, and although the Supreme Court may have pronounced it constitutional, yet it is nevertheless no law at all, if he, in his good pleasure sees fit to deny its effects; in other words to repeal and annul it. . . . Statutes are but recommendations, judgments are no more than opinion. Both are equally destitute of binding force. Such a universal power of judging over the laws and over the decisions of the judiciary, is nothing else but pure despotism. If conceded to him, it makes him at once what Louis the Fourteenth proclaimed himself to be when he said, 'I am the State.'"

Webster, in the heat of the debate, exaggerated the danger of despotism and it is almost certain that he misrepresented and may have even misunderstood the meaning of the passage quoted above from the President's message. Jackson lacked capacity for clear and accurate expression of his ideas and on this occasion evidently failed signally to say just what he intended. Close attention to the phrasing in the passage quoted from the veto message reveals that he must have meant to say that the mere fact of Marshall's having given the opinion that the establishment of a bank was within the constitutional competence of Congress did not place Congress and the President under the necessity of considering any and every proposed bill for a bank constitutional. That is to say, the opinion of Marshall placed them under no obligation to recharter the bank and in no manner hindered them from terminating its existence. Congress was still free to exercise its policy-determining function in this field.

Although Jackson here appeared to be defending Congress and the Executive against the assumption of dominating authority by the courts, he was really striking at the attitude of the Senate, which seemed to be seeking to force acceptance of the bill by invoking the compelling power of the Court's opinion. . . .

The National Republicans could not see that after the long eclipse of Presidential power, President Jackson was only vigorously asserting the independence of the Executive and placing the co-ordinate branches of the government in a position apparently more nearly like that intended by the framers of the Constitution. . . .

Martin Van Buren was the intimate friend of President Jackson and had developed a sympathetic understanding of his brusque old chief. He has given an illuminating interpretation of the controversy under consideration. He admitted that the President was not on his guard as to his language when he wrote, "Each public officer who takes an oath to support the Constitution swears that he will support it as he understands it and not as it is understood by others." But Van Buren pointed out that the only reasonable interpretation of the President's meaning was that he had in mind those officers "who singly as was his own case, or in conjunction with others as was the case with some, constituted the three great departments of the government whilst acting in their respective official capacities. . . . The plain and well-understood substance of what he said was that in giving or withholding assent to the bill for the recharter of the bank it was his right and duty to decide the question of constitutionality for himself, uninfluenced by any opinion or judgment which the Supreme Court had pronounced upon that point further than his judgment was satisfied by the reason which it had given for its decision." In short, we might say, President Jackson considered that he had the right in the exercise of his discretionary power to reach the conclusion: "This particular bill which Congress has submitted to me is, in my opinion, not constitutional and I shall accordingly veto it."

Mr. Van Buren maintained that if Mr. Webster was correct in his claim that the final decision of all constitutional questions belongs to the Supreme Court, then "the incumbents of the legislative and executive departments in respect to questions of constitutional power are *ministerial officers only.*" Jackson's words consequently appear to be just the kind of a protest to be expected from the leader of a party claiming to represent the doctrines of Thomas Jefferson. That statesman had expressed himself on this very point a dozen years before the bank veto in words of which Jackson's sound almost like an echo. "My construction of the Constitution," Jefferson explained, "is that each department is truly independent of the others and has an equal right to decide for itself what is the meaning of the Constitution in cases submitted to its action; and especially where it is to act ultimately and without appeal."

President Jackson regarded his re-election in 1832, following the thorough public discussion of his bank veto, as a vindication of his veto and he slowly and deliberately matured the determination to withdraw the public funds from the bank three years before the expiration of the charter. Since Congress had already refused to pass a measure authorizing him specifically to do this, he decided to act through the Secretary of the Treasury under the authority conferred upon that official by the statute chartering the bank. Attorney General Roger B. Taney had advised the President that sufficient authority for such action existed. The particular passage of the charter invoked for the purpose provided that: "the deposits of the money of the United States in places in which the said bank and branches thereof may be established shall be made in said bank or branches thereof *unless the Secretary of the Treasury shall at any time otherwise order and direct,* in which case the Secretary of the Treasury shall immediately lay before Congress, if in session, and, if not, immediately after the commencement of the next session, the reason for such order or direction." Taney claimed that according to the terms of the statute Congress could not remove the deposits but the Secretary of the Treasury could do so.

Before the President could get a Secretary of the Treasury willing to execute his decision on the removal of the government deposits from the bank he had to transfer the incumbent of that office to another department and appoint W. J. Duane who, however, resolutely refused to accept the President's persistent and patient advice on this matter. Dismissing Duane, Jackson then transferred his Attorney General, Taney, to the treasury. Because of the peculiarly close relationship that had always obtained between Congress and the Treasury Department the President's dismissal of Duane in order to force the removal of government deposits appeared to the Whigs a particularly audacious and violent act of executive "usurpation." The astonishment and indignation the Senate had manifested over the bank veto seemed mild indeed when compared with the later wrath and fury of the Whigs at the Executive usurpation of what had long been considered as undoubted congressional prerogative. Jackson was assuming power over the acts of the Secretary of the Treasury which neither the Constitution nor Congress had granted. Not only had Congress assigned the duties in question specifically to the Secretary of the Treasury with the direction that he report his activities in this line directly to Congress, but the Supreme Court in one of its famous decisions had held that Congress could thus assign duties to officers who would then be solely responsible to them for their execution. Thus the existence of the power Jackson was indirectly exercising had apparently been expressly denied by the Supreme Court.

The question at issue now became: Can the President of the United States, through his constitutionally implied power of dismissal, dictate to the Secretary of the Treasury how he shall exercise the discretionary power vested by Congress exclusively in the latter? The dismissal of Duane because he would not obey Jackson and remove the deposits was apparently based on the assumption that this officer was without question subject to the orders of the President. With Jackson's view Congress, and particularly the Senate, could be depended on to take issue. Accordingly, no sooner had Congress assembled in December, 1883, than Henry Clay opened the contest. His first move was a resolution introduced and promptly approved by the Senate, inquiring of the President whether a certain paper reported to have been read at a Cabinet meeting and later published was genuine.

This was the famous paper in which the President had revealed to his Cabinet his determination to have the government deposits removed to state banks. . . . Such an inquiry as Clay's resolution made on the part of either house of Congress in our day respecting a Cabinet meeting would be simply incomprehensible and the resolution becomes intelligible only when considered against a background of almost a quarter of a century of subordination of the Executive to Congress. . . .

When Clay introduced his resolution he took occasion to condemn the governmental revolution in progress in the intemperate language that has been heard in every struggle of Congress with the Executive. "We are in the midst of a revolution," said he, "rapidly tending toward a total change of the pure republican character of our government, and to the concentration of all power in the hands of one man. The powers of Congress are paralyzed, except when exerted in conformity with his will, by frequent and extraordinary exercise of the executive veto, not anticipated by the founders of our Constitution and not practiced by any predecessors of the present Chief Magistrate."

Clay's resolution proved to be a strategic blunder, in fact, a boomerang. Few shrewder American politicians ever lived than Andrew Jackson and he knew how to employ the legal talents and political sagacity of his lieutenants in turning the attacks of his enemies back upon themselves. The Senate resolution proved to be an excellent opportunity to confound the opposition to the President while giving the Whigs an elementary lesson in constitutional law as interpreted by the new political school. In a burning message the President informed the upper house that: "The Executive is a co-ordinate and independent branch of the government equally with the Senate, and I have yet to learn under what constitutional authority that branch of the legislature has a right to require of me an account of any communication, either verbal or in writing, made to the Departments acting as a Cabinet council. As well might I be required to detail to the Senate the free and private conversations I have held with those officers on any subject relating to their duties and my own. . . . Knowing the constitutional rights of the Senate, I shall be the last man under any circumstances to interfere with them. Knowing those of the Executive, I shall at all times endeavor to maintain them agreeably to the provisions of the Constitution and the oath I have taken to support and defend it."

Three months later Clay carried the war against the President a step further by putting through the Senate the famous resolution of censure: "Resolved that the President, in the late executive proceedings in relation to the public revenue, has assumed upon himself authority and power not conferred by the Constitution and laws and in derogation of both."

The President countered the new challenge with a protest to the Senate worthy of the occasion and with a skill that put the Senate Whigs at a disadvantage before the country. He declared that a charge as serious as that made in the resolution of censure called for impeachment, in which case the Senate could act only as judges: "The President of the United States has been by a majority of his constitutional triers, accused and found guilty of an impeachable offense, but in no part of this proceeding have the directions of the Constitution been observed." Of course the President was ignoring the very patent fact that the Senate had resorted to censure instead of waiting for impeachment because Jackson's partisans controlled the lower house and there was consequently not the slightest possibility of getting that procedure in motion.

The President closed his protest with words that exasperated the Whig senators at the same time that they inspired his followers with renewed enthusiasm for their chief. "I do hereby solemnly protest against the aforementioned proceedings of the Senate as unauthorized by the Constitution, contrary to its spirit and to several of its express provisions, subversive of that distribution of the powers of the government which it has ordained and established, destructive of the checks and safeguards by which those powers were intended, on the one hand to be controlled and on the other to be protected, and calculated by their immediate and collateral effects, by their character and tendency to concentrate in the hands of a body not directly amenable to the people a degree of influence and power dangerous to the liberties and fatal to the Constitution of their choice." Thus while Clay and his colleagues were trembling at executive usurpation and threatened despotism the President, with a better understanding of the mood of the American people, struck a more popular chord by raising the specter of a senatorial oligarchy.

It was during these conflicts between Congress and the President that the heterogeneous aggregation and anti-Jackson men came to assume the party name of "Whig." Historically the term carried the connotation of opposition to executive prerogative, particularly on the part of the king, and on the other hand an attachment to parliamentary or, in this case, congressional superiority to the Executive. No doubt the Whigs meant by their name to imply that their opponents were Tories, the "King's Friends," as the party of King George III had been named, friends of "King Andrew the First." These Whigs claimed to be the only genuine disciples of Thomas Jefferson, true exponents of constitutional government with its separated powers and checks and balances. With a sort of strange political blindness the great Whig chieftains had convinced themselves that they were the champions of a popular movement. They were in reality fighting the rear-guard actions of the retreat of the old Republicanism that had begun its career resisting the Hamiltonian system with its executive initiative in legislation, the Republicanism that had culminated in the supremacy of Congress during the administrations of the Virginia dynasty. In a sense these American Whigs, like the English Whigs, constituted an aristocracy and, like aristocracies throughout history, when they could not govern directly, they sought to control the Executive through the legislature.

The debate over Jackson's formal protest against the resolution of censure was long and bitter. . . . The solemnly presented arguments of the Whigs betray their astonishing lack of touch with the main currents of popular opinion. Every one of these conflicts with Jackson reveals their inability to comprehend the character of the democratic revolution in progress. The great Whig statesmen were lawyers, experts in refinements of juristic analysis. Is it too much to suggest that Jackson and his lieutenants with their keen awareness of political realities were better political scientists than Clay and Webster? A profound change had taken place in the very nature of the American body politic in this era so aptly designated, "The rise of the common man." This common man was beginning to look to the one official of the federal government who was not only chosen by his vote but could speak the voice of the people of the whole nation. Clay and Webster had certainly not sensed this change. They could not conceive of the President as a popular representative. To these disciples of John Locke that particular function was, by tradition, by philosophy, by the nature of things, they thought, monopolized by the legislature. When Webster contended that the Senate was standing as the guardian of the people against the tyranny of President Jackson his blindness to reality and his insensibility to the prevailing popular conception of things placed him in a position of almost pathetic absurdity. [And] Clay could not see that in exercising the veto power President Jackson was endearing himself to the people by expressing quite precisely their sentiments. . . .

9

The Presidency And National Crisis: The Civil War

James G. Randall   **ABRAHAM LINCOLN: THE CONSTITUTION STRETCHED**

From James G. Randall, *Constitutional Problems Under Lincoln*, rev. ed., (Urbana, Illinois: Univ. of Illinois Press, 1963), 513–522.

It is indeed a striking fact that Lincoln, who stands forth in popular conception as a great democrat, the exponent of liberty and of government by the people, was driven by circumstances to the use of more arbitrary power than perhaps any other President has seized. Probably no President has carried the power of proclamation and executive order (independently of Congress) so far as did Lincoln. It would not be easy to state what Lincoln conceived to be the limit of his powers. He carried his executive authority to the extent of freeing the slaves by proclamation, setting up a whole scheme of state-making for the purpose of reconstruction, suspending the *habeas corpus* privilege, proclaiming martial law, enlarging the army and navy beyond the limits fixed by existing law, and spending public money without congressional appropriation. Some of his important measures were taken under the consciousness that they belonged within the domain of Congress. The national legislature was merely permitted to ratify these measures, or else to adopt the futile alternatives of refusing consent to an accomplished fact. The first national use of conscription, in connection with the Militia Act of 1862, was an instance of Presidential legislation. [In addition,] Lincoln or those acting under his authority exercised judicial functions in regions under martial law, in Southern territory under Union occupation, in the application of military justice, in the performance of quasi-judicial functions by executive departments, and in the creation of "special war courts" such as the "provisional court of Louisiana." It thus appears that the President, while greatly enlarging his executive powers, seized also legislative and judicial functions as well.

Lincoln's view of the war power is significant. He believed that rights of war were vested in the President, and that as President he had extraordinary legal resources which Congress lacked. For example, he promulgated the "laws of war" to regulate the conduct of the armies; and in vetoing the Wade-Davis bill of 1864 he questioned the constitutional competency of Congress to abolish slavery in the States at a time when his own edict of emancipation had been in force for eighteen months. Lincoln tended to the view that in war the Constitution restrains Congress more than it restrains the President. Yet the view of the Supreme Court was that Congress may exercise belligerent powers and that in the use of these powers over the enemy the restraints of the Constitution do not apply. Lincoln's view, under pressure of severe circumstance, led naturally to that course which has been referred to as his "dictatorship"; and, as illustrated in the *Prize Cases*, it produced uncertainty as to the legality of the war. Though the validity of Lincoln's acts was sustained by a majority of the court—which could hardly have decided otherwise on so vital a political question—yet four dissenting judges held that the President's action alone was not sufficient to institute a legal state of war. Lincoln's plea in defense, to the effect that his acts within the legislative domain could be legalized by congressional ratification, could hardly be accepted as consistent with the constitutional separation of powers; and this whole phase of the President's conduct illustrates not so much a permanently acceptable principle, but rather Lincoln's ability to retain popular confidence while doing irregular things. It should be added that Lincoln excelled in human reasonableness, and that his character included not only a readiness to act in an emergency, but also a high regard for the rule of law.

In all this extension of governmental power there was a noticeable lack of legal precision. A tendency toward irregularity may be observed as a characteristic of the period, in military and civil administration, in legislation, and in legal interpretation. Congress did its work loosely and various of its laws were never carried out; while others produced bewilderment in the officers who sought to apply them. The Southern states were taxed as if part of the United States; yet the property out of which such tax must be paid was declared confiscable as belonging to enemies. The Unionist government of Virginia was considered competent to authorize the disruption of the state; but later this same government (removed from Wheeling to Alexandria) was denied representation in Congress and rejected as the instrument of reconstruction. Eight states of the former Confederacy, after assisting in ratifying the antislavery amendment of the Constitution, were treated as outside the Union. Legal interpretation in the 'sixties often smacked of sophistry—so much so that to many men an open confession of unconstitutionality appeared preferable to the labored reasoning that was all too common. Much of the legal inconsistency arose from confusion as to what the war was, whether it was extramural or within the family. Was the government facing something like a magnified Whiskey Insurrection, or was it dealing with war in the international sense? Confronted with this dilemma, the Supreme Court adopted the convenient and practical solution of accepting both alternatives.

The conflict was defined as both a public war and a rebellion, with the result that in Southern territory the United States claimed both belligerent and municipal powers. Many bootless and mystifying discussions resulted from this acceptance of two inconsistent viewpoints.

Yet there was nothing more natural than that these two opposite theories of the war should both be adopted. As to the insurrectionary theory, its adoption resulted from the government's unwillingness to accept disunion as justified and to give up federal sovereignty in the South; while the recognition of the struggle as a public war arose from the practical necessity of dealing with a nation in arms as a regular belligerent. The existence side by side of two opposing legal principles is understandable if we remember that the insurrectionary theory was not in fact applied as against Southern leaders and their adherents. They were not held personally liable as insurrectionists as were the leaders of the Whiskey Insurrection; instead, the Confederacy was in practice treated as a government with belligerent powers.

If we were to ask how far our usual constitutional checks operated during the Civil War to prevent an extreme use of power, we would find that neither Congress nor the Supreme Court exercised any very effective restraint upon the President. Congress specifically approved the President's course between April and July, 1861; and, as to the *habeas corpus* question, after two years' delay, Congress passed an ambiguous law which was at the same time interpreted as approving and disapproving the doctrine that the President has the suspending power. The net effect, however, was to support the President; and immunity from prosecution was granted to officers who committed wrongs during the suspension. It is true that the Habeas Corpus Act of 1863 directed the release of prisoners unless indicted in the courts. This was equivalent to saying that the President's suspension of the privilege, which was authorized by this act, was to be effective in any judicial district only until a grand jury should meet. On paper this law radically altered the whole system regarding political prisoners, making arbitrary imprisonment illegal after grand juries had examined the prisoners' cases. The significant fact, however, is that the law was ineffective. It did not, in fact, put an end to extra-legal imprisonments; nor did it succeed in shifting the control of punishments from executive and military hands to judicial hands.

As to the courts, a careful study will show that they did not function in such a way as to control the emergency. In dealing with disloyal practices, the courts played a passive rather than an active role. They dealt in a hesitating way with cases that were brought to them; but the President, through the Attorney General and the district attorneys, controlled the prosecutions, and where it appeared that treason indictments were being pushed toward conviction, the administration at Washington showed actual embarrassment at the government's success. Its way of dealing with dangerous citizens was not by prosecution in the courts, but by arbitrary imprisonment, followed by arbitrary release. The terrors of the old treason law proving unsuitable to the emergency, its penalty was softened; but even the softened penalty was not enforced. There is a striking contrast between the great number of arbitrary arrests and the almost negligible amount of completed judicial action for treason, conspiracy, and obstructing the draft. It was widely argued that the courts could not deal with the emergency, and that this inability justified an extraordinary extension of military power.

The Supreme Court of the United States did not, during the war, exert any serious check upon either Congress or the President. In the *Prize Cases* the court approved Lincoln's acts in the early months of the war. Such an extreme measure as confiscation was upheld by the court, though its validity, both in the international and the constitutional sense, was seriously questioned. It was not the Supreme Court, but Chief Justice Taney, . . . who denounced the President's suspension of the *habeas corpus* privilege. After the war, it is true, the court, in the Milligan case, declared a military régime illegal in regions remote from the theater of war; but while the war was in progress the court had declined to interfere with the action of a military commission in a similar case, that of Vallandigham. On the whole it appears that, while extreme measures were being taken, neither Congress nor the courts exerted any effective restraint. Instead of the "rule of law" prevailing, men were imprisoned outside the law and independently of the courts; and governmental officers were given a privileged place above the law and made immune from penalties for wrongs committed.

This is one side of the picture. There is, however, another side; and we must note certain factors which at least partly redeemed the situation. The greatest factor, perhaps, was the legal-mindedness of the American people; and a very great factor was Lincoln himself. His humane sympathy, his humor, his lawyerlike caution, his common sense, his fairness toward opponents, his dislike of arbitrary rule, his willingness to take the people into his confidence and to set forth patiently the reasons for unusual measures—all these elements of his character operated to modify and soften the acts of overzealous subordinates and to lessen the effect of harsh measures upon individuals. He was criticized for leniency as often as for severity. Though there were arbitrary arrests under Lincoln, there was no thoroughgoing arbitrary government. The government smarted under great abuse without passing either an Espionage Act or a Sedition Law. Freedom of speech was preserved to the point of permitting the most disloyal utterances. While a book could be written on the suppression of certain newspapers, the military control of the telegraph, the seizure of particular editions, the withholding of papers from the mails, and the arrest of editors, yet in a broad view of the whole situation such measures appear so far from typical that they sink into comparative insignificance. There was no real censorship, and in the broad sense the press was unhampered though engaging in activities distinctly harmful to the government. As to Lincoln's attitude in this matter, it should be remembered that in general he advised non-interference with the press, and that he applied this policy prominently in the case of the Chicago *Times*.

To suppose that Lincoln's suspension of the *habeas corpus* privilege set aside all law would be erroneous. The suspension was indeed a serious matter; but men were simply arrested on suspicion, detained for a while, and then released. The whole effect of their treatment was milder than if they had been punished through the ordinary processes of justice. As to the military trial of civilians, it should be noticed that the typical use of the military commission was legitimate; for these commissions were commonly used to try citizens in military areas for military crimes. Where citizens in proximity to the Union army were engaged in sniping or bushwhacking, in bridge burning or the destruction of railroad or telegraph lines, they were tried, as they should have been, by military commission; and this has occasioned little comment, though there were hundreds of cases. The prominence of the cases of Vallandigham and Milligan should not obscure the larger fact that these cases were exceptional: in other words, the military trial of citizens for non-military offensses in peaceful areas was far from typical. It was thus a rare use of the military commission that was declared illegal in the Milligan case.

Legally, the Civil War stands out as an eccentric period, a time when constitutional restraints did not fully operate and when the "rule of law" largely broke down. It was a period when opposite and conflicting situations coexisted, when specious arguments and legal fictions were put forth to excuse extraordinary measures. It was a period during which the line was blurred between executive, legislative, and judicial functions; between state and federal powers; and between military and civil procedures. International law as well as constitutional interpretation was stretched. The powers grasped by Lincoln caused him to be denounced as a "dictator." Yet civil liberties were not annihilated and no thoroughgoing dictatorship was established. There was nothing like a Napoleonic *coup d'état*. No undue advantage was taken of the emergency to force arbitrary rule upon the country or to promote personal ends. A comparison with European examples shows that Lincoln's government lacked many of the earmarks of dictatorial rule. His administration did not, as in some dictatorships, employ criminal violence to destroy its opponents and perpetuate its power.

It is significant that Lincoln half expected to be defeated in 1864. The people were free to defeat him, if they chose, at the polls. The Constitution, while stretched, was not subverted. The measures taken were recognized by the people as exceptional; and they were no more exceptional than the emergency for which they were used. Looking beyond the period called "reconstruction," the net effect, as Lincoln had said, was not to give the nation a taste for extreme rule any more than a patient, because of the use of emetics during illness, acquires a taste for them in normal life. In a legal study of the war the two most significant facts are perhaps these: the wide extent of the war powers; and, in contrast to that, the manner in which the men in authority were nevertheless controlled by the American people's sense of constitutional government.

10

The Presidency And National Crisis: The Depression

Emmet John Hughes   **FDR: THE HAPPIEST WARRIOR**

From *Smithsonian*, Vol. 3, No. 1 (April 1972), 30–33. Copyright Smithsonian Institution, 1972.

Less than a fortnight after Franklin D. Roosevelt's inauguration in 1933, William Allen White was writing to historian Allan Nevins: "My feeling about Roosevelt [is] that it is not so much what he does as the way he does it. The people will forgive mistakes. They will not forgive inaction, debate, cowardice, dilettante hesitation, splitting hairs."

Months before, FDR had given the nation, immediately upon his nomination, a clear sign of his sense of the *way* to do things politically—and dramatically. Discarding the venerable ritual of all previous Presidential nominees—frozen in a pose of silence, until formally advised of their selection some weeks later—he had flown to the Democratic Convention in Chicago to become the first Presidential nominee ever to deliver a speech of acceptance in person. He left the delegates happy and hoarse from cheering his vow: "I pledge you, I pledge myself, to a new deal for the American people." And while his future biographers might debate the merits of many aspects of the New Deal, all would have to agree that, after him, the Presidency itself could never be quite the same.

Roosevelt's Presidential style was not unstudied, for he and his counselors shared an almost joyous sense of political theater. "No cosmic dramatist," Robert E. Sherwood said long after, "could possibly devise a better entrance for a new President—or a new Dictator, or a new Messiah—than that accorded to Franklin Delano Roosevelt.... Hereberet Hoover was, in the parlance of vaudeville, 'a good act to follow.' Roosevelt rode in on a wheel chair instead of a white horse, but the roll of drums and the thunderclaps which attended him were positively Wagnerian...." The political setting was perfect, indeed, for letting a President loose. "The whole country is with him, just so he does something," as Will Rogers said. "If he burned down the Capitol, we would cheer and say, 'Well, we at least got a fire started anyhow.'"

This sort of franchise for leadership was not wasted on a Roosevelt. He took due note of it, and gave soft warning of ventures to come. One declaration in his first inaugural sounded deceptively innocent: "Our Constitution is so simple and practical that it is possible always to meet extraordinary needs by changes in emphasis and arrangement without loss of essential form." In plainer words, this President was ready at once to reach for the joker in the deck of Constitutional powers.

To rally "the credulous crowd" so distrusted by Hoover, FDR relied on the readiest weapons—his own words—with the cry, "The only thing we have to fear is fear itself." An aphorism that was more a sound than a thought, it nonetheless was delivered with a zest that exhilarated the same millions of Americans who would have discarded it, if murmured by a Hoover, as one more reason to suspect their President of mindless euphoria. With the soar of slogans and the series of "fireside chats" to the nation, Roosevelt courted and mastered the press that had left Hoover so estranged. *The New York Times'* Arthur Krock judged him the shrewdest reader of newspapers he had ever seen in the Oval Office. Welcoming direct oral questions in press conference, despite the nervous disapproval of his own advisers, he came close to mesmerizing the correspondents with his commanding personality. As Leo Rosten later recalled: "His answers were swift, positive, illuminating.... He was lavish in his confidences and 'background information.' He was informal, communicative, gay."

But the apparent political magic was not wrought by words alone. Quite as swiftly, there came the astonishing array of New Deal proposals that sent the 73rd Congress into 100 days of frenzy. The sequence began with an emergency banking bill dispatched with such speed that it was never properly printed; rushed to Capitol Hill in some half-dozen typewritten texts, bearing penciled notes and corrections, it passed the House of Representatives in less than 40 minutes.

Headline writers could barely keep pace with lawmakers: AAA subsidies to farmers, NRA codes for business, relief for unemployed, loans for homeowners, safeguards of "Truth in Securities," promises of the Tennessee Valley Authority. Amid the Congressional fireworks, some Senators fretted over the long-range implications of this carnival of Presidential initiatives. But Harry Hopkins, who would become Roosevelt's closest counselor, once snapped the retort: "People don't eat 'in the long run.' They eat every day."

Hopkins' words caught Roosevelt's spirit of relentless pragmatism. "Let's concentrate upon one thing," he said to Secretary of Commerce Daniel C. Roper, "save the people and the nation and, if we have to change our minds twice every day to accomplish that end, we should do it." He told the White House press corps that he fully intended to play the Presidential role like a football quarterback, unburdened by any rigid game plan, since "future plays will depend on how the next one works." This was the kind of talk that long since had driven Hoover, with a rare flash of wit, to call his successor a "chameleon on plaid." And it impelled H. L. Mencken to report of Roosevelt: "If he became convinced tomorrow that coming out for cannibalism would get him the votes he so sorely needs, he would begin fattening a missionary in the White House backyard come Wednesday."

Both the exuberance of FDR and the exasperation of his critics celebrated, with opposite feelings, the driving force of the New Deal. At its heart, as Richard Hofstadter later observed, "there was not a philosophy but a temperament." Once asked by a reporter to state his philosophy, Roosevelt jauntily described himself as "a Christian and a Democrat—that's all." Such nonchalance only increased the torment of his opponents. They might hope to expose an obnoxious "philosophy," but how fight an insidious "temperament?"

This President's sovereign purpose was not to create a national program, but to quicken a national mood. On his renomination in 1936, he raised a toast to his own first term: "Better the occasional faults of a government that lives in a spirit of charity than the constant omissions of a government frozen in the ice of its own indifference." This confident self-absolution—and the popular acceptance of it—allowed FDR to practice his political artistry, shifting speed, changing course, swerving without breaking loose from the trust of most of the electorate. He could proclaim in the mid-1930s America's perpetual neutrality, yet stand forth in the 1940s as the happiest warrior of the Western world. He could pursue, as late as 1935, economic policies that left labor leaders in a fury, yet convert these same leaders into a dedicated Democratic coalition.

The audacity and inventiveness of this Presidential style accomplished something more important than the political endurance of Franklin Roosevelt: It made probable the survival of the two-party system of government. Even as FDR was being attacked for subverting the system he was, in fact, saving it. The economic crisis at the end of the 1920s had driven not merely the impoverished and jobless, but also a legion of liberals and intellectuals, to despair of a political solution. The most impassioned liberal critics—from John Dewey and Stephen Vincent Benét to Reinhold Niebuhr and Lewis Mumford—had announced the death of the "old politics" and dismissed Roosevelt as a sign of all that was vain and gone. To Heywood Broun, he had been no more than "the corkscrew candidate." To Walter Lippmann, he had appeared "a pleasant man . . . without any important qualifications for the office." Yet, by 1939, Harold Laski saluted Roosevelt: "He has dramatized the issues upon which men know that their lives depend."

This achievement might be judged this President's greatest service: the holding of the wide American audience to witness the repertoire of programs performed by a versatile democracy—in a theater that seemed afire. There was no undue arrogance in Roosevelt's boast to Orson Welles that they were the two best actors in the nation.

11
President vs. Congress

THE CRACK IN THE CONSTITUTION

From *Time*, Vol. 101, No. 3 (January 15, 1973), 12–17. Reprinted by permission of *Time, The Weekly Newsmagazine;* Copyright Time Inc.

The U.S. is facing a constitutional crisis. That branch of government that most closely represents the people is not yet broken, but it is bent and in danger of snapping. A Congress intended by the framers of the Constitution to be the nation's supreme policy setter, lawmaker and reflector of the collective will has been forfeiting its powers for years. Now a President in the aftermath of a landslide seems intent upon further subordinating it and establishing the White House ever more firmly as the center of federal power.

Whatever the merits of Richard Nixon's intentions in trying to hold down federal spending or seeking peace in Vietnam in his own way, his actions represent, among other things, a serious challenge to Congress as an institution. In Vietnam, he has mined harbors and turned the massive bombing on and off like a spigot with no advance consultation with Congress and with explanation, if at all, only after the fact. He has vetoed congressional appropriations, which is his right. But he has also ignored Congress when it overrode his veto, refusing to spend the money appropriated—which is not his clear right. He has used a brief recess of Congress to "pocket veto" bills, extending a power intended only as an end-of-session action. Even as he centralizes more powers of the executive branch within his White House staff, he has drawn a cloak of executive privilege around his men, refusing to allow key decision makers to be questioned by congressional committees. The trend could be ominous for the future of representative government.

As the 93rd Congress convened, there were signs that the lawmakers are finally aroused, determined to meet the White House challenge. While Nixon had his landslide, 96% of incumbent congressmen seeking re-election and 80% of such senators also won. Predominantly Democratic, they feel they have a mandate of their own.

Although the institutional integrity of Congress is more than a partisan concern, the Democratic leaders of both chambers—often criticized for their meekness in letting their powers erode—sounded especially angry. "If there is one mandate to us above all others," Senate Majority Leader Mike Mansfield told the Senate Democratic caucus, "it is to exercise our separate and distinct constitutional role in the operation of the federal government. The people have called for the reinforcement of the checks and balances." House Speaker Carl Albert similarly vowed to "work harder than I have ever worked in my life . . . to safeguard the constitutional role of the House as a strong and influential branch of our national government."

More concretely, members of both houses expressed stronger sentiment than ever to cut off funds for the Vietnam war unless Nixon quickly negotiates peace. Indignant at Nixon's bombing tactics while Congress was in adjournment, Mansfield proposed that it never again adjourn sine die, retaining instead the right to call itself back into special session—a brusque indication that Mansfield does not trust Nixon. Rather than waiting for the President to present his legislative requests, Mansfield and Albert both listed priorities of their own—mainly bills that Nixon had vetoed last year.

Turning to the judicial branch for help, more than 20 senators, including such fiscal conservatives as Mississippi's James Eastland and John Stennis, signed a brief asking a federal court to force Nixon to spend impounded highway trust funds, as demanded by the state of Missouri. North Carolina Senator Sam Ervin, the Senate's leading constitutional expert, declared that the Constitution gives "the power of the purse exclusively to Congress," and that Presidential impounding of funds is "contemptuous" of both the the Congress and the Constitution.

These new demands that Congress reassert itself only dramatize how far the national legislature has fallen; those lost powers were once taken for granted as congressional prerogatives. Nor can the protests be considered merely the customary complaint of the out party over the fact that the other party controls the White House. The decline of Congress began years ago.

Yet a further challenge to congressional rights was posed by Nixon last week as he shifted the powers of key Cabinet members in order to present as almost a *fait accompli* a reorganization of the executive branch that Congress has so far declined to approve. He elevated three of his Cabinet appointees to the title of White House Counsellor, and gave them broader authority. Caspar W. Weinberger will not only be HEW Secretary but will also supervise all of the "human resources" functions now scattered in various departments. James T. Lynn, the HUD Secretary, will administer all community-development programs, and Earl Butz, Secretary of Agriculture, has a new mandate over all "natural resources" activities. Democratic Senator Abraham Ribicoff has warned that any attempt by the President to reorganize the executive branch by decree poses a constitutional issue.

In comparison with other national assemblies, Congress still stands out as relatively stable and more representative than most. Tennessee's Republican Senator William Brock may be right in calling it "one of the most remarkable institutions known to man," and Ervin may not be off base in terming it "the most powerful political legislative body on the face of the earth." Indeed, the individual quality of senators and congressmen has never been higher. Yet in relation to the Presidency and within the unique American system of balanced arms of government, Congress has been failing. It no longer effectively checks the President, as required by the Constitution. . . .

In its earliest days, Congress had less cause to quarrel with the White House; elected indirectly by what was then a truly independent electoral college, the President existed almost solely to carry out the congressional will. He was regarded as a national administrator, and did not even dare veto a bill he personally opposed unless he believed that signing it would violate his oath to uphold the Constitution. The early fights came instead between the congressmen, elected by popular vote in their home districts, and the senators, selected by state legislatures.

The House may have been, as De Tocqueville said, "remarkable for its vulgarity and its poverty of talent." But it was dominant, having the sole power to initiate revenue legislation and impeach federal officials, including the President. The Senate's role, as Alexander Hamilton described it, was to "correct the prejudices, check the intemperate passions and regulate the fluctuations" of the more democratic House. Actually, the Senate was generally too cowed by the popular clout of the House—and too conceited—to object. It was largely the House, through its influential Speaker Henry Clay, that led the U.S. into the War of 1812—despite the reluctance of President James Madison. Clay was the kind of autocrat who, upon leaving a party at sunrise and being asked how he could preside over the House that day, replied: "Come up, and you shall see how I will throw the reins over their necks."

The erosion of House dominance began with the grass-roots movement that elected Andrew Jackson in 1828. Jackson conceived the argument that he was the only representative of all the people. He also introduced patronage, thereby enhancing the role of the Senate, which alone had the right to approve or reject Presidential appointees. The great debates over slavery that preceded the Civil War were staged in the Senate rather than the House, which was fragmented over the issue. Yet even Abraham Lincoln, who emancipated slaves by fiat, sometimes deferred to Capitol Hill. Said he: "Congress should originate, as well as perfect, its measures without external bias."

The Civil War's divisions helped create a strong two-party system in which a succession of powerful House Speakers used positions of party leadership to restore the supremacy of that chamber. These men—first James G. Blaine, then Samuel J. Randall, John G. Carlisle, and finally Tom Reed—appointed committee chairmen, dictated legislative priorities, and then determined the fate of their bills by the simple power of whom to recognize on the floor. By 1890, Reed was so contemptuous of the White House that he spurned presidential invitations to discuss his congressional plans. It was Reed who told a colleague in 1892: "I have been 15 years in Congress and I never saw a Speaker's decision overruled, and you will never live to see it either." . . .

The first serious 20th century assault on congressional power was made by Theodore Roosevelt, who took the novel step of outlining his own Square Deal program, although he had no great success in getting it enacted. Without asking Congress, he intervened to protect the Panama Canal Zone from Colombian forces, boasting later: "I took the Canal Zone and let Congress debate, and while the debate goes on, the Canal Zone does too." Yet when his successor, President Taft, had the temerity to have a bill drafted and presented to Congress, House Democrats haughtily objected to the notion that they should consider any legislation "drawn at the instance and aid of the President and declared to be the President's bill."

Woodrow Wilson was the first President to enjoy much success with a domestic legislative program of his own creation. But in foreign affairs, the field now so completely a Presidential province, he was humiliated by the Senate's post-World War I rejection of his proposed League of Nations. Complained Wilson bitterly: "Senators have no use for their brains, except as knots to keep their bodies from unraveling." No President thereafter was able to mount a serious challenge to Congress until Franklin Roosevelt, who was aided immensely by the crisis urgencies of the Depression and World War II. Roosevelt appealed directly to the people in his fireside chats; radio, and later television, did much to focus the nation's attention on the presidency.

The notion of the Congress as the originator of legislation was reversed by Roosevelt, who began summoning Democratic leaders of both chambers to his office for weekly instructions. This made them political lieutenants of the President. Yet Congress could rebel, as when he tried to pack the Supreme Court. Strong congressional leaders still carried heavy weight after F.D.R., notably Lyndon Johnson in the Senate and Sam Rayburn in the House, but they held a more cooperative attitude toward the White House. Declared Rayburn at one point: "I haven't served *under* anybody. I have served *with* eight Presidents."

With the outbreak of World War II, the President became a dominant international figure, and Congress assumed more and more the status of acolyte. The cataclysmic cloud of the atomic bomb immeasurably enhanced the life-and-death powers of the President in world affairs. Although there had been some legislative protests when various Presidents had ignored the constitutional war-making powers of Congress by sending troops briefly into Latin American republics in the 1920s, there was little complaint when Harry Truman committeed U.S. forces to Korea and Dwight Eisenhower ordered Marines to Lebanon. John Kennedy kept Congress ignorant of his plans to invade Cuba, and Lyndon Johnson merely informed Congress that he was sending troops in huge numbers into Vietnam. The Gulf of Tonkin resolution, giving Johnson a free hand and later repealed under President Nixon—but without any practical effect in either case—only illustrated the congressional impotence in matters of war. For practical purposes, Presidents have moved away from the treaty-making processes, using executive agreements and grants-in-aid, thus undercutting the Senate's old dominion in this field.

It is, of course, the long frustration of the Vietnam war more than any other factor that has fed the growing reaction against Presidential power. Indeed, there has been an ironic turnabout by academics and liberals who once excoriated members of Congress as moss-backed obstructionists retarding the social legislation of F.D.R., Truman and Kennedy. Now such critics attack congressmen for acquiescing in the war policies of Johnson and Nixon, and for not obstructing more. The rationale of legislators has long been that the President "knows better" than they about a complex problem like Vietnam through the executive's intelligence and military bureaucracy. But as the Pentagon papers suggested, all of the expertise does not necessarily yield sound policy; the decision-making apparatus can achieve a blind momentum of its own. Worse, the White House may deceive Congress about its true intentions. Congressional intervention might well have averted, or shortened, some of the travail— the need to make a case for Congress might have improved the quality of executive decision-making.

Despite its doubts, Congress has continued to support the war through its military appropriations, partly because it has completely lost its grip on the nation's budget-making machinery. This, even more than the loss of war powers, may be the most debilitating congressional deference to the executive branch. Congress once determined, item by item, what the government should spend for what purpose, then dutifully raised the revenue to do so. It has attempted to deal with the growing complexity of spending and taxing by creating a multiplicity of committees and subcommittees. As a result, Congress has no overall view of either function, and thus no means of rationally setting priorities. The Bureau of the Budget, created in 1921 to aid both Congress and the President, has been captured by the executive, reducing Congress to the role of making minor alterations in a hand-me-down budget produced by each administration. . . .

Maryland Senator Charles Mathias claims that Congress is so narrowly concerned with each single piece of legislation that it ignores a broader perspective and fails to notice when it is "at a Rubicon, facing a great constitutional watershed." [TIME] correspondent Neil MacNeil agrees that the legislators "live, like many people, on the razor edge of right now. They are parochial in time; they lack a sense of the past or a care for the future."

One reason for this, as Ohio's Republican Senator William Saxbe sees it, is that "Congress has declined into a battle for individual survival" in which few members think about the welfare of Congress as a whole. Each reasons that "if you don't stick your neck out, you won't get it chopped off." Thus when a decision is rough, argues Oregon's Senator Packwood, Congress may be more than willing to pass the buck to the President. "We can delegate powers to the President, then sit back and carp or applaud, depending on whether what he does is popular or unpopular. If it's unpopular, we can say, 'What a terrible thing. We wouldn't have done that.'"

Berkeley Political Scientist Nelson Polsby, author of *Congressional Behavior,* finds legislators hampered simply by their needs to get re-elected. While the public expects congressmen to be generalists, competence in a complex age requires specialization—a dilemma Polsby would resolve by urging constituents to expect less "omnicompetence" in their representatives so they can concentrate on their specialized committee work. Polsby considers committee competence the key to a strong Congress.

Another dilemma working to the disadvantage of Congress is described by University of Rochester Political Scientist Richard Fenno, who wrote *The Power of the Purse: Appropriations Politics in Congress.* Fenno claims that most people "love their congressmen, but not Congress." It is easy to like a legislator for his personal style and policy views, Fenno notes, but difficult to admire a Congress because it is expected to solve national problems—and it rarely can. Moreover, many congressmen "portray themselves as the gallant fighters against the manifest evils of Congress; they run *for* Congress by running *against* Congress." As Congress thus loses prestige, its effectiveness can decline in a self-perpetuating spiral of criticism.

Among the specific areas of congressional decline:

Budget. Despite political charges that Congress has been spending the government into heavy debt, it has actually altered the administration's budget in recent years by less than 5%. Saxbe illustrated congressional inadequacy in analyzing just one part of the budget: that of the Defense Department, which spends more money on the staff to prepare its budget alone than the whole Congress spends for all of its operations. Against the Pentagon, the Senate Armed Services Committee has only 15 staff members, who, says Saxbe, also "spend a lot of their time campaigning for the committee members, running their offices and hauling their wives around."

Senator Abraham Ribicoff of Connecticut, among others, makes a persuasive proposal: Congress should have its own budget bureau to keep up with the overall spending totals, as well as to analyze specific funding needs and set up general priorities. Tennessee's Brock, a conservative who helped organize the Nixon re-election campaign among youth, has introduced a bill to set up a joint House-Senate committee that would propose a legislative budget, apart from the administration's request, and create its own priorities. The joint committee, moreover, would periodically review the programs it has funded to see if they are working as intended. But Scholar Ralph Huitt worries that such a centralized committee would be easier for a President to control, and that "these people elected by no national group would have no responsibility to anybody."

Impounding. There is no more direct challenge to congressional power than Nixon's refusal to spend money Congress has appropriated. This issue apparently is headed for a momentous collision in the courts. Presidents have refused to spend funds in the past as far back as Thomas Jefferson, who withheld some $50,000 that had been authorized for gunboats to patrol the Mississippi River. But this was generally done then because the need had passed or a project cost less than had been expected. Nixon has used this device as an expanded veto power, impounding some $6 billion in water-pollution control money and $5 billion in highway funds. Moreover, he asked Congress for the right to select which appropriations he could reject, in an effort to keep spending within $250 billion this fiscal year—and the House meekly agreed. Mathias claims the House did so because it saw the matter "as a mere housekeeping item,"—while Ribicoff termed the Senate's rejection of this request "its most significant action in modern times." Approval would have given the President unprecedented authority to thwart congressional will.

Priorities. Congress has fallen into the habit of mainly reacting to the President's legislative requests, rather than setting its own agenda. Huitt argues that Congress simply does not have the machinery to do so now. Ervin distrusts any effort to change that, contending that Congress is too disparate a body, and each member would have his own priority preferences. "I would set a priority on moonshine liquor," he quips, "because a lot of my constituents still make it up in the hills." [But] as Mansfield and Albert indicated, current attempts to set legislative priorities are taking place within the caucauses of the controlling Democratic Party.

Staffs. Congressional committees, as well as most legislators, have inadequate staffs to compete with the administration and what some consider a fourth branch of government: the huge bureaucracy that neither the President nor Congress can control. Despite a 1946 law requiring all committees to hire only professional staff experts, many still use political pals or unskilled generalists. Minnesota's Democratic Senator Walter Mondale noted that when he held a hearing to argue against more aicraft carriers, it was a case of "myself and one college kid versus the U.S. Navy and everybody who wanted to build a carrier, or who had a friend who was an ensign or above. We foolishly handicap ourselves by failing to properly staff ourselves."

General William Westmoreland, on the other hand, assailed congressmen for not even using administrative-supplied information at committee hearings. He charged that they do not do their homework and are more interested in "stagemanship, self-aggrandizement and demagoguery" than in analyzing "extremely complex" issues. TIME's MacNeil contends that legislators are afraid to hire more help because of adverse public reaction, but that if they forthrightly stated their need, the expense would be accepted.

Information. Congress needs more help from computers in order to retrieve information and analyze complex statistics. Brock noted that twelve state legislatures have such equipment, while the University of Pittsburgh's Charles Jones *(Minority Party Leadership in Congress)* estimated that Congress has "the computer capability, roughly, of the First National Bank of Kadoka, S. Dak." Declared Mondale: "Whenever I am on the side of the administration, I am surfeited with computer printouts that come within seconds to prove how right I am. But if I am opposed to the administration, they always come late, prove the opposite point, or are on some other topic. He who controls the computers controls the Congress." Congress should be provided with a modern computer capability.

Leaders. Despite the new spirit shown by Mansfield and Albert, the leadership in both chambers [has been] widely criticized as too conciliatory or gentlemanly to be effective. What is required, argues Correspondent MacNeil, is some of "the arrogance" of past taskmasters who ran Congress with heavy hands. Jones suggested that there is perhaps no greater congressional need than to strengthen the leaders of each party within Congress and thus pin down responsibility. He cited Woodrow Wilson's dictum that "somebody must be trusted, in order that when things go wrong it may be quite plain who should be punished."

Seniority. The academic experts generally argue that the seniority system of selecting committee chairmen has been attacked much too broadly as a central evil when in fact it is a minor matter. Henry Hall Wilson, president of the Chicago Board of Trade, even contends that if the seniority system were abolished, the same men would be chosen as leaders. "Why? Because they are abler." Senator Ervin concedes that the system is bad in some respects, "but the only thing that is worse is every alternative that has ever been proposed for it." Such views are challenged by Massachusetts Congressman Robert Drinan, who charges that seniority and some other House rules produce "tyranny and tyrants." Arizona Congressman Morris Udall says wryly: "My God, this is the only institution on earth where you can lead a 'youth rebellion,' as I was accused of doing, at age 47."

Udall attacks the system as giving "national power to people who are responsible to a limited constituency; Wilbur Mills, one of the most able men in Congress, is not chairman for Little Rock, but for Los Angeles and Long Beach and Prescott, Ariz." Udall has proposed a plan for the majority-party caucus to elect committee chairmen from among the three senior members on each committee, and by secret ballot. In sum, it may well be necessary to drop or at least modify the seniority system in order to encourage more legislators to develop expertise, with the expectation of gaining influence sooner.

Re-election Pressures. The need for Congress to be constantly seeking re-election was deplored, although some scholars argue that it actually keeps them better informed on the desires of their constituents than any other federal officials. Also assailed was the dependence of many legislators on campaign contributions from donors with potential special interests. Mondale termed this "the dark side of the political moon, tragic and dangerous." Saxbe said a donor almost always expects a return favor. "It is like the boy who buys a girl a beer and then expects the right to squeeze it out of her." There is a strong need for public funding of campaigns.

Secrecy. While deploring the spreading use of executive privilege by recent administrations, [experts can] suggest little that Congress can do to check it. Another problem, of course, is the excessive secrecy of Congress itself. The House Appropriations Commitee opened only 33 of its 399 meetings last year, the House Ways and Means Committee closed 48 of its 76 sessions, the Senate Finance Committee held 85 of its 110 meetings behind closed doors and the Senate Armed Services Committee went into secret session in 109 of its 152 meetings. It is at committee meetings that most of the key decisions of Congress are made. Declares John Gardner, head of Common Cause: "These matters are secret only to the public. The Public Works Committee holds no mysteries for the highway lobby, nor the Agriculture Committee for agri-business. The deliberations of the Ways and Means or Finance Committee are accessible to a whole swarm of loophole lizards." More of the crucial committee deliberations should be opened to the press in order to improve public understanding of congressional action and problems.

The Press. [The press has been] criticized for its overconcentration on the White House, its relatively superficial coverage of Congress, and its oversimplification of the reforms necessary to make Congress more effective. "If Henry Kissinger is the best national journalists can do for a sex symbol in national politics," noted Jones, "then they have not completed the search." Mondale claimed that reporters follow a "star system," and fail to spot talented and courageous newcomers, many of whom quit politics when they see no one supporting their efforts.

Other possible reforms would involve improving the public image of legislators by tightening conflict-of-interest rules, including the banning of outside work (the $42,500 annual salary, plus expense allowance, should be adequate to make the job worthy of a member's full time). The overseer functions of committees should be emphasized, to determine whether the congressional intent of programs is being carried out by the executive branch.

Some argue that the problems on the Hill are psychological, having to do with the sheer will of Congress to make itself felt. Perhaps more than any specific set of reforms, the Congress needs only to use more fully the tools and potential it has long possessed. "Reforms are not going to make any difference unless there is the will in Congress to want to govern," contends Packwood. "We can set policy, we can take back the powers if we want. But we have said 'can't, can't, can't' so long it has become an excuse for 'won't.'" Sums up MacNeil: "I have never seen Capitol Hill so alive to its problems, so anxious to begin the restoration. Yet whether that will can be sustained for an extended time—time enough to accomplish the ends—is debatable. Carrying the hard commitment for the necessary months and years is not easily done."

In an age of growing complexity—and in an era when momentous global decisions might have to be made in an instant—a strong Presidency is necessary. But not a Presidency made strong with the usurped powers of another branch. As a former senator and congressman, it seems strange that Nixon does not fully appreciate this. The shape in which Congress emerges from its crisis, whether regaining its lost luster or continuing to recede, to function as a kind of windy Washington sideshow, may be determined by what the public demands of it. Ultimately, the nation gets the kind of Congress it deserves. As Charles Jones observes: "Whatever is wrong with Congress may also reflect ills in the society. And if the legislature fails, democracy fails."

Presidential Also-Rans

John Bell
John Bell was the candidate of the Constitutional Unionist Party in 1860. He got 39 electoral votes in a four-way race in which Lincoln emerged victorious.

John C. Breckenridge
John C. Breckenridge of Kentucky, was nominated by the 'deep South' democrats in the 1860 campaign. The regular democrats nominated Douglas.

William Jennings Bryan

William Jennings Bryan, populist spokesman for the agrarian South and West and tireless worker for progressive legislation throughout his political career, was the unsuccessful candidate for President on the Democratic ticket three times. He was defeated by William McKinley in 1896 and again in 1900, and lost to William Howard Taft in 1908. However, he remained influential and active in Democratic politics until 1920. Bryan is perhaps best known for his involvement in the Dayton, Tennessee trial of John Scopes for teaching evolution in the Tennessee public schools. Bryan, a fundamentalist, aided the prosecution. Although Scopes was convicted, Bryan suffered a humiliating cross-examination at the hands of defense lawyer Clarence Darrow and died shortly after the trial.

20

b. 1777
d. 1852

Henry Clay

Henry Clay was one of the outstanding political figures of his time. An ambitious and pleasure-loving lawyer from Kentucky, he served for over 40 years in the House of Representatives and the Senate. He never made any secret of his desire to be President and was nominated three times; losing each time—to John Quincy Adams in 1824, to Andrew Jackson in 1832, and to James K. Polk in 1844.

James M. Cox

James M. Cox, former Governor of Ohio, was the Democratic candidate for President in 1920. He and his running mate, Franklin D. Roosevelt, were defeated in a landslide that elected the Republican ticket of Warren Harding and Calvin Coolidge.

On November 3, 1948, Thomas Dewey went to bed believing himself elected President, as did many other Americans. The Chicago Tribune, published early on election night, proclaimed Truman the loser, providing the President with a hearty laugh the next morning.

Thomas E. Dewey

Thomas E. Dewey, twice the unsuccessful Republican candidate for President, is shown here accepting his party's nomination in 1948.

Stephen Douglas

Stephen Douglas, the "little giant", was the candidate of the Northern Democrats in the election of 1860. Elected to the U.S. Senate from Illinois in 1846, he was active in trying to compromise the disputes over the spread of slavery and was largely responsible for the passage of the Kansas-Nebraska Act of 1854. In 1858, while running for reelection to the Senate, he engaged in a series of debates with his then little-known opponent, Abraham Lincoln. The debates catapulted Lincoln into national prominence and set the stage for their Presidential contest two years later. In defeat, Douglas tried to rally his followers around the new administration. He believed in the Union, exhausted himself in a strenuous campaign to preserve it, and died while on a speaking tour in Chicago.

Gus Hall

Gus Hall, candidate of the Communist Party, was on the ballot in 15 states in the 1972 election and received 25,222 votes. He was born in Iron, Minnesota on the Mesabi Range in 1910. His father, a miner and strike leader, was one of the founders of the Communist Party, U.S.A. At the age of 16, Hall was an organizer for the Young Communist League and joined the Party a year later. Although a navy veteran of World War II, in the 1950's Gus Hall was sentenced to serve an eight-year term at Leavenworth under the Smith Act, which makes it a crime to advocate the violent overthrow of the government. In 1959, he was first elected General Secretary of the Communist Party and has been reelected at succeeding party conventions. The 1972 campaign was his first try for the Presidency.

Dick Gregory

Dick Gregory, comedian turned activist turned politician, was on the Freedom and Peace and New parties ticket in 1968. Gregory and Eldridge Cleaver, running as the candidate of the Peace and Freedom party, were the first two black Presidential candidates in the country's history. Cleaver got 195,134 votes; Gregory, 148,622. The size of their combined vote does not reflect significant ethnic support, but does demonstrate hard-core dissatisfaction within the system.

Hubert Horatio Humphrey

Before running for the Presidency on the Democratic ticket in 1968, Hubert Humphrey had served 12 years as U.S. Senator from Minnesota and four years as Vice-President in the Johnson administration. His defeat at the hands of Richard Nixon did not end his political career, in 1970, he was re-elected to his fourth term in the Senate. Humphrey tried unsuccessfully for the Presidential nomination in 1972.

George McGovern

Senator George McGovern campaigned, officially and unofficially, almost two years to gain the 1972 Democratic Presidential nomination. He forged an unorthodox coalition of young people, blacks, women, and anti-war activists, which enabled him to win the nomination. However, his campaign alienated such traditional and conservative power blocs in the party as organized labor and many ethnic groups, and he was badly defeated in the election.

Alfred E. Smith

"Al" Smith, four-term Democratic Governor of New York, made history in 1928 by being the first Roman Catholic to run for the Presidency. Although the campaign degenerated at times into emotional attacks on Smith's religious convictions and his morality—he opposed prohibition—he polled over 15 million votes—the most ever won by a Democrat up to that time. However, it was not enough to defeat his opponent, Herbert Hoover, who swept to victory with a plurality of 6 million votes.

29

30

Wendell Wilkie

Wendell Wilkie was the Indiana Republican who ran against Franklin D. Roosevelt in the 1940 Presidential election. Wilkie was the dark horse candidate at the Republican convention and won the nomination on the sixth ballot. He proved to be a strong candidate with great charm and personal magnetism. Even though he was no match for Roosevelt—losing by 5 million votes—his 22 million votes were the most ever cast for any Republican up to that time. After the election, Wilkie—a strong internationalist—went on a goodwill trip around the world for Roosevelt. He also remained active in Republican politics until his death in 1944.

Norman Thomas

Norman Thomas, the Socialist party's perennial "also-ran" for the American Presidency, made a significant contribution to social progress in the United States. Many of the policies he proposed during his six campaigns were adopted by the Democratic and Republican parties and ultimately became the law of the land. Thomas, the son and grandson of ministers, was himself the minister of a church in East Harlem. His daily involvement with the poor and underprivileged convinced him that the existing political parties offered no solution to the problems of poverty and social injustice. As early as 1917, he became active in Socialist politics—campaigning for the party's candidate in the New York City mayoralty election. He was his party's Presidential candidate in every election from 1928–1948.

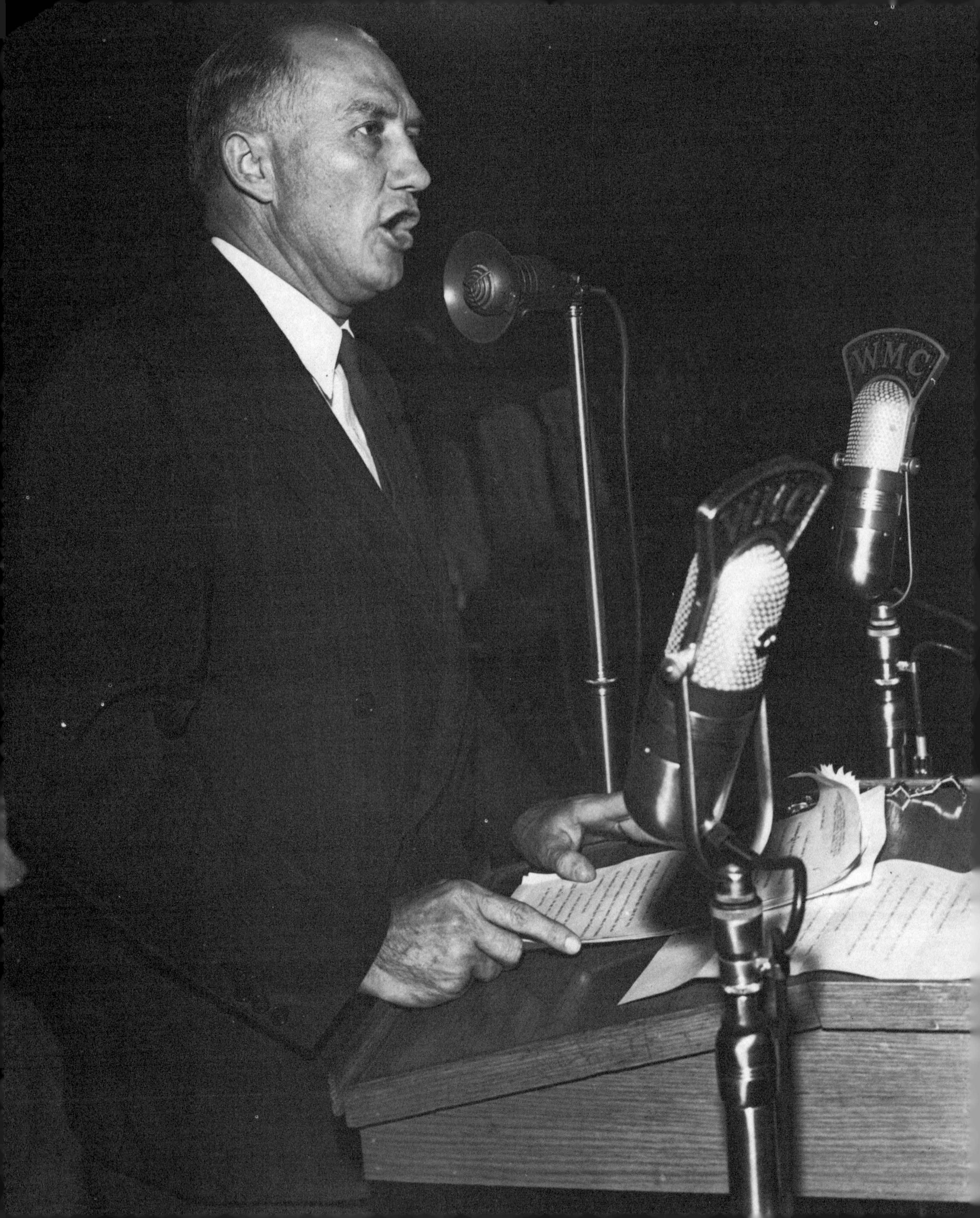
WMC

George Corley Wallace

The candidate of the American Independent party in 1968, Wallace hoped to throw the election into the House of Representatives. He failed, but received almost 10 million votes and carried five Southern States.

J. Strom Thurmond

J. (James) Strom Thurmond of South Carolina was the candidate of the States Rights Democrats (Dixiecrats) in the 1948 Presidential election. He and his followers left the regular Democrat party in opposition to the Civil Rights planks in the party platform. Although Thurmond failed to achieve his spoiler's goal of throwing the election into the House of Representatives, he did carry four states and won 39 electoral votes.

Governor of his state from 1947–1951, Thurmond won election to the U.S. Senate in 1954 as a write-in candidate. A nominal Democrat, he disagreed with his party's position on many issues and in 1964, he changed to the Republican party. He was instrumental in shaping the Nixon "Southern strategy" in 1968.

BE SAVED BY FREE LOVE

Victoria Woodhull

Victoria Woodhull, first woman Presidential candidate, ran in 1872 for the Equal Rights party, a rump group that had bolted from the National Woman's Suffrage Association.

Her colorful past involved her with such famous financial figures as Cornelius Vanderbilt, who set her up in a stock brokerage business.

Along with her sister, Tennessee Claflin, she began publishing a New York weekly in 1870 which advocated a single standard of morality for both sexes and equal rights for women. They also published in their paper the first English translation of Karl Marx and Friedrich Engel's Communist Manifesto.

Part 4
Filling The Office

12

The First Step– The Presidential Primary

Wilfrid Sheed **MEMOIR OF A CAMPAIGN DROP-IN**

From *The Atlantic Monthly,* Vol 222, (September 1968), 48–53. And by permission of the author.

An Easterner arrives in Los Angeles armored with notions. You feel your brain beginning to rot as you hit the runway. And the people in the airport look tanned out of their minds, offensively bland, and desperately superficial. The main impression, if you shed the one you came in with, is no impression at all. If someone had said to me, ha-ha, this is really Detroit, I would scarcely have known what to answer, except to wave weakly at some palm tree.

However, the mind never steps working. A city that leaves no impression is sinister, too, right? This would not seem quite so silly later. Meanwhile, there was nothing for it but to stare with frozen horror at the spastic taximeter and at the nameless pastels sliding past the window. The Beverly Hilton itself is a fine figure of a hotel, with a front someplace in the middle and a string of off-mustard terraces to refresh your spirit on; but what you see from there is more of the same, pale greens and sickly beiges, and signs saying "Esther Feather's Reducing Salon," and Somebody's custom-made hats, operating out of dirty chartreuse warehouses; and beyond that—well, more of that . . . .

I moseyed over to the Westwood CDA headquarters to see what work there was for a diffident, low-road speaker. This was the Wednesday night, a week from the primary. I got the impression that the smart writers had mostly headed for San Francisco already for the balmy cultural weather. Anyhow, they weren't here, in this vague, cheerful barn of a headquarters.

The girl in the speaker's bureau seemed confused and willing, the hallmark of a McCarthy student worker. The kids who had made the trek from New Hampshire had developed a style by now, flip, tired, gallant. Items: boy spread-eagled center floor in the Crenshaw headquarters taking the most ostentatious midday nap you ever saw —whacked out, poor devil; a girl staggering off from a party at 2 A.M. "to work the mimeograph for a few hours" (but Dame Mitty, you *can't!*). And all the other Weary Warriors with their eighteen-hour days and tired grins.

The speaker's bureau girl was not of the theatrical persuasion, but she did have one thing in common with most of the others: she knew practically nothing about Los Angeles. This most labyrinthine of urban sprawls was being blitzkrieged by kids who couldn't tell a boulevard from a freeway. My first assignment was to a gentle middle-aged Jewish household, hardly my schtik, where I believe I was introduced as Wilbur Snead, or one of its variants, and then (quick glance at card) as literary editor of *Life* magazine and *The New York Times*. The first question I got concerned McCarthy's attitude toward Israel.

That night, as on others, I found the speaker's kit from headquarters more or less useless. I had dutifully memorized all the stock answers about oil depletion, poll tax, and so on, but found that my little audiences didn't even know the questions. The famous distorted version of McCarthy's voting record (concocted by a New York group of Kennedy backers) was still circulating briskly in Negro neighborhoods; but the white folks didn't know or didn't care. How was McCarthy going to end the war in Vietnam?, did he have executive ability?, or (fringe stuff) what was wrong with the CIA anyway? were the questions they asked.

I found myself sinking quickly into the deepest fens of demagoguery. How far to the left or right was this particular group was all I needed to know. Did they dig adventure, or was responsibility in goverment their thing? As proxy brood sow, I was there to serve. As to the enemy, Bobby became more two-faced and Hubert more ludicrous every night. Until one sobered up on Tuesday and looked at the mess. Unfortunately, I had not followed the sound advice of Leonard Lewin who had grown gray stumping the country for Gene: to wit, ignore the other fellows, be positive out here.

They do, I believe, like you to be positive in the L.A. area; might stomp you if you were not. It is interesting, as you leave some resolute sunniness with the vicious, in-turned quality of the Los Angeles driving that waits for you outside. There seems to be no continuity between life in the car and life in the house....

A chronological rundown of the next few days would be misleading, because the mind has long since jumbled them, and that's the form they now take. Speaking, driving, more speaking, more driving; Sunday now comes before Thursday, because that's the logical order. Prejudice gave ground slowly to glib observation. You notice right away the cool proto-movie-star routines of garage attendants, busboys, of the fellow who rents you the inevitable car, so stylized after New York, where manners are formed by abrasion and erosion, and where the doormen are old rock formations. You notice the fact that people not only have no accents but use no slang to speak of (this may not go for special groups, beach-and-bike enclaves, but it does for the middle-class students and such that I met). There is no common speech because there is no city. With so many people, it seems dangerous not to have a city.

These are thoughts to drive by. To Anaheim for a small give-'em-hell rally in an improvised Eugene's. To Santa Paula for a Mexican-American picnic, where you wish you could stay but can't—the stern demands of the stump whisking you from good scenes and bad alike. And through the airless Simi Valley in Ventura County, where the physical facts of campaigning became a little clearer.

A formidable motorcade had rolled up outside the local bowling alley, twenty to thirty cars covered in gorgeous bunting, and Michael McCarthy, the senator's sixteen-year-old son, perched on a back seat for display. With horns blasting and loudspeaker braying (bring our boys back, vote for Senator McCarthy), we set off through the desolate streets. Occasionally a stray dog would follow us. A small child would wave. Otherwise, silence, shuttered windows. It couldn't be every day that they had a motorcade out this way, yet they responded like people jaded, sick, with excitement.

One soon wearied of waving v-signs at stony-faced men who rubbed their cars in response, at stray gardeners who would not look up or around, even in anger. Occasionally on that long ride I thought I saw people actually lurking in their garages, peering from the shadows. All right, paranoia, but paranoia is modest good sense in the Simi Valley on a Sunday.

Meanwhile, a fellow in our car was trying to make a pitch to young Michael McCarthy. It seemed he wanted a civil service job, had written to Michael's dad about six months ago, maybe the letter had been mislaid. I know your dad's been awful busy (laugh), but maybe he could find just a moment, used to be friends back in Minnesota, sixteen years ago. Roots still in Minnesota, you know, Dad's a wonderful man. "Mother would go back tomorrow if we could sell the house."

Michael is a boy of great poise, and he dealt with the matter gracefully. But this bleak cry for help combined badly with the dry sun, and the cheerless wind and the endless bungalows—which, two days before the primary, showed no signs of preference, no bumper stickers, no anything. The man told us he had been a salesman for twenty-seven years, had learned from selling that you had to believe in your product, that's why he believed in McCarthy; it was like religion or anything else, you had to sell it. Yet this Willie Loman of the Far West was one of the valley's live ones.

For a Presidential candidate, this would have been an off day. But for an out-of-shape dilettante, it brought the illuminations of fatigue. The first secret of campaigning must be to regulate your thermostat, to avoid excitement and depression equally, to save yourself for the next meeting and the next and the next. You cannot afford to feel like God, that would take too much out of you. Every excess must be paid for. Watch those naps, snacks, toilet habits. Remember the name of this man, and his wife, listen to his prattle and be prepared to prattle back in kind. I had always wondered at the steady, humming vitality of politicians, from breakfast rally to midnight caucus, but now I saw how it worked: the kind, empty eyes, the firm, indifferent handshake, everything economized on except appearances.

That evening, I returned to L.A., passing on the way something described as the world's largest shopping center, set in a great vacuum, to talk to a group of, I think, Italian Catholics, more communal and New Yorky than anything I had struck so far. But all resilience was gone. I read the basic speech woodenly and hacked through the questions somehow. A professional politician would never have let this happen. He would not have wasted energy brooding about the denizens of the Simi Valley or about huge shopping centers where small ones would do, or about all the failures and solitaries who cluster about Los Angeles looking on the bright side and driving like werewolves.

All the while, this microscopic private campaign was trotting alongside the real one, and following its contours. Senator McCarthy had come to Los Angeles and gone, making his usual mild but favorable impression. Private observation informed me that he looked wretched before breakfast, an excellent thing in a candidate (how else could he represent the interests of my group?). More significantly, in some ways, Clarence Jones, Martin Luther King's legal adviser and co-chairman of McCarthy's New York campaign, had come to town, snapped his fingers at the easygoing Westwood staff, and had set to work making an eleventh-hour pitch to the racial minorities, which the McCarthy workers had prematurely conceded to Kennedy.

Jones's scheme included talking to as many Negro ministers as possible before they hit their pulpits on the Sunday before Tuesday's primary, and circulating reprints of an editorial endorsement of McCarthy by the influential Negro newspaper the *Sun Reporter* outside the churches. McCarthy workers were reluctant to enter Watts at all, where pro-Kennedy fervor could, if inclined, wreak much damage to cars and sound trucks. But as it turned out, the editorial was circulated safely enough, and so was Louis Lomax's endorsement of McCarthy after the Saturday night debate. And who knows, perhaps a percentage point was affected by this frenetic activity.

Meanwhile, one had had at least one glimpse of the incurable triviality of history. I went to a party on Thursday thrown by the Negro head of the CDA headquarters in Crenshaw, hoping to meet whatever other black supporters were around, only to find some sort of boycott in progress. A wistful spread was laid on, but only a few white workers and Myrna Loy showed up for it. Later a couple of Negro friends dropped in. With a lifetime to feud in, the matter had chosen primary week to erupt.

But the important thing now was the Saturday night debate. We had high hopes for this. McCarthy was reported to be indignant over the ground rules, and if his face shows a weakness, it is for petulance. But he was resting well and looked strong as a lumberjack. He would cream their boy.

Thank God (I suppose), he did not. For their own different reasons, the two men dealt gently with each other. The group I was with laughed when Senator Kennedy brought Israel into a question where it didn't strictly belong: a routine political stunt, no hard feelings. His reference to the 10,000 Negroes who might descend on white-Republican Orange County if McCarthy had his way was not so well received. We took that to be a backlash pitch, and hoped that Negroes picked it up. Otherwise, the mildness of the occasion was unbroken. Kennedy might have lost, by looking less Presidential and all that, but McCarthy had hardly won.

It was obvious that the big question the next day would be, what is the difference between them anyway? I thought the debate had revealed some significant ones, notably on the question of negotiating with the NLF, but it was hard to tell whether Californians cared about this, or anything else in particular. The task suddenly seemed to be to interest them in their own primary. There were on the margins random signs of Bobby-love and Bobby-hatred, both echoing through the squeal that followed him everywhere; but of serious political feeling, there seemed to be surprisingly little. Eighteen percent Undecided in a Saturday night poll. Eighteen percent, after all this.

On Monday, I talked to a bunch of Catholic colleges, plus the normal allotment of housewives. It took an act of faith to believe that this was still making a difference. I was told of one student who had changed his mind as a consequence of my harangue, but he was probably under voting age. Otherwise the important question now was whether to ring doorbells, or to phone up the neighbors and bother them that way. The activists in the audience threshed this out while the rest of us listened. I had no thoughts on the subject. Los Angelenos seemed infinitely inaccessible by any means at all.

That evening, the senator ambled around the seventh (McCarthy) floor chatting with his cohorts, and I had a chance to gauge him up close. He is physically imposing, and I could understand why his admirers had wished him to be photographed standing next to Kennedy. Americans would always like an extra few inches of President, all else being equal. He has a politician's memory—I had met him briefly some seven years before, and he remembered this without faking. He listens fairly well, for a politician, looking beyond you, but picking up the drift. He seemed sharper and more concentrated than I remembered, as if the campaign had summoned his wits together.

Beyond that, he is the kind of wry Irishman that I have known more than my share of, feel comfortable with, would trust crossing a bog. The famous cynicism is *de rigueur* with this Irish-uncle type—emotions being for special occasions and cynicism for everyday wear; at any rate, a matter of style, not of moral conviction, and nothing to worry about. I felt no doubt that he would make a good President, if he wanted to; there remained some small doubt about that, however. We talked briefly about the debate, and he said that he thought Kennedy had made one or two mistakes. "Put him on bread and water for forty days and he'll blurt out the truth," he said, smiling. When I reminded the senator that he had been on that same diet himself, he said, still smiling, "Yes, but I'm tougher than he is." Not hostile, but decidedly scrappy.

Robert Lowell (without whom no account of this sort would be complete) also turned up that evening, but our conversation was not noteworthy. The Boston Brahmin and the Roxy dropout sparred briefly, using the light gloves, is probably the simplest way to put it. There was nothing to do now but wait. At the Westwood headquarters next morning, a parking-lot attendant tried first to stop me, then, failing that, to extort an unprecedented fee. I pointed out that the lot was half-empty, and he said, "It's as full as I want it to be." When I rejoined rather pompously that people like him were hurting McCarthy's cause, he said, "I don't give a — about McCarthy. I'm for Kennedy." And a smirking crony drove this home: "We just want to get you people out of here."

Upstairs, one of the sillier girls was going on about last night's sniping mission—a couple of delirious hours spent tearing down Bobby posters and slapping up Gene ones. So the eighteenth-century spirit, bullyboys, street goons, and vandalism, was alive in both sides, the more grotesque because there were no special interests involved to speak of, only personalities—and in a sense, only one personality, Kennedy's, followed by that weird squeal. The speaker's bureau was closed. There was some action downstairs, dubious small boys from Port Said and the Levant collecting stickers and hats, and so on, but upstairs it was like the last day of school, feet on the desk, detective story out, last-minute gossip.

This prompted a few last thoughts about the scholar-gypsies who had followed the McCarthy caravan from coast to coast.

Some of the McCarthy youth corps had run through a life cycle, from zealous to slightly smug, in a few months. The best of them, including their leader, Curt Gans, kept their heads down all the way; the worst would chat while a phone went unanswered, or would pick it up and sound ineffably bored into it. "She isn't in. I don't know. Yes, why don't you do that." Office work was clearly not their thing, and it was probably time for the more languid of these to be phased out and replaced by semipros, yet how could you fire them? They had gone to God knows what sacrifices in order to be able to lounge around here; they came at bargain prices —always a factor in the McCarthy campaign; they represented McCarthy's appeal to youth, which Kennedy was alleged to envy; and their departure, however tactfully managed, would be interpreted as an erosion of this.

That evening I invited Lowell to my room for a drink. The usual election-day liquor crisis was raging, and I had to advertise up and down the corridor for a tooth-mug of bourbon. After a bit, the senator himself appeared, along with Blair Clark, both looking noncommittally morose. Although the polls were still open, the word was in from the killjoys at the networks that McCarthy had already lost by nine percentage points; a miracle could shave this to six.

McCarthy accepted a cigar and a small scotch and went out on the terrace with Lowell. Being as snoopy and star-struck as the next man, I wanted badly to follow them, but it was one of those scenes—the two tall men motionless, leaning on the rail looking out at Esther Feather's Reducing Salon—that you don't intrude on. I stayed inside and talked instead to Blair Clark (a man destined from birth to smoke a pipe). I had not quite gathered until now how precarious our man's position actually was. If Kennedy lost and dropped from the race, enough of his delegates would split to Humphrey to scuttle McCarthy for good. If Kennedy won, our puny funds would dry up still further, and some of our workers would defect. The closest thing to a success would be what we finally got, a close defeat. But, of course, when we got it, it wasn't worth having.

I finally did go out, on some ruse, and did a little light eavesdropping. They were talking about how the Indians lived in Arizona (McCarthy had spent the day there) and the virtues of living out of a canoe. The senator looked wistful. "Everyone should try living out of a canoe," he said. "Do them good." The talk turned to poetry, and he brightened. Lowell had been a good poet once upon a time, he conceded, before taking up obscurity; now, who could tell?

It was not a typical conversation, I gathered, but a sensible attempt to ward off stress, the banter of athletes or soldiers. McCarthy knows how to handle the nerves—he couldn't have come so far otherwise—and talking with Robert Lowell is part of his strategy. They talked about which of his own poems he should read tonight if the mood was on him; Lowell had helped him with one or two of them and made his recommendation meticulously, liking the rhythm of this one, the imagery of that one.

For something to say, I asked McCarthy about his sports metaphors. He didn't seem to understand the question at first; his eyes were tired and withdrawn, and it occurred to me that he had probably been thinking politics all along, deciding when and how to concede, while humoring Lowell and me with small talk. Lowell asked if he would join us for dinner, and he said, sadly, "You know I can't do that. I'm a public figure now." Charlie Callinan, his tiny bodyguard, came up to tell him he was wanted someplace or other, and he said, "Charlie has graduated from a presence to a force," and left us. I noticed that he had smoked his cigar twice as quickly as I had mine.

That brings us almost back to the beginning. I had dinner with Lowell after that, and he talked about the Catholic politeness of the TV debate, and the Catholic nastiness. Every culture has its own forms of the virtues and vices. Then he talked about whether McCarthy would make a good President. Well, there were only two great ones in our whole history (I forget which). McCarthy would be a lot better than most. He also spoke fondly of Kennedy, and was sorry to have to choose between them. Earlier in the evening, a Washington correspondent had been asked to compare the Kennedy boys. "Next to Jack, Bobby is all heart," he said. These scraps came back to mind later in the evening.

I saw the senator twice more that night. The first time was in Mary McGrory's room, where he was watching television. He seemed severe now, bordering on the vexed—possibly over the incredible CBS projection of the final vote, which had him losing 52 percent to 39 percent or thereabouts. A mistake like that must play hob with a candidate's blood pressure. But I fancy he was simply saving his strength and doing a little light planning. Because the next time I saw him, down in the ballroom, he was as serene as ever. They were having voting machine trouble in Los Angeles County (some were stolen), so we were still leading by a thin margin at midnight. To hell with the projections. We would stage a miracle during the night. "I want to be in that number," we sang, and waved our fingers aloft. On to Chicago. . . .

13
Choosing The Candidate

Paul O'Neil   **CONVENTIONS: NOMINATION BY RAIN DANCE**

From *Life Magazine*, (July 5, 1968), © 1968 Time, Inc.

No American institutions so fascinate and so appall the citizenry of the Republic (and so absolutely flabbergast foreigners) as do those vulgar, those quarrelsome, those unspeakably chaotic rites by which U.S. political parties choose candidates for the Presidency. The quadrennial conventions assume the loftiest of partisan obligations; but no other such convocations anywhere in the civilized world perform their functions amid such torrents of hoarse and lamentable oratory, such displays of hypocritical bedlam and such barefaced recourse to the mores of the poker table and the flea market. They are motivated by an arrant opportunism, will seize upon a Warren G. Harding as ecstatically as upon an Abraham Lincoln, and are such natural incubators of bathos and low comedy that their functionaries sometimes seem to be engaged in some large-scale revival of nineteenth century burlesque.

To illustrate this last aspect of the American nominating process, one need only recall the pigeons which took so dramatic a part in the Democratic Convention of 1948 at Philadelphia.

The hapless birds, which were delivered on stage in two large wicker hampers, were expected to 1) sweep upward past a huge, floral Liberty Bell and 2) behave like "doves of peace" during a speech by Mrs. Emma Guffey Miller. . . . Not a soul questioned the wisdom of this curious project—although it held up the Presidential acceptance speech—and Chairman Sam Rayburn surrendered the stage to it without a moment's hesitation. Mrs. Miller bustled importantly through a women's club talk on "world peace," paused dramatically, held up one hand, and looked pointedly around at a helpful chauffeur—who proceeded, thus cued, to fling up the lids of the hampers. The pigeons, however, refused to budge. The unhappy deputy began scooping them up and heaving them frantically into the air, and the torpid and heat-stricken conventioneers were galvanized, in an instant, into paroxysms of laughter and outbursts of violent applause. The sound grew . . . and grew . . . and grew.

The pigeons, once airborne, circled drunkenly in search of roosts, undeterred by the fact that the flower of the party—Alben Barkley, Mrs. Eleanor Roosevelt, and President Harry Truman himself—were arrayed on chairs below them. They teetered precariously on the big, wire-housed floor fans which stood about the stage, committing nuisances and threatening at every instant to reduce themselves to pigeonburger. They flew out over the audience by the dozen and then, apparently revolted by what they saw, zoomed back once more to harass the quivering dignitaries on stage. Some flapped about the rafters. Some clung to the draperies. When Sam Rayburn began banging his gavel to restore order, a pigeon attempted to land on his bald head. He ducked wildly and, when the bird lit on the lectern before him, flung it savagely away. Pandemonium!....

The Democrats could hardly have avoided the convention embarrassments of 1948—the U.S. being the kind of country it is—even if someone had bothered to anticipate them. The pigeons, for one thing, had been donated by the Allied Florists of Philadelphia and one does not connive for elective office by offending florists, or barbers, or patternmakers. Mrs. Miller, more importantly, was not only a party worker—and former Senator Joe Guffey's sister—but a WOMAN! And the convention, it must be noted, achieved its larger purpose just as well with an intrusion of birds as it could have without them; it not only nominated Harry Truman on schedule but provided a forum for the first of the "give 'em hell" speeches which won him the Presidency.

The absurdities and shortcomings of the Presidential convention, like faults inherent in other aspects of the democratic process, are more evident to the casual eye than are its uniqueness of concept and its underlying utilitarianism. Many of its failings, moreover, are actually the failings of those who participate in it—of politics itself—and could not necessarily be expected to vanish if they were transferred into some other channel of expression. If one considers the nominating devices of other nations, if one takes a realistic view of politics and politicians, if one contemplates the American past, and if one is willing to admit the impossibility, in a nation of 200 million people, of often achieving truly representative government, it is hard not to conclude that the convention is one of history's most ingenious and practical political inventions. Beyond that, it is a kind of potlatch or rain dance by which political parties and populace are reminded of tradition and assured of identity....

Every convention, of course, is a receptacle for monkey business; but the convention has ways of utilizing it or rejecting it according to circumstances. It is the rare delegation which is not controlled, in one way or another, by state bosses or natural leaders or fiat from a primary back home. But in many cases—if the convention is simply renominating a President or even if it is picking a sure loser in a bad year—it has only one choice to make. In more fluid situations, however, the schemes of one fixer can neutralize the schemes of another.... And in times of genuine crisis and genuine contest ... a convention can behave so aberrantly that the most intransigent of bosses must abandon greed for reality or go down with a dead horse.

The convention is not simply vulgar; it is, like Mt. Rushmore or the beer-splashed locker room of a World Series winner, supremely, uniquely, even inspirationally vulgar.... Neither the Republicans nor the Democrats have any real "national organizations"; both parties are a hodgepodge of 50 almost unrelated and often quarreling state organizations. The convention —and this is its most marvelous attribute—is a kind of mold or form or template in which these diverse mobs can shape themselves into a reasonably coherent whole and can engage, once their intraparty differences are resolved, in false though binding and hideously sentimental expressions of solidarity and love....

The convention puts party power above the

national welfare and can mistake mediocrity for revelation, but in times of need still has picked great leaders with remarkable regularity. It is a sort of advertisement, a commercial (now fully televised) for partisan politics. It links the American present with the American past—with the Whigs, the Jacksonians, the Barnburners, the Know-Nothings, the Greenbackers, the Populists, the Abolitionists, the slave Democrats, the Bull Moosers, the sachems of Tammany and the old Western Republicans from whom it has inherited its flavor, its peculiarities, its memories of vanished frontiers....

Most Americans nurse an innate suspicion of political parties but, for better or for worse, would hardly deny them the function of selecting and electing Presidents. Not so the Founding Fathers, who did their level best to keep the office absolutely uncontaminated by politics. They were certain that private citizens of worth and intelligence—chosen in their own states as members of a college of electors—could accomplish the whole process of selection if each simply scribbled the names of two eminent Americans on a piece of paper and sent it off to Congress. The fellow who got the most votes was—presto!—President and the runner-up Vice President. This splendidly nutty idea backfired almost instantly and is responsible for our present system....

Conventions did not evolve, however, until the evolution of a "popular" Presidency and this materialized only as the country itself developed and grew....

The first Presidential convention was inspired by a New York stonecutter named William Morgan and conceived by as curious a bunch of rubes and hayshakers as ever conspired in a henhouse. History is rather vague about the life, the times and even the fate of William Morgan —beyond the fact that he was credited with writing an "exposé" of Masonry in the 1820s and vanished forthwith and forever. This literary production concerned itself solely with the passwords, door-knocks, highfalutin' titles and other rigmarole involved in Masonic meetings, and any two pages of it would put a speed freak to sleep for 23 hours. The "Freemasons of Batavia and Rochester" were, nevertheless, incensed and—at least according to rumor which swept the countryside—not only kidnaped the incautious muckraker but rowed him across the Niagara River, festooned him with sinkers, and heaved him, yelling, into the depths.

Local indignation over this tale was accentuated, in the autumn of 1827, by the discovery of a male body floating near the southern shore of Lake Ontario. The corpse, like the stonecutter, boasted a broken tooth. Hundreds of upstate clodhoppers, assuming it was Old Bill, formed an Anti-Masonic party and eventually—since Andy Jackson was a Mason, too—set out to avenge the martyr by throwing Old Hickory out of the White House.

In the fall of 1831, to dramatize their cause, they sent 114 delegates to a meeting in Baltimore and nominated William Wirt of Pennsylvania, a former attorney general, for President. This first gesture was also the last gasp of the Anti-Masons—but not of their political idea. Jackson himself, who had gotten the legislature of Tennessee to nominate him for the first term, adopted a convention as a means of launching his second campaign for office. Thus sanctioned, it was a part of Americana for good....

Hoopla and expansiveness ... were the hallmarks of the nominating process. The streets of downtown Baltimore were a "fairyland" of arches, signs and silken banners when the Whigs nominated Henry Clay of Kentucky for President in May, 1844. The delegates restrained themselves during the convention itself—perhaps because it was held in the Universalist Church—but having "recommended" their hero "to the people *with one voice*," they cut loose with a roar. Delegates, bands and innumerable Clay Clubs (bearing such signs as: Star of the West We Hail Thy Rays) paraded through the city to "continued applause." So did a horde of Allegheny County "mountain boys" in hunting shirts, who pushed a "rolling ball," a huge wooden sphere with a pole protruding from either end of its horizontal axis, as a curious feature of Clay's campaign (and inspired the phrase: "Keep the ball rolling!"). A mob of 65,000 met them in a suburban pasture, gave "three deafening cheers and a blast on the bugle" and listened to praise of the candidate by Daniel Webster.

These noisy exercises were less peripheral than they seemed; they reflected the optimism, the naiveté, the energy and prejudices of the young republic so accurately as to make the convention a barometer of national as well as partisan aspiration. The Democratic Convention of 1860 provided more tragic proof of this sensitivity. No single event of the years before Fort Sumter so demonstrated the inevitability of the Civil War. The participants gathered at Charleston, S.C. in April as if determined to preserve conviviality in the face of tension. Southerners and Northwesterners slept on long rows of cots set up in high-ceilinged public halls and commiserated amicably over the rascality of the locals, who had raised the price of pie from 6¢ to a dime for the duration. The New England delegations camped aboard their means of arrival—the iron, sidewheel steamship *S.R. Spaulding*, which not only boasted two brass cannon said to have been fired at Bunker Hill, but also a supply of whisky guaranteed to last until all delegates were returned to Boston. Moderates from both sides of the Mason-Dixon line agreed on Stephen A. Douglas as the candidate best calculated to preserve unity. But the climate of the convention was nevertheless the climate of war.

Southern "Ultras" . . . demanded that the party stand for slavery, a "divine" institution, in territories. Northerners balked. The Southern hotheads were adamant—in part because they were reacting to years of abuse from Abolitionists like Boston's Wendell Phillips, who described the South as "one great brothel, where a half million of women are flogged to prostitution." Delegates from Alabama, Mississippi, Florida, Texas, South Carolina, Louisiana, Georgia, Arkansas, Delaware and North Carolina walked out. The convention struggled through 57 ballots without them, "adjourned" to Baltimore, attempted to win the Southern delegations back, and then split apart again. Northern splinter groups eventually nominated Douglas and Southern splinter groups Vice President John C. Breckenridge of Kentucky . . . who carried most of the South in the election and left the Union to become a Confederate general.

The convocation of new Republicans, by contrast, reflected a kind of prairie exuberance and a confidence, even a sort of "evangelism," in the cause of the party and the cause of the Union. Chicago was a city of 110,000 in 1860; it built a huge, flag-topped wooden hall—the famous Wigwam at Lake and Market Streets—simply to accommodate the convention. The North flexed its industrial might to salute it: 40,000 visitors came to Chicago by railroad alone. . . .

The convention seemed to have no more idea of what it was about than most: William Henry Seward got 173½ votes to Lincoln's 102 on first ballot and lost most of his advantage on second, largely because Abe's floor managers made a trade with Pennsylvania's Boss Simon Cameron —a cabinet seat for 50 delegates. But 1860 proved that such convention crudities can fuel a kind of mass wisdom and that convention politicos will respond to intuition.

Lincoln grew on the convention, in no small part because of intangibles. His lieutenants were moved by an irascible industry which set them apart. Horace Greeley seemed "feverish" as he hurried from room to room through the first night exhorting the doubtful, and Lincoln's grassroots backers were obviously motivated by an extraordinary enthusiasm. Most of them came to Chicago lugging fence rails and the piles of lumber they deposited around the Wigwam were visual proof of unusual faith. And they howled in the galleries. The Lincoln bandwagon, once started, was beyond halting and the roar which greeted his nomination expressed a unanimity felt far beyond the Wigwam. Observed Lincoln's friend Leonard Swett: "Ten acres of hotel gongs, a tribe of Comanches might have mingled in the scene unnoticed." Steam engines whistled in the railroad yards outside, cannons were fired at the Tremont House and church bells began a clangor which went on for 24 hours.

Presidential conventions have, in their century and a half of history, demonstrated a tendency to repeat themselves—to behave, given a certain set of circumstances, roughly as they behaved when they last dealt with similar problems. Washington Political Scientist Richard Montgomery Scammon uses the capital's newest "In" word—scenarios—to describe the patterns into which convention proceedings may fall:

▶ "One guy gets ahead and everybody tries to gang up on him: John Fitzgerald in 1960.

▶ "Man comes up from behind: Wendell Wilkie in 1940.

▶ "Outstanding candidates battling neck and neck down to the finish line: Dwight D. Eisenhower and Robert Taft in 1952.

▶ "Dark horse wins: Warren G. Harding in 1920.

▶ "Candidate far out in front—no contest: Herbert Hoover in 1928, Alfred Landon in 1936.

▶ "Incumbent President to nominate—nothing to do but parade in the aisles: Calvin Coolidge in 1924, Franklin Roosevelt in 1936, Lyndon Johnson in 1964."

But there are variations on these themes. Some conventions seem to have been so chaotic —so subject to irrationality, coincidence and conflicts of ambition—as to have been controlled by the hand of fate, rather than the hand of man. None has produced a candidate by means more unpredictable, more confusing or more raucously hilarious than those by which the Democratic Convention of 1912 selected Woodrow Wilson at Baltimore's Fifth Regiment Armory.

Few politicians have ever owed as much to chance as Wilson. He became governor of New Jersey only 1) because George Harvey, editor of *Harper's Weekly,* convinced Democratic Boss James ("Jim") Smith that the party needed a candidate "with no past and no present" and 2) because a set of enormously practical underlings—"Big-jaw" Jim Nugent, "Planked Shad" Thompson and "Little Napoleon" Bob Davis—rigged the state convention in his favor. Not that "the professor" lacked a certain sanctimonious instinct for the jugular; he wrapped himself in a mantle of "instant statesmanship" and cut the throats of his sponsors at the moment of summons from Princeton University to public life. He owed nothing, he told the astonished state delegates, to any combination of leaders or bosses. It took him only three months as governor to destroy Boss Smith (by refusing to back him for re-election as U.S. senator), only a few more to take over the state organization, and only a year to dump backer Harvey, replace him with Colonel E. M. House—who promised him political influence in the Midwest—and to start running for President.

But Wilson, for all this, was not exactly the sort of fellow most Democrats pined to see in the White House. The Republicans were hopelessly split between Taft conformists . . . and the bolting Bull Moosers of Teddy Roosevelt. A Democratic victory seemed deliciously certain. "We propose to name a straight-out organization man," said Democratic National Committee Chairman Norman E. Mack. "It is our first opportunity since the Civil War to have a President willing to recognize his obligations to the party workers. Cleveland never did. It looks like Champ Clark."

Missouri's congressman, Speaker James Beauchamp Clark, might have been especially designed for old-line delegates and the yahoos out yonder. He opposed protective tariffs, monopolies, Eastern bankers and the get–rich–quick schemes of railroad magnates. He looked right: big, thick-browed, gray and homespun in his frock coats, dark alpaca trousers, gates–ajar collars and black ties. He was Western. He was regular. He was Folks. His backers sang:

> "Every time I come to town,
> The boys start kicking my dawg aroun'.
> Makes no difference if he is a houn,'
> They gotta quit kicking my dawg aroun'."

Clark led from the start. He had 556 votes to Wilson's 350½ by the 10th ballot . . . and his floor manager, W. J. Stone, wired Woodrow Wilson at Sea Girt, N.J. for capitulation to "the choice of the majority." Wilson agreed. "Stone's logic is correct," he said. He picked up a telephone, told his own manager, W. J. McCombs, to scratch his name from the lists and sat down to compose a telegram of congratulation to the front runner. It was never delivered. Manager McCombs—who hung up muttering, "Not on your life!"—told not a soul about Wilson's decision to withdraw. And it became apparent, almost immediately, that the convention had hardly begun—that it was not being dominated by Clark at all but by that jealous old egomaniac William Jennings Bryan, one-time Boy Orator of the Platte and perennial Democratic Presidential aspirant. . . .

Although he had been three times a presidential candidate, Bryan came to the convention in the humblest of roles—a simple delegate from Nebraska committed to vote for Clark. But he also came with a scheme for creating havoc, out of which he hoped to emerge once more as the hero of the hour. He began by trying—thousands hissed, howled, or applauded—to grab the temporary chairmanship of the convention. He failed. But he was soon making a nuisance of himself again with a resolution attacking Tammany Hall and the New York delegation: "We hereby declare ourselves opposed to the nomination of any candidate for President . . . under obligation to J. Pierpont Morgan, Thomas F. Ryan, August Belmont or any other member of the privilege–hunting and favor–seeking class'" This triggered genuinely frightful scenes of mass complaint.

The convention hall rang to thunderous volleys of booing, cries for order, whistles, laughter and noisy waves of applause. . . . The Democrats, who had heard Bryan rant against the "interests" before, felt they were being victimized by rhetoric from a tiresome has-been and began—mostly because The Peerless Leader seemed intent on making himself a figure of fun—to vote "aye" for his proposition. It passed, with even New Yorkers approving, by 883 to 201½. Not a soul seemed to realize that Bryan had set a trap until—with New York having swung its 90 votes to Clark—the Nebraska delegation was polled on the 14th ballot.

Bryan stepped into the aisle and began bawling: "Mister Chairman!"

"For what purpose does the gentleman rise?"

Bryan yelled: "To explain my vote!"

"Under the rules," cried Chairman William Sulzer, banging furiously into a recurrence of the horrible din which Bryan alone seemed to inspire, "nothing is in order but the calling of the roll." He was eminently correct. But Bryan persisted: "As long as Mr. Ryan's agents . . . as long as New York's 90 votes are recorded for Mr. Clark, I withhold my vote and cast it . . ."

His voice was engulfed in a hurricane of boos, catcalls, whistles and impassioned cries of "Regular order! Regular order!" But now Clark's manager, certain that his man was too far ahead to be beaten, certain that Bryan would make himself harmlessly ludicrous if given the chance, waved at the platform and indulged himself in one of the century's most ringing errors of political judgment.

"I move," he called grandiloquently, "that unanimous consent be given Mr. Bryan to explain his vote." Bryan insistently began fighting his way through struggling men to the stage. He stood silent, waving his fan, for 15 minutes while a deafening tumult expended itself on the floor below. But he had a point: the delegates *had* voted opposition to any Tammany-backed candidate and Clark *had* accepted New York votes. And, old or not, Bryan was still an orator of rare skills. No man, he finally cried, should be nominated to whom, if elected, the "money trust" could say, "Remember thy creator!" He went on: " I refuse to obey the instructions of my state to vote for Mr. Clark."

That—by the peculiar chemistry which sometimes governs the minds of politicians arranged en masse—was the end of Missouri's favorite son. Alabama's Candidate Oscar W. Underwood made it plain that he would not throw his votes to Clark, and since this involved that period (1832–1936) in which Democrats did not nominate with less than a two-thirds majority, every delegation was forced to a reassessment of strategy....

The convention turned to Wilson—with glacial deliberateness. "The professor" did not edge ahead until the 28th ballot....But the delegates had decided, and, on the 46th ballot, sent him on his way to the White House....

It is hard not to wonder whether the convention, by its very informality, by its confident and impromptu assumption of such awesome power, may not symbolize some larger and more ephemeral quality of the American experiment than is contained within the diameter of simple politics; whether turn-of-the-century political analyst, Russian-born Moisei Ostrogorski, may not have spoken less sardonically than he thought when he concluded that a convention—"15,000 people all attacked at once with St. Vitus' dance"—was certain proof that God in his infinite wisdom watches benevolently over drunkards, children, and the United States of America.

14

A Vanishing Phenomenon– The Whistle-Stop Tour

Irwin Ross **THE LONG CAMPAIGN TRAIL**

From *The Loneliest Campaign: The Truman Victory of 1948* by Irwin Ross. Copyright © 1968 by Irwin Ross. Reprinted by arrangement with The New American Library, Inc., New York, New York.

Truman's first major tour of the campaign got underway on the morning of Friday, September 17. The President, trimly turned out in his tan double-breasted suit, was animated and self-confident as he said goodbye to Secretary of State George Marshall and Senator Alben Barkley. "Mow 'em down, Harry!" Barkley boomed. Truman grinned. "I'm going to fight hard," he vowed. "I'm going to give 'em hell!"

The exchange set the tone of the tour.... The President was to cover eighteen states, cutting through the heart of the Midwest, crossing the mountain states to San Francisco, swinging south to Los Angeles, then returning east via the southern route, through Arizona, New Mexico, Texas, up to Oklahoma, and across Missouri, Indiana, Kentucky and West Virginia to Washington, D.C. Truman would make a maximum number of back-platform appearances, responding to what he assumed was an insatiable curiosity to see the President.

Two advance men went on the road—Oscar Chapman, the Under Secretary of the Interior, and Donald Dawson, a Presidential administrative assistant who normally handled personnel matters. They traveled several days in advance of the train and took care to check out all details of local arrangements. The political chores on the train were generally handled by Matt Connelly and by William M. Boyle, Jr., an old friend of Truman who was later to be chairman of the Democratic National Committee....

Truman was at his best, everyone agreed, in his whistle-stop appearances. He subjected himself to an exhausting schedule, occasionally speaking a dozen times or more each day. On September 18, his first full day on the road, he began at 5:45 A.M. in Rock Island, Illinois ("I don't think I have ever seen so many farmers in town in all my life") and was not through until after an 8:10 P.M. appearance in Polo, Missouri. ("I didn't think I was going to be able to do it but the railroad finally consented to stop.")

Truman's impromptu talks held to no set sequence, but they usually contained the same ingredients: a plug for the Democratic candidate for Congress or the Senate, a passing reference to the local college or baseball team (sometimes only the local weather was worthy of note), a brief exposition of some problem of local or national concern (housing, farm price supports, public power) which the Republicans had managed to muck up, and a plea for his audience to register and vote. The final turn in his routine was to introduce his wife and daughter. "And now I would like you to meet Mrs. Truman," he would say, at which point the blue velvet curtain behind him would part and the First Lady would appear to smile at the crowd. "And now my daughter Margaret" or, in southern states, "Miss Margaret." Margaret was an object of great curiosity because of her well-publicized singing career.

Truman combined invective with folksy informality. No language was too extravagant to characterize the misdeeds of the Republicans. He informed the throng in Roseville, California, that the Republican Congress "tried to choke you to death in this valley" by cutting off appropriations for publicly owned electric power lines. In Fresno, he announced that "You have got a terrible congressman here in this district. . . . He is one of the worst obstructionists in the Congress. He has done everything he possibly could to cut the throats of the farmer and the laboring man. If you send him back, that will be your fault if you get your throats cut."

Truman always voiced an uncomplicated view of the economic philosophy of the opposition. In Merced, California, he remarked that the "Republican policy is to let the big fellows get the big incomes, and let a little of it trickle down off the table like the crumbs fell to Lazarus." In Colton, California, he put the matter more pungently: "Republicans are simply tools of big business. They believe that there is a top strata [sic] in the country that ought to run the government and that ought to profit from the government. . . . They'll tear you apart."

He could be equally blunt when it came to lecturing the voters on their responsibilities. In Colorado Springs, on September 20, he reminded his audience that "In 1946, you know, two-thirds of you stayed at home and didn't vote. You wanted a change. Well, you got it. You got the change. You got just exactly what you deserved. If you stay at home on November the second and let this same gang get control of the government, I won't have any sympathy with you."

Truman's informality was often startling; no other President within memory could so readily shed the dignity of office before a crowd. He frequently ended his exhortation on a personal note. In Provo, Utah, he urged the crowd to exercise "that God-given right . . . to go to the polls on the second of November and cast your ballot for the Democratic ticket—and then I can stay in the White House for another four years." In Ogden, Utah, he suggested that if the voters did the right thing "that will keep me from suffering from a housing shortage on January 20, 1949." In Colorado Springs, he made a neat equation of public and private interest: "If you go out to the polls . . . and do your duty as you should I won't have to worry about moving out of the White House; and you won't have to worry about what happens to the welfare of the West. Those two things go together." . . .

Truman was full of surprises. Sometimes an odd braggadocio emerged. At Truckee, California, on September 22, he announced, "I am glad that so many people at this place deemed it advisable to come out and take a look at the next President of the United States." In Denver, at a luncheon of the Colorado Truman-Barkley Club, he startled his audience by reminding them of the dump-Truman movement of the previous spring. Occasionally he indulged in reminiscences about his family. In Salt Lake City, he recalled how his grandfather Young, a freight forwarder, had driven an ox-train of merchandise to Salt Lake City and had difficulty disposing of it. He went to see Brigham Young, who advised him "to rent space down on the main street here in Salt Lake City, place his goods on display, and he would guarantee that my grandfather would lose no money, and he didn't."

Toward the end of his trip, in Shelbyville, Kentucky, Truman delighted the crowd with a story of how his grandfather Truman had eloped with a local farm girl. Fearing her father's wrath, they moved to Missouri after the marriage; not until three or four years later, when the in-laws wanted to see their first grandchild, was a reconciliation effected. "You all know my daughter Margaret," the President said jovially. "She was down here several years ago, looking up the records to see if my grandparents were legally married." The train then pulled away. Soon afterward, press secretary Ross hastened back to the press car with assurances that the President had been speaking facetiously.

It all made for an entertaining show, but most reporters present had no reason to believe that Truman was gaining votes. Crowds were large, curious, good-natured, but not especially enthusiastic. As Earl Richert wrote in the Scripps-Howard papers, "The President . . . has called the Republican congressional leaders just about everything but horse thieves. But his epithets do not stir his audiences. They're the kind of words that need to be roared or snarled to bring crowd responses. But the President just says them in his dry, matter-of-fact way." On the other hand, Richert reported that the phrase, the "do-nothing Congress," had become widely known as Truman's campaign theme. "The people come to the railroad stations expecting to hear him say these words. And, whether they agree or not, they chuckle or applaud when he says them." . . .

Midway in the Truman trip there was also a good deal of press criticism of the mechanical arrangements aboard the train, which worked a disservice both on the candidate and on the fifty-member press party. Truman's prepared texts were often available only an hour or so before delivery; this meant that for the principal evening speech delivered on the West Coast, text would be available too late to be printed verbatim in the first editions of the morning papers in the East, where it was three hours later. Reporters were dismayed at the lack of a loudspeaker in the press car, which compelled them to dash back to the end of the train to catch the President's words at a brief whistle-stop. They were also not allowed in the last three cars of the train, where the Presidential staff worked and local politicians were received; a useful news source was thus cut off. The same lack of forethought also extended to such housekeeping details as laundry arrangements and baggage pickups; when the Truman train stopped overnight in a city, it was every man for himself. . . .

On Saturday the 25th, Truman quickly covered New Mexico, speaking twice and offering generous endorsements of Clinton Anderson, who had resigned as Secretary of Agriculture to run for the Senate against General Patrick J. Hurley. Anderson was regarded as the front-runner. By 11 A.M., Truman was in El Paso for the start of an intensive four-day tour of Texas, the first state he visited where the Dixiecrats were on the ballot. He made a speech on public power in El Paso, then addressed five more whistle-stop audiences in the next ten hours. He was in jolly humor. "It has been an education to see these bright and shiny faces," he told the crowd in Valentine. "Everybody seems to be happy and everybody seems to be interested in the welfare of the United States because you have come out to meet your Chief Executive and look him over and see what you think of him." A new note of optimism appeared in his comments. The Republicans, he twice exclaimed, "are on the run now! We've got them scared and we want to keep them that way."

He arrived in Uvalde at daybreak on Sunday the 26th to have breakfast with seventy-nine-year-old John Nance Garner, F.D.R.'s first Vice-President. Garner, the high school band, and some 4,000 citizens were on hand at the railway station. So was an angora goat, clothed in a gold blanket with red lettering bearing the legend "Dewey's Goat." Truman posed for pictures with the animal, telling the press, "I'm going to clip it and make a rug. Then I'm going to let it graze on the

White House lawn for the next four years." (He was forced, however, to leave the goat behind, there being no facilities on the train for it.)

Truman's visit to Uvalde was billed as purely a social affair, but it represented a small political coup: if old "Cactus Jack" Garner, a very conservative gentleman, found Truman palatable, he was clearly no threat to the Texas Democracy. Garner served Truman an enormous breakfast, lovingly detailed in the press: white-wing dove and mourning dove, bacon, ham, fried chicken, scrambled eggs, rice and gravy, hot biscuits, Uvalde honey, peach preserves, grape jelly and coffee. When the feast was over, Garner introduced Truman to the crowd waiting outside as an "old and very good friend." Truman responded: "Mr. President—that's the way I used to address him in the Senate—I haven't had such a breakfast in forty years.... John Garner and I have been friends for a long time and we are going to be friends as long as we live. I'm coming back for another visit sometime. I fished around for another invitation and got it." At this point Mrs. Truman broke her long-standing rule against speaking in public and told the throng: "Good morning and thank you for this wonderful greeting." Garner then urged everyone to go to church.

On Monday, traveling north through Texas, Truman opened a new attack on Dewey's unity theme. "Republican candidates," he said in Dallas, "are apparently trying to sing the American voters to sleep with a lullaby about unity in domestic affairs.... They want the kind of unity that benefits the National Association of Manufacturers.... They don't want unity. They want surrender." In Bonham, he charged that under the Republicans the country would have "the unity of the Martins and Tabers and the Wherrys and the Tafts. Then it would be unity in giving tax relief to the rich ... unity in letting prices go sky high ... unity in whittling away all the benefits of the New Deal ..."

Large and friendly crowds greeted Truman everywhere—15,000 at Waco, another 15,000 outside the railroad station in Fort Worth, 20,000 or more at the Rebel Stadium in Dallas. Initially, advance man Donald Dawson had wanted to hold the Dallas rally at the railway station, fearing that Rebel Stadium would look empty. He was wrong. At Dallas, before Truman spoke, Attorney General Tom Clark introduced him at some length, winding up with the declaration, "And I was with him when he stopped Joe Louis in the courts." Truman was still laughing when he got to the microphone. "Tom, you gave me too much credit," he said. "It wasn't Joe Louis I stopped—it was John. I haven't quite that much muscle." Texas was altogether a triumph. In Fort Worth, Governor Beauford Jester, who had bitterly opposed Truman's civil rights program, took a prominent part in the festivities, promising that Texas would again go Democratic in November. Truman had the discretion not to mention civil rights once during his tour of the state.

Next on Truman's schedule was Oklahoma, where he was again met with large crowds for his back-platform talks; at most stops he boosted the candidacy of Robert S. Kerr, a former governor now running for a Senate seat being vacated by a Republican. At Oklahoma City Truman delivered a major speech on communism and national security, seeking to answer Republican charges that he had "coddled" Communists in government. He made much of his administration's record in combating communism abroad and argued that the FBI was doing an effective job eradicating domestic subversion. He denounced the Republican congressional committees, maintaining that they were more interested in political propaganda than national security.

"I charge that the Republicans have impeded and made more difficult our efforts to cope with communism in this country.... I charge that they have not produced any significant information about Communism espionage which the FBI did not already have.... I charge them with having recklessly cast a cloud of suspicion over the most loyal civil service in the world. . . . I charge that in all this they have not hurt the Communist party one bit. They have helped it."

It was a strong speech, more crisply written than most of Truman's orations. Its impact was difficult to gauge, but it was agreeably received by the 20,000 persons in the state fair grounds; scattered applause interrupted Truman eighteen times. The speech was regarded as sufficiently important for the Democratic National Committee to pay for a "live" radio broadcast for the first time on this tour. Considerable thought had also been given to the setting for the speech, with Oklahoma finally being selected because Truman's strategists had the impression that the Republicans were exploiting the Communist issue most effectively in the Midwest.

The Oklahoma City speech on September 28 was the high point of the second week of Truman's tour. On the following day, he finished his tour of Oklahoma and crossed into southwest Missouri, delivering sixteen speeches between 7:35 A.M. and 11:15 P.M., most of them from the rear platform of the train. He arrived in Mount Vernon, Illinois, early on the morning of September 30, made a 7:40 A.M. speech, and then switched from the train to a motor caravan for a 141-mile trip through southern Illinois; in five and a half hours he spoke nine times. This was farming and coal country, largely Republican in its politics, but there was a great outpouring of spectators. *The New York Times* estimated that at least 75,000 people saw the President; he put the figure at half a million. He delivered his familiar message, but in Carbondale, where he spoke at the University of Southern Illinois, he made a brief comment about civil rights; he was in the North again. A new metaphor also appeared in the Carbondale speech. The Republicans, he said, "have begun to nail the American consumer to the wall with spikes of greed." By late afternoon, Truman was whistle-stopping through Kentucky; that evening in Louisville, he gave a prepared speech in large part devoted to an attack on the National Association of Manufacturers.

The following morning, in Lexington, Truman's public show of optimism took the immodest form of likening himself to the famous horse Citation, a frequent winner despite being a slow starter. "It doesn't matter which horse is ahead or behind at any given moment," he assured his admirers. "It's the horse that comes out ahead at the finish that counts. I am trying to do in politics what Citation has done in the horse races." The first lap of the race was over that night after three appearances in West Virginia. His last major speech of the tour, broadcast over nationwide radio from Charleston, West Virginia, was a recitation of most of his stock themes, enlivened by the prediction of "a headlong dash toward another depression" if a Republican President as well as a Republican Congress was elected.

By the time Truman returned to Washington on Saturday morning, October 2, he had covered 8,300 miles and delivered 140 speeches; he estimated that he had been seen by 3,000,000 people. The journalists who had accompanied him had difficulty assessing the impact of the tour. However inflated Truman's estimate might be, there was no question that large crowds had turned out to hear him; but was this an indication of political preference? As Robert J. Donovan wrote in the *New York Herald-Tribune*. "The American people have a very high regard for the office of President of the United States and a very great curiosity about the man who occupies it. When he comes to town they turn out in droves, tack up the welcome signs, bring out the bands, and drag all the children out of school to see the President and, if possible, to shake hands with him. But does that mean they are going to vote for him?" The reporters agreed, however, that the President appeared confident of victory wherever he appeared. To his advisers, he never expressed anything but optimism about the final outcome. Clark Clifford's testimony is emphatic: "From the beginning of the campaign until election day I never heard him express a doubt about his winning. I don't know, of course, whether this was a deep conviction or his idea of the attitude a leader should take. But he certainly had no patience with gloomy reports. I've seen him ashen with fatigue, but never discouraged."...

15

The Campaign Train Doesn't Stop Here Anymore

CAMPAIGN '72: SURROGATES AND T.V.

From *National Journal*, Vol. 4, No. 44 (October 28, 1972).

"The irony of campaigning is that when a candidate is on a whistle-stop tour, meeting the people personally, he is usually out of touch with what is going on in the country at large."

". . . What determines success or failure in handling a crisis is the ability to keep coldly objective when emotions are running high."

—Richard Nixon
Six Crisis (Doubleday, 1962)

[George] McGovern has stated, "The real issue of this campaign is Richard Nixon." Equally aware of this, Nixon strategists have shielded the President from the potential vulnerability of exposure. This has led to charges by the Democrats that Mr. Nixon is "hiding" from the electorate. White House spokesmen, however, insist that the most responsible—and most effective—way for the President to campaign is to attend to the business of the Presidency.

Nonetheless, both John Ehrlichman, assistant to the President for domestic affairs, and Charles Colson, a key figure in the President's re-election campaign, acknowledge that some Presidential assistants advocate more personal campaigning on the part of Mr. Nixon and that he probably will take a more visible role in the homestretch leading to election day.

Ehrlichman reported that Mr. Nixon is in very good form. "The intensity of his campaigning has been dictated by the amount of work on his desk," Ehrlichman said.

"We have over a hundred bills on his desk right now. His attitude is that he has a big job of work and that he owes it his responsibility and energies. So we've been spending a lot of time bringing decisions to him that he has to make. . . . He's really been pinned down. I've already been in his office four times today talking to him about decisions involving congressional action. It's just impossible for him to stop being President of the United States."

Claiming that an incumbent President runs on his record and the vision he holds out to the voters for the next four years, Colson said he favors communications campaigning (press conferences, radio addresses and television speeches) by Mr. Nixon.

He said "old-fashioned campaigning," including ticker-tape parades and motorcades, is "not the way to get a candidate's message across to the voters. The voters are concerned with the character of the man and his ability to handle the toughest job in the world. . . . They assess the man, not the number of cities visited or rallies attended. Traditional campaigning with all the hoopla may soon be a thing of the past."

Ehrlichman said that while Mr. Nixon keeps a close check on the progress of the campaign, he does not make every significant campaign decision. The President, he said, has "complete confidence" in his campaign managers.

Referring to the "hiding" charge, Ehrlichman said, "I was surprised to learn that at this point in the campaign (three weeks before the election), Mr. Nixon has campaigned in 11 states and McGovern in only 20 since the conventions. It's true that until Congress adjourned the President has not made a lot of campaign starts and stops in the conventional sense, but he does enjoy campaigning that way because it gives him a chance to meet people."

Nonetheless, Mr. Nixon's campaign trips so far have been swift-striking, tightly controlled forays that have afforded him little opportunity to rub shoulders with the mass of the electorate. His appearances, for the most part, have been before invitation-only audiences.

[And] although partisan in tone, his speeches never mention McGovern by name, nor does he attempt to rebut or reply to charges by the opposition.

Mr. Nixon's major campaign trips have included a fast visit Sept. 22 to the Texas ranch of former Treasury Secretary John B. Connally, chairman of the Democrats for Nixon Committee. There he met and dined with more than 200 wealthy Texans, mostly Democrats who have indicated their support of the President.

Late in September, Mr. Nixon went on a three-day, cross-country swing that took him to New York, Los Angeles, and San Francisco. While in New York he made a brief appearance at the Statue of Liberty to dedicate the American Museum of Immigration, a courtesy not unnoticed by ethnic voters. He also attended closed-door meetings with Jewish contributors and New York campaign officials.

On Oct. 12, the President went on a motorcade through downtown Atlanta during a one-day campaign visit, a gesture generally interpreted as appreciation for the solid support he almost certainly will receive from Deep South voters.

Then on Veterans' Day, Oct. 23, Mr. Nixon went on a motorcade through highly affluent Westchester County outside New York City and met with Northeast regional campaign officials at the estate of New York Governor Nelson A. Rockefeller near Tarrytown, N.Y. That same evening he delivered a speech in Nassau County, Long Island, after which he returned to Washington.

Most of the places visited by the President in his campaign are considered "safe districts" that enthusiastically back his reelection. Asked why Mr. Nixon chose to go to Westchester County, for example, Ehrlichman replied, "It's a traditional hunting ground for Presidents in an election year. In every national campaign, it's been a motherlode of Nixon support."

The tenor of Mr. Nixon's 1972 campaign oratory was reflected in an address he made in Atlanta at the Regency Hyatt House before a select audience. Barely alluding to the Nov. 7 election except in broad, general terms, Mr. Nixon spoke of the need for national unity—or what he refers to as a "new American majority" —because the problems that afflict the nation cross political, state, and regional lines.

Typically, he listed the five great issues facing the country as:

—maintenance of a strong defense second to none in the world;

—peace with honor in Vietnam;
—improved economic conditions;
—justice and respect for law and order;
—implementation of his revenue sharing plan, whereby money and power would be returned from the federal government to the states and cities.

Nowhere in the speech did the President refer to counter-proposals made in these areas by McGovern. Consequently, there has been no dialogue between the two candidates in the campaign. This, however, is to Mr. Nixon's advantage since, as he stated in his Atlanta speech, "What I am trying to do is to appeal to all. That is why we seek what I call a new American majority."...

White House officials are concerned, however, that the President's lead might quench the motivation among his followers to rush to the voting booths on election day. Mr. Nixon recognized this in a statement made during an Oct. 5 press conference in his Oval Office. He said:

"The problem with a candidate who is ahead in the polls ... is the problem of getting his vote out. What we need above everything else is a big vote. In order to get a big vote, it means that people have to be stimulated to vote."

Along the same lines, the re-election committee's Albert Abrahams said, "The problem is our people don't get excited enough. We must fight apathy. You can get so confident that you stay off the phone banks and fail to do enough voter canvassing. It's possible to blow the election by lying down.

"Admittedly, our kind of problem is nicer to have than George McGovern's; his is apathy because it looks hopeless. With us, it is not a matter of impoverishment but of having it too good. ... Yet, it cuts both ways and the embarrassment of too much of a lead is not a totally unmixed blessing. Still, it's better to have a sense of confidence than a sense of foreboding."

Abrahams said that the predictable shrinkage in the gap between the two candidates as election time draws near will "rev our people up." On several occasions, H. R. Haldeman, the assistant to the President who runs the Nixon campaign from the confines of the White House, has reminded re-election officials not to let the drive bog down because of overconfidence.

At the peak of the Nixon campaign organization stands Haldeman, acting on behalf of Mr. Nixon. "Word from Haldeman is the same as getting it from the President," observed a White House aide.

Beneath Haldeman, who operates behind the scenes, are the three principal levers of the re-election committee supervised by campaign Colson as the chief political operative: the re-election committee supreviced by campaign director Clark MacGregor; and the Republican National Committee, headed by Sen. Robert Dole of Kansas. Integrated at the top in special capacities are Ehrlichman and former Commerce Secretary (1969-72) Maurice H. Stans, chairman of the Finance Committee for the Reelection of the President.

These officials virtually are in command of a small army, which includes Cabinet resources and personnel, state party members, and a legion of volunteers.

Since the Republican National Convention at Miami Beach in August, almost all White House personnel, totalling almost 600 persons, have been involved in one way or another in the campaign. The re-election committee currently numbers about 575 professionals and the Republican National Committee lists a roster of 245, about 100 above the normal level.

The White House's double-edged blade in the campaign consists of a planning group of senior Presidential assistants and a so-called Attack Group. The senior aides include Haldeman, Ehrlichman, MacGregor, and Colson, with John Connally, Sen. Dole, and John N. Mitchell, former Attorney General (1969-72) and campaign director, occasionally sitting in on the meetings. These sessions generally are held in Haldeman's or Ehrlichman's office and are concerned with overall campaign strategy.

The Attack Group, presided over by Colson, is involved mostly with tactical strategy: what action to take in certain circumstances, how to counter charges from the opposition and what responses to give, where surrogate speakers should go and what items should be inserted in their briefing books.

Colson also runs a clearing house for the re-election campaign's media operation. This covers press and information sections in the Cabinet departments, those at the Republican National Committee and those at the reelection committee, as well as the office of Herbert G. Klein, director of communications for the executive branch. Essentially Colson's role is to coordinate what is being said by the various voices of the Administration.

Ehrlichman, who, in addition to being assistant to the President for domestic affairs, is also executive director of the Domestic Council staff, has a unique position in Mr. Nixon's campaign entourage. His campaign chores are to keep track of the issues and make sure that the President's speeches are accurate in content and are faithful to administration policy. He also travels with the President on campaign trips "to be available," he said, "in the event someone in government needs to bring something to his attention and to serve as a point of contact for people in the communities where we go who need to talk to someone or desire to talk to someone associated with the Office of the President."

Although all are working for the same objective—the re-election of the President—the individual segments of the Nixon campaign trinity do not always see eye to eye.

Officials of the re-election committee tend to resent intrusions by White House aides in their operations. But the most vocal complaints are sounded by officials of the Republican National Committee.

"There is a certain amount of friction," conceded an RNC spokesman. "Mostly it involves personality conflicts between a member of one organization and his counterpart in the other. It stems from the fact that at election time the national organization does not run the campaign. We feel we should. For three years we work up to this and then a new organization is formed and takes over. They make mistakes. But they want to take credit for what is right and slough off their mistakes."

The RNC official added, "Ninety-nine percent of the Republican National Convention was planned, developed and arranged by the RNC. We put together the convention but you would never know it. Today, those people (re-election committee officials) could not operate without our research division."

Probably the most celebrated case of internecine warfare involved Colson and Franklyn C. Nofziger, then the RNC deputy chairman for communications and former White House aide, Washington political writer, and press assistant to California Governor Ronald Reagan. Following repeated disagreements between the two, Nofziger was transferred to California to head the state's re-election committee. Commenting on the family feuding, Craig R. Maurer, RNC director of public information, said, "All of us like to think we're playing the most important role in the campaign."

Taking advantage of the privileges accorded the incumbent, the Nixon forces have inaugurated several innovative techniques. Recently put on display at national parks are free pamphlets containing a subliminal political message. Called "Bringing Parks to the People," the documents, published by the Interior Department, carry on the cover a quotation by President Nixon:

"Among the most important legacies that we can pass on to future generations is an endowment of parklands and recreational areas that will enrich leisure opportunities and make the beauties of the earth and sea accessible to all Americans."

Inside, the reader is informed that President Nixon initiated the "legacy of parks" and is told of other accomplishments by the administration in the environmental and recreational areas.

Beginning in September, the Selective Service System printed 300,000 letters to be sent to potential draftees, telling them that their chances of being inducted were exceedingly slim. One of the two form letters, sent to young men facing possible induction in 1973, noted that "the President and Secretary Laird (Defense Secretary Melvin R. Laird) have indicated that inductions beyond July first are not likely to be required."

The second letter, sent to those who escaped the 1972 draft, were told, "Unless there is a major mobilization in future years, you will no longer be an active candidate for induction."

Earlier, the administration came under fire from a group of Democratic senators for taking credit for increased social security benefits in notifications sent to 28 million recipients, even though the White House had opposed the hike.

In other innovations:

The RNC research division published a 137-page *McGovern Manual*, pointing up the inconsistencies in the Democratic candidate's record. As part of the foreword, the researchers wrote, "It is hoped that the *McGovern Manual* will be of particular benefit to campaign managers and speech writers."

The re-election committee announced a "Host (or Hostess) for the President" program in which every Nixon supporter "is invited to have his friends to a dinner, cocktail party, cookout, reception, etc., asking each guest to contribute to the President's campaign." The announcement said each host or hostess "will receive an appointment in the form of a formal commission suitable for framing."

Frederick V. Malek, deputy chairman of the re-election committee, has instructed the ethnic voter bloc division not to overpress the ethnic issue by appealing to Italians, Poles and other national origin groups solely on the basis of their heritage.

The press as adversary

As part of their campaign arsenal, the Nixon forces have assembled a huge press and information apparatus. Abrahams' operation at the re-election committee numbers more than 22 staff members. Some divisions, such as the black and youth sections, have their own press liaison official.

In the meantime, the White House press office, Klein's branch and the RNC's communications setup are all geared to the campaign. Yet, . . . the natural adversary position between the press and the White House has become accentuated. After more than three and a half years of daily briefings by Presidential press secretary Ronald L. Ziegler, the White House press corps only recently challenged his method for ending the sessions.

Since the beginning of the Nixon Administration, the White House briefings have been terminated at the discretion of the senior wire service reporter. Now, however, the White House press corps contends that while this traditional system is followed at Presidential press conferences, it does not apply at the daily briefings. When Ziegler appointed a committee of newsmen to study the matter, some reporters argued he had no right to take such action.

At the re-election committee, Abrahams has been criticized by some members of the press for the failure of committee officials to see them or even answer their telephone calls. Early in September, campaign director Clark MacGregor cautioned his staff against discussing internal affairs with outsiders. And several secretaries have told reporters that, in line with committee policy, all questions had to go through the press office. Abrahams, however, denied this.

"We have decided," he said, "that the campaign's interest is best served if we try to route all information questions through the press office. Any policy questions, we also handle. But if a reporter wants to see an official for an in-depth discussion on substantive matters, we will try to arrange it."

Abrahams, nonetheless, conceded that some committee officials were not adequately acquainted with the press policy and might have turned away requests by newsmen. . . .

In another incident involving the media, the White House drafted a list of questions to be asked of McGovern on ABC's "Issues and Answers" program Oct. 22. Despite the irregularity of the procedure, one of the questions was put to McGovern concerning his alleged comparison of President Nixon with Adolf Hitler.

Denying he had likened Mr. Nixon to Hitler, McGovern explained that he had said that bombing civilians in Indochina "is the most barbaric thing that has been done by any great power since the Nazis were in office, and I personally hold Mr. Nixon responsible for that."

ABC officials said that the questions were forwarded by Alvin Snyder, an aide to Herbert Klein who serves as liaison with television networks and stations. Other sources confided that the questions were drawn up by Colson. . . .

16
The Electoral College: An Imperfect Institution

Louis C. Kleber   **THE PRESIDENTIAL ELECTION OF 1876**

From *History Today*, Vol. 20, No. 11 (November 1970), 806–813. Copyright © 1970 by Louis C. Kleber.

In the summer of 1876 the United States celebrated a centenary of independence. Although it was a jubilee year, the American Republic was also deeply troubled. The desperate battles of the Civil War had ended more than a decade before; yet Abraham Lincoln's call for 'malice toward none' remained an unfulfilled appeal, as Federal troops continued to occupy some of the former Confederate States. President Ulysses S. Grant's second term of office was drawing to a close under a barrage of criticism directed at corruption in his government. The coming Presidential election would take place in November. It promised to be an exciting fight, but no one foresaw that the struggle between Republican Rutherford B. Hayes and Democrat Samuel J. Tilden would result in an unparalled scandal and bring America perilously close to another civil conflict. Indeed, the roots of the dispute were firmly woven into the Civil War and its tragic aftermath.

On April 9th, 1865 General Robert E. Lee surrendered the Army of Northern Virginia and the guns at Appomattox stopped firing. The Civil War drew to a close.... The day after the surrender, Abraham Lincoln returned to Washington after a visit to Richmond. A wildly cheering crowd called for a speech, but the President demurred. Instead, he asked the military to strike up 'Dixie.' For a brief moment there seemed to be hope of genuine reconciliation. It was unquestionably Lincoln's fervent hope. Then, only days later, John Wilkes Booth fired a fatal bullet into the President's head at Ford's Theatre in Washington.

With Lincoln's death, the 'Radicals' in the Republican Party gained the upper hand. For them, men like Thaddeus Stevens of Pennsylvania and Charles Summer of Massachusetts, the South fully deserved the revenge they intended for her. The bitter years of Reconstruction followed.... Gradually, however, the South returned to the control of its native white population. In doing so, it became more solidly attached to the Democratic Party than ever before.

Due to the presence of Federal troops and 'carpet-bagger' officials in positions of power, Ulysses S. Grant was able to carry eight southern states for the Republican Party in the Presidential election of 1868. Grant won a second term in 1872, but this time only six southern states were in the Republican camp. The grip of Radical Republican power was fading. Perhaps more significant, the immediate post-war zeal in the North for Negro welfare had diminished.

As the election of 1876 approached, Grant's Republican administration reeled under a heavy attack by the press when a great whisky scandal broke. Western distillers had been flagrantly evading Federal taxes, and Grant's own private secretary, General Babcock, was implicated. The President's enemies gleefully pointed to corruption in the White House. Instead of dissociating himself from Babcock, Grant leaped to his defence. Indeed, Grant displayed an almost incredibly loyalty to dubious colleagues during his Presidency. His support of Babcock largely contributed to an acquittal. But this was just part of the rapidly mounting troubles faced by the Republican Party. In March 1876, just eight months before the election, Secretary of War William Belknap was charged with malfeasance in office by the House of Representatives. Rather than remove Belknap from his post, Grant merely accepted the cabinet members' resignation. One month later it was James G. Blaine's turn to embarrass the Administration. As Republican leader in the House of Representatives, Blaine was in a most influential position. When the press charged that he had taken favours from the Union Pacific Railroad, the tag of 'Grantism' received new life as a synonym for political avarice.

The scandals could not have come at a more inopportune time, for the Republicans desperately needed a politically untarnished standard-bearer in the coming election and Blaine was a strong candidate. Despite the publicity, Blaine's name was prominent when the Republicans met at Cincinnati, Ohio, on June 14th to nominate a contender for the Presidency. Recognizing that public attention had to be focused on something other than the Administration's record, Blaine attacked the South and stirred up fears of a new war. In doing so, he alienated those members of his party who sought a genuine rapprochement with the old Confederacy. On the seventh ballot, he lost the nomination to a 'dark horse' candidate, Rutherford B. Hayes of Ohio. Hayes was a compromise between the extreme wings of the Party. Above all, his personal record and political integrity could not be seriously challenged.

The fifty-three-year-old Hayes had a good, if not spectacular, background. Born in Delaware, Ohio, he had been raised by a widowed mother who, fortunately, enjoyed financial security. He received a degree from the Harvard Law School in 1845 and subsequently accepted a number of fugitive slave cases. . . . During the Civil War, Hayes rose to the rank of brevet major-general of volunteers, participated in many actions, and was severely wounded. While the war still raged he was elected to Congress. He was later elected Governor of Ohio on three separate occasions and put through a number of reforms.

In accepting the nomination, Hayes vowed to end the spoils system and called for an end to 'the distinction between North and South in our common country.' . . .

The Democrats had no problem in devising their campaign strategy. The entire nation was aware of the administration's shortcomings. Corruption was the issue and the Democratic party promised reform. On June 27th they held their convention in St. Louis, Missouri. In an auditorium jammed with 5,000 people, Governor Samuel J. Tilden of New York scored a landslide victory on the second ballot.

Tilden was a unique figure, and certainly one of the most interesting to cross the American political scene. This frail, articulate bachelor commanded a crusading zeal for his supporters. As a boy, Tilden was withdrawn and showed little inclination to mix with young people. Politics, however, fascinated him and his father fostered that interest. . . . By 1841, he was a qualified lawyer with a continuing and consuming interest in politics. His brilliant grasp of political matters brought him to the attention of Democratic leaders who sought his counsel. For some time Tilden studiously avoided candidacy for high public office, but his own abilities soon brought him national recognition. A particularly significant event was Tilden's exposure and prosecution of New York's notorious racketeer, 'Boss' William M. Tweed. His popularity soared and he was elected Governor of New York. Then he broke up the 'Canal Ring,' a group of crooks and unscrupulous politicians. Tilden's name became associated with integrity in politics. This was just what the Democratic party wanted as a contrast to the Republican administration.

The battle lines were clearly defined. Left to themselves, it is possible that Hayes and Tilden might have kept the election campaign free from distortion of facts and bitter personal invective, but it was not to be. Tilden was subjected to a potpourri of charges. There seemed to be no limit—liar, swindler, perjurer, counterfeiter and even an absurd claim that he had been in league with the infamous Tweed. In line with their basic campaign strategy, the Republicans allowed that Tilden had supported the Confederacy, the right of secession, and the system of slavery. This all stemmed from his opposition to Lincoln in 1860, but that was because he was a Democrat and feared a Republican victory would bring disaster to the United States. This feeling had no bearing on his fundamental loyalty to the Union, for once the war began he urged the quick suppression of the Confederacy.

As election day approached, excitement grew with each rally and parade. It was, after all, the centenary of American independence. . . . But on November 7th, calm prevailed as people made their way to [the polls.] It was a stillness soon to be shattered. Hayes' hopes began to sink as doubtful states such as Connecticut, Indiana, and New Jersey went to Tilden. When New York finally fell into Tilden's camp, Hayes admitted defeat to those around him and went to bed. Tilden was not only leading in the popular vote, he had 184 of the far more important electoral votes to Hayes' 166; and it was the electors from each state who decided the Presidency. The 19 votes of South Carolina, Florida, and Louisiana were in some dispute, but they were in the heartland of the Democratic South. Samuel J. Tilden had been 'elected' President of the United States.

In Republican national headquarters, exhausted and dispirited party workers began to go home. On the morning of November 8th, the press of both parties was crowded with news of Tilden's victory. Even the militantly Republican *New York Tribune* conceded the election. *The New York Times*, however, would do no more than admit a Democratic lead. Two days after the election, John C. Reid, editor of that influential paper, sat in the editorial room with two assistants. It was after 3 A.M. when a message arrived from the State Democratic Committee: 'Please give your estimate of the electoral votes secured by Tilden. Answer at once.' Reid was astounded. If they urgently needed such information, then the Democrats were not certain of victory. In a matter of minutes he conceived a scheme to wrest the election away from Tilden and put Rutherford B. Hayes into the White Houes. Tilden had 18 more electoral votes than Hayes, but if the 19 from South Carolina, Louisiana, and Florida were secured by the Republicans, Hayes would win by one vote, 185 to 184. Reid, accompanied by a Republican official, hurried into the night and awakened Zachariah Chandler, National Republican Chairman. Chandler agreed to Reid's proposal—telegrams must be sent immediately to Republican officials in the three states.

'Hayes is elected if we have carried South Carolina, Florida, and Louisiana. Can you hold your state? Answer immediately.' That message did not require translation: Those states were to be held at any cost. At the same time, Republican headquarters claimed Hayes' election. From this moment, America began to slide toward the abyss of another civil war.

The key to the plot's success lay in the state canvassing boards. They had the power to certify the votes and cast out those that, in the board's opinion, were questionable. The need for absolute honesty by the boards in exercising their power was self evident, but even the personnel of some made comedy of that requirement. Louisiana, for example, had a board composed of a Negro saloon-keeper, a Negro undertaker, and two totally dishonest white men. Of course, all of the boards were Republican and backed by Federal troops.

Hayes must be given full credit for dissociating himself from the plan: 'I think we are defeated . . . I am of the opinion that the Democrats have carried the country and elected Tilden.' Hayes made the statement, despite his belief that many Negro votes were not cast for Republican electors due to fear and intimidation. A few weeks later, however, he changed his mind: 'I have no doubt that we are justly and legally entitled to the Presidency.'

From the beginning there was an outside chance that Hayes could have carried South Carolina and Louisiana on the strength of a combined Negro and carpetbagger vote. Florida's heavily Democratic white majority, however, made that state a dim prospect for Republican hopes. But they had to have Florida or Tilden would win by 188 to 181.

During the actual election campaign, all three states witnessed a wide variety of attempts by both sides to cow voters and fraud was rampant. In one shameful tactic, the Democrats tried to distribute ballots with the Republican emblem prominently displayed over the names of Democratic candidates. It was worth the chance in the hope of picking up votes from illiterate Negroes. On the Republican side, one inspired person devised 'little jokers'. These were tiny Republican tickets inside a regular ballot. A partisan clerk could slip them into the ballot box with little chance of being detected.

In Louisiana, Tilden held a comfortable majority over Hayes. And in New Orleans, the Democratic elector with the smallest plurality had more than 6,000 votes over his Republican opponent. The canvassing board solved the problem in that state by simply throwing out 13,000 Tilden votes against only 2,000 for Hayes. Then the electors for Hayes were certified.

The prelude to the election in South Carolina was a bloody affair. The Governor was Daniel H. Chamberlain of Massachusetts, a strict dogmatist on the race question and thoroughly loathed by white South Carolinians. In addition to the Presidential election, there was a gubernatorial race. The Democrats were running a war hero, former Confederate General Wade Hampton. 'Rifle clubs' were organized over the entire state by Hampton's supporters and there were numerous clashes with Negro groups. As far back as July 8th, there had been a sharp fight in Aiken County at which Negroes suffered a severe defeat. Grant described the rifle clubs as 'insurgents' and sent all readily available troops to South Carolina. The resultant fury at this action was compounded when the Republican canvassing board ensured the certification of Hayes' electors.

Florida was the most critical problem. As the polling booths closed, each side claimed victory. Once again, the canvassing board held the decision in its hands. The three-man board was dominated by two Republicans, Florida's Secretary of State and its Comptroller. The third man was the Democratic Attorney General. The board had the right to exclude 'irregular, false or fraudulent' votes. In a complete travesty of integrity, the board voted for Hayes by virtue of its Republican majority. Thus, Florida's key electoral votes went to Hayes. The Republican Governor certified them with the official blessing of the state. The outraged Democrats held a meeting and had the Attorney General certify the Tilden electors. With this action, a new and dangerous complication entered the scene. Democrats, claiming dishonesty by the canvassing boards, were certifying their own electors by whatever legal or quasi-legal means they could. To further complicate matters, Florida Democrats elected G. F. Drew as Governor and he appointed a new board of canvassers who promptly judged Tilden's electors to be victorious. In South Carolina, where Wade Hampton had been elected Governor, there were unqualified demands to disenfranchise the Hayes electors.

As a precaution, General Grant ordered Federal troops into all three state capitals, directing General Sherman 'to see that the proper and legal boards of canvassers are unmolested in the performance of their duties'. That meant Hayes would win. . . .

The Senate and House of Representatives convened for the second session of the Forty-fourth Congress on December 4th, 1876. It was just two days before the date set for Presidential electors chosen in each state to meet and declare their choice for President and Vice-President of the United States. It was the responsibility of each state Governor and Secretary of State to affix the official state seal to the voting certificates and send them to the President of the Senate in Washington, D.C., who would then count them before a joint session of Congress. Since the Senate was controlled by Republicans, the Democratic House demanded the right to decide which votes were valid. The Senate, understandably, refused. Here was an incredible situation; each day bringing the United States closer to March 4th, the date when Grant's term expired. Who would succeed him and how would it be done?

Rumblings of a new civil war rolled ominously across America. There were drills and parades and wartime units began to reform. Even cool heads discussed the possibility of the National Guard, under the command of Democratic Governors in most states, marching on Washington to install Tilden by force, if necessary. In that case, the Regular Army under Grant would oppose the Guard as Hayes had been 'legally' elected. It was an unthinkable prospect. Fortunately, there were men of influence on both sides who saw that a peaceful solution was absolutely mandatory. On December 14th, the House appointed a committee to approach the Senate in the hope that a tribunal could be created; one 'whose authority none can question and whose decision all will accept as final'. After much debate, an Electoral Commission was approved. Congress proceeded to set up a group of fifteen men; five from the Senate, five from the House and five from the Supreme Court. Presumably, the Court Justices would be nonpartisan. Both Hayes and Tilden declared the Commission unconstitutional, but they reluctantly agreed to accept its verdict.

It was clear to everyone what would happen without the Commission. Republican Senator Thomas Ferry of Michigan, presiding officer of the Senate, would open the certificates before a joint session and declare Hayes the winner by 185 to 184 electoral votes. The House would then immediately adjourn to its own chambers where Speaker Samuel Randall would declare no electoral majority and throw the election into a vote by each state delegation in the House. That would assure Tilden's victory, and on March 4th, 1877 both Hayes and Tilden would be in Washington to be inaugurated as President of the United States. Senator Roscoe Conkling of New York described this route as a 'Hell-gate paved and honeycombed with dynamite'. It was no understatement.

The Commission held its first session just four weeks before the inauguration. Democratic members of the Commission pressed for a searching examination of the honesty of the canvassing boards. The Republican members claimed that the legal authorities had filed legitimate certificates and Congress had no power to interfere. The Commission finally voted along party lines with the decision going to Hayes, 8 to 7. On Friday, March 2nd at 4 A.M., the Senate awarded the last certificate to Hayes. It was just two days before the inauguration. The fury of the South was matched by its Democratic allies in the North. All eyes turned to Samuel J. Tilden. If he claimed that the will of the American people had been frustrated by partisan duplicity and fraud, then America faced civil war. Instead, Tilden said: 'It is what I expected.'

Open conflict might still have been a possibility except for a meeting that has since been the subject of much speculation. One week before the inauguration, Southern Democrats and Republicans met at the Wormley Hotel in Washington in an effort to find some compromise before it was too late. There is ample evidence to suggest that a quid pro quo was reached; the South to agree to Hayes' election if the North would agree to abandon all efforts to maintain carpetbag régimes in the South. That meant withdrawal of Federal troops. In return, the South presumably agreed not to take reprisals against Negroes or carpetbag officials. For that matter, the South and its Democratic friends in the North already held a powerful sword over the head of the United States Army. They attached a clause to the Army Appropriations Bill that outlawed the use of Federal troops to sustain state governments in the South without congressional approval. When the Senate refused the clause, the House simply adjourned and left the Army without funds to pay soldiers. Morale collapsed and the end of Reconstruction was at hand.

After the decision, Tilden commented: 'I can retire to private life with the consciousness that I shall receive from posterity the credit for having been elected to the highest position in the gift of the people, without any of the cares.' That summer he sailed for Europe for a year's vacation. Rutherford B. Hayes took the oath of office in private, kissing the open Bible at Psalm 118.13 '... the Lord helped me'. There was no inaugural parade or ball. There was little to celebrate.

17

The Office Filled

Gary M. Maranell **RATING THE PRESIDENTS**

Excerpted from *The Journal of American History*, Vol. 57, No. 1 (June 1970), 104–113.

In 1948 and again in 1962, Arthur M. Schlesinger asked panels of historians and political scientists to rate the Presidents of the United States in categories ranging from "great" to "failure." ... This essay enlarges upon the Schlesinger polls, as well as updates them. The two Schlesinger studies, which created the interest in this line of inquiry, found the following ordering of Presidents (see Table 1). ...

The participants in the present study were ... randomly drawn from the membership of the Organization of American Historians. This group clearly includes historians who are most interested in American history. The total sample selected was 1,095, and the questionnaire designed to secure the ratings was sent to the respondents in March 1968. A single follow-up questionnaire was employed. The questionnare was returned by nearly 600 historians, and it was discovered that 571 were sufficiently complete to be included in the analysis. The scores obtained and presented here are the standardized responses of these 571 historians. ...

A comparison between Schlesinger's 1962 poll (see Table 1) and the present poll (see Table 2) reveals some interesting changes in the ordering of the Presidents. This is especially evident in the rank order of the Presidents appraised by both studies (excluding John F. Kennedy and Lyndon Johnson,). For example, Thomas Jefferson and Theodore Roosevelt have moved ahead of Woodrow Wilson, and Harry S. Truman has moved ahead of Andrew Jackson and James Polk. Numerous other changes have also occurred. Herbert Hoover, Dwight Eisenhower, James Monroe, and Andrew Johnson have moved up; and William McKinley, among others, has moved down. The rank order also indicates that at this point in time Kennedy is listed among the top ten Presidents.

An examination of the arrangement and scores of the Presidents demonstrates that general prestige and strength of role played by the President, although similar, are not the same thing (see Table 3). Therefore, general prestige is not simply a reflection of strength of role played. Some interesting observations include the fact that Franklin D. Roosevelt, Jackson, and Lyndon Johnson secure much higher scores on strength

Table 1
Schlesinger Polls of Presidential Greatness

1948 poll (Responses from 55 experts)	1962 poll (Responses from 75 experts)

Great

1. Abraham Lincoln	1. Abraham Lincoln
2. George Washington	2. George Washington
3. Franklin D. Roosevelt	3. Franklin D. Roosevelt
4. Woodrow Wilson	4. Woodrow Wilson
5. Thomas Jefferson	5. Thomas Jefferson
6. Andrew Jackson	

Near Great

7. Theodore Roosevelt	6. Andrew Jackson
8. Grover Cleveland	7. Theodore Roosevelt
	8. James K. Polk ⎫ tie
	9. Harry S. Truman ⎭
9. John Adams	10. John Adams
10. James K. Polk	11. Grover Cleveland

Average

11. John Quincy Adams	12. James Madison
12. James Monroe	13. John Quincy Adams
13. Rutherford B. Hayes	14. Rutherford B. Hayes
14. James Madison	15. William McKinley
15. Martin Van Buren	16. William Howard Taft
16. William Howard Taft	17. Martin Van Buren
17. Chester A. Arthur	18. James Monroe
18. William McKinley	19. Herbert Hoover
19. Andrew Johnson	20. Benjamin Harrison
20. Herbert Hoover	21. Chester A. Arthur ⎫ tie
	22. Dwight D. Eisenhower ⎭
21. Benjamin Harrison	23. Andrew Johnson

Below Average

22. John Tyler	24. Zachary Taylor
23. Calvin Coolidge	25. John Tyler
24. Millard Fillmore	26. Millard Fillmore
25. Zachary Taylor	27. Calvin Coolidge
26. James Buchanan	28. Franklin Pierce
27 Franklin Pierce	29. James Buchanan

Failure

28. Ulysses S. Grant	30. Ulysses S. Grant
29. Warren G. Harding	31. Warren G. Harding

---

[1] The respondents were asked to evaluate thirty-two Presidents. Two Presidents, William Henry Harrison and James A. Garfield, were excluded because both served in the Presidency less than a year.

Table 2
General Prestige

Abraham Lincoln	+2.10*	Herbert Hoover	− .09
George Washington	+1.78	Dwight D. Eisenhower	− .29
Franklin Roosevelt	+1.57	Andrew Johnson	− .30
Thomas Jefferson	+1.47	Martin Van Buren	− .37
Theodore Roosevelt	+1.18	William McKinley	− .39
Woodrow Wilson	+1.01	Chester A. Arthur	− .52
Harry Truman	+ .94	Rutherford B. Hayes	− .59
Andrew Jackson	+ .87	John Tyler	− .78
John Kennedy	+ .63	Benjamin Harrison	− .89
John Adams	+ .61	Zachary Taylor	− .96
James K. Polk	+ .30	Calvin Coolidge	− .99
Grover Cleveland	+ .25	Millard Fillmore	−1.19
James Madison	+ .23	James Buchanan	−1.28
James Monroe	+ .17	Franklin Pierce	−1.29
John Quincy Adams	+ .16	Ulysses S. Grant	−1.50
Lyndon Johnson	+ .06	Warren G. Harding	−1.84
William Howard Taft	− .05		

* A high positive score is high in prestige.

Table 3
Strength of Action

Franklin D. Roosevelt	+1.98*	Herbert Hoover	− .23
Abraham Lincoln	+1.74	William McKinley	− .30
Andrew Jackson	+1.37	Martin Van Buren	− .34
Theodore Roosevelt	+1.36	Andrew Johnson	− .40
Woodrow Wilson	+1.35	Dwight D. Eisenhower	− .43
Thomas Jefferson	+1.18	Chester A. Arthur	− .68
Harry Truman	+1.06	Rutherford B. Hayes	− .69
Lyndon Johnson	+1.00	John Tyler	− .716
George Washington	+ .89	Zachary Taylor	− .72
John F. Kennedy	+ .68	Benjamin Harrison	− .97
James K. Polk	+ .55	Calvin Coolidge	−1.17
John Adams	+ .41	James Buchanan	−1.19
Grover Cleveland	+ .18	Millard Fillmore	−1.22
James Madison	+ .05	Franklin Pierce	−1.33
James Monroe	− .02	Ulysses S. Grant	−1.36
William Howard Taft	− .17	Warren G. Harding	−1.66
John Quincy Adams	− .22		

* A high positive score is strength; a high negative score is weakness.

than prestige, and that Washington has a much higher prestige score than strength score. . . .

The similarity of the ordering and scores of the Presidents on the dimension of accomplishments (see Table 4) and the general prestige dimension (see Table 2) suggests that this is a major area in the evaluation of general prestige. The fact that Presidential accomplishment is of major importance in (or highly related to) Presidential prestige should add confidence to an assessment of the meaningfulness of the initial evaluations. . . .

Table 4
Accomplishments of Their Administrations

Abraham Lincoln	+2.07*	John Quincy Adams	− .24
Franklin D. Roosevelt	+1.91	Herbert Hoover	− .29
George Washington	+1.72	Dwight D. Eisenhower	− .32
Thomas Jefferson	+1.31	Andrew Johnson	− .40
Theodore Roosevelt	+1.26	Martin Van Buren	− .46
Harry Truman	+1.12	Chester A. Arthur	− .52
Woodrow Wilson	+1.11	Rutherford B. Hayes	− .64
Andrew Jackson	+ .83	John Tyler	− .80
Lyndon Johnson	+ .53	Benjamin Harrison	− .86
James K. Polk	+ .50	Zachary Taylor	− .99
John Adams	+ .37	James Buchanan	−1.136
John F. Kennedy	+ .36	Millard Fillmore	−1.14
James Monroe	+ .13	Calvin Coolidge	−1.20
Grover Cleveland	+ .11	Franklin Pierce	−1.25
James Madison	+ .10	Ulysses S. Grant	−1.38
William Howard Taft	− .01	Warren G. Harding	−1.61
William McKinley	− .21		

* A high positive score is great accomplishment; a high negative score is little accomplishment.

18

Thoughts Of A Professional President-Watcher

Richard H. Rovere   **EISENHOWER REVISITED**

The New York Times Magazine, (February 7, 1971). © 1970–1971 by The New York Times Company. Reprinted by permission.

It has been slightly more than a decade since Robert Frost greeted the dawn of a "next Augustan age . . . of poetry and power" and Dwight D. Eisenhower, ex-President, left Washington for Gettysburg—still an immensely popular figure who, had the law permitted and the spirit and the flesh been willing, could easily have been the man taking the oath of office on January 20, 1961, thus deferring the Augustan age for at least four more years. Eisenhower was held in high esteem for the rest of his life, but throughout most of the sixties those amateurs who sit in more or less professional judgment on Presidents—other politicians, historians, journalists—came more and more into agreement that his eight years in the White House had been a period of meager accomplishment and lackadaisical leadership. The greatest failure, the consensus seemed to be, was one of anticipation. What a prescient statesman could have foreseen in the fifties, the argument runs, was that the ship of state was headed for a sea of troubles, and this the 34th President conspicuously failed to perceive. He lacked foresight and imagination and thus bore considerable responsibility for the difficulties of the three men who succeeded him in the sixties.

Many of those who judged him most harshly until only a few years ago are now having second and third thoughts about the man and his Presidency—thoughts that should ring most agreeably in the ears of those whose faith had never never wavered. Such nay-sayers on the left as Murray Kempton and I. F. Stone are finding virtues in him they failed to detect while he served, and others are making claims for him that not even his partisans made when he sought office or held it. Garry Wills, the eminent Nixonologist, advises us in *Nixon Agonistes* that Eisenhower was "a political genius." Walter Cronkite, who first knew Eisenhower in France during the war and saw him often in subsequent years, recently said that he never thought highly of Eisenhower "either as a general or a President" but that in the post-White House years he discovered that Eisenhower was in actuality a "brilliant" man—indeed, "more brilliant than many brilliant men I have met."

A political genius? A brilliant man? Who ever said or thought that about Eisenhower in his own time? Certainly not Eisenhower himself. It was not that he was lacking in vanity; he had his share, but there is no evidence that he ever thought of himself as possessing a great talent for politics or a towering intellect, and the aspect of his "genius" that Wills calls "realism" would have deterred him from this kind of self-appraisal. He was, and we can be sure that he knew he was, no slouch politically (had he been below average in this respect, he would not have risen in the Army), and he was certainly not lacking in intelligence. But his real strengths lay elsewhere, and the Wills and Cronkite superlatives seem, one has to say, silly. . . .

For my part, I think the revisionist phenomenon as a whole can be rather easily accounted for—though I do not wish to suggest that new judgments are erroneous simply because they are new or, at least as I see it, obvious in their origins. Seen from 1971, the most important single thing about Dwight D. Eisenhower was that, through luck or good management or some combination of both, *we did not go to war while he was President.* To be sure, we came close on occasion, and his Secretary of State practiced a brand of cold-war diplomacy in which what was called "brinkmanship" at the time—risking war, including nuclear war—was an indispensable strategy. It can also be argued that Dulles's and Eisenhower's Indochina policy made Kennedy's and Johnson's and Nixon's all but inevitable and that, had Eisenhower held office for a third term, he would have found himself at war in Vietnam. The contrary can also be argued, but it does not matter; we were at war when he came to office, and six months later we were out of it, and we did not enter another war during his tenure. Eight years of Eisenhower: seven and a half years of peace. Ten years of Kennedy, Johnson, Nixon: almost ten solid years of war.

What else is there to celebrate about the Eisenhower years? I can think of a few things but they are of far less consequence and, moreover, they are not blessings of the sort that can be appreciated only in hindsight—unless one chooses to include among them such engineering projects as the St. Lawrence Seaway and the interstate highway system. Though I have myself altered some of my views about Eisenhower over the years, I have felt since 1958 or thereabouts that the country benefited from his first term but would have been better off if he had not had a second. I think I can defend the view in 1971. By 1953 we had made our point in Korea—the expulsion of the invading armies—and it was time for a settlement. It required a Republican President (not necessarily Eisenhower, though of course it helped that he was a successful military man) to end that war on terms short of the "victory" for which Gen. Douglas MacArthur said there was "no substitute." As Harry Truman was to say, he or any other Democrat would have been "lynched" for agreeing to the settlement Eisenhower so cheerfully accepted. It also required a Republican in the White House (though, again, not necessarily Eisenhower) to bring about the downfall of Senator Joe McCarthy.

Eisenhower, to be sure, never took the initiative against McCarthy. He declined to "get into the gutter" with the demagogue, and he tolerated, for a while, a certain amount of high-level appeasement. But the fact remains that 15 months after Eisenhower took office McCarthy was done for. With an active, military President, the job might have been done somewhat sooner and with less loss of dignity all around. However, a Republican President did not have to be an activist to draw McCarthy's fire. Though nominally a Republican, McCarthy was bound by the nature of his mission in American political life to attack any administration, and when in time he attacked his own party's stewardship of affairs, resistance was bound to be offered. It tends now to be forgotten that McCarthy scored most of his triumphs when the Democrats controlled both the White House and Congress, and he would probably have been more difficult to deal with had they remained in control. It has always seemed to me that the election of Adlai Stevenson in 1952, however desirable it might have been in certain respects, would have prolonged both the Korean war and McCarthyism, and I have reason to think that, in later years, Stevenson believed this, too. The country was bitterly divided in 1952, and 20 years of Democratic governance was one of the causes of disunity.

Putting Eisenhower in the White House seemed a way of promoting national unity, which, though hardly the highest of political values, is not one to be disregarded. But by 1956 Eisenhower had achieved just about all that it was in his power to achieve. The war was over, McCarthy was a spent force and the President had, at the Geneva Summit Conference of 1955, helped negotiate a limited but nonetheless helpful *détente* in the cold war.

The second term was anticlimax almost all the way. It was also rather melancholy and at times squalid. The President was not a well man. The Democrats, growing in power in the Congress and knowing that no one would ever again ride Eisenhower's coattails, were openly seeking to embarrass him and passing bills he felt he had to veto. In midterm, he lost the two men he had relied on most heavily. John Foster Dulles left office and soon died, and Sherman Adams, who was general manager at the White House, had to retire because of a clear conflict of interest. Eisenhower began on his own to practice some of Dulles's peripatetic diplomacy, but it didn't work. In 1960, he started for another summit meeting, in Paris, but Nikita Khrushchev refused to make the final ascent because of the unpleasantness over the U-2 affair. Eisenhower set out for Japan, but for security reasons (rioting anti-American students, etc.) was advised to turn around and go home.

There is more to being a President than entering or ending wars—and more than instituting or failing to institute political and social change. Style and character are important and closely related aspects of leadership. Eisenhower came to us as a hero—not in the old sense of a man who had displayed great valor but in the newer sense of having been an organizer of victory. His style, though, was anything but heroic. It was in part fatherly, in larger part avuncular. He was not an exhorter—except now and then in campaigns—and as a counselor his performance was as a rule inadequate. He had difficulties with language, particularly when he extemporized. Readers of press-conference texts found his syntax all but impenetrable and often concluded that his thinking was as muddled as the verbatim transcripts. Actually, he was seldom as unclear as he appeared to be when encountered in cold type. Those who listened and watched as he talked were rarely in doubt as to what he was saying. Inflection and expression conveyed much of what seemed missing or mixed up in print. But he was never, to put it mildly, eloquent, never a forceful persuader. He never influenced, or sought to influence, American thought.

Eulogizing Eisenhower in April, 1969, President Nixon said of his late mentor: "For more than a quarter of a century, he spoke with a moral authority seldom equaled in American public life." Nixon did not explain how, when or where the impact of this "moral authority" was felt. Eisenhower was an upright man, a believer in the Protestant ethic he seemed to embody. But the man he twice defeated was no less honorable, and Stevenson had a moral vision that seemed somewhat broader, deeper and less simplistic than Eisenhower's. Do any survivors recall the Eisenhower years as a period notable for elevated standards of morality in public life or elsewhere? In our public life, there were two issues full of "moral" content—McCarthyism and race. On neither did the President personally exercise any of the kind of authority Nixon attributed to him. He was not a McCarthyite or a racist, but he conspicuously failed to engage his personal prestige or that of his office in the struggles against demagogy and racial injustice.

A President can also provide leadership by improving the quality of public life—the quality of the people he appoints and associates himself with, the quality of the acts he and they perform, the quality of the ideas his administration espouses. If in the future, the brief Presidency of Eisenhower's successor is well regarded, it will be largely because of his quest for "excellence." Kennedy brought many first-rate people to Washington, and if one of the lessons they taught us is that first-rate people can sometimes mess things up as badly as third-raters or fourth-raters, it is nevertheless true that some of them performed brilliantly and should continue to serve the Republic for some years to come. No such praise, so far as I am aware, accrues to Eisenhower—except in the case of one institution, the Supreme Court.

He appointed a Chief Justice and four Associate Justices, and all but one of the five (Charles Whittaker, who sat only briefly) served with high distinction. In this respect, Eisenhower's record may be as good as any in history. There was about it, though, a kind of inadvertent quality —as if some architect had achieved splendor while seeking only mediocrity. The President was surprised and in some cases hugely disappointed by the performance of the institution he had created.

In the executive branch, mediocrity was the rule. The one Cabinet member of stature was John Foster Dulles, an imposing man in many ways but also a stiff, self-righteous Calvinist who intensified the cold war as an ideological conflict and sometimes seemed bent on making it a theological one as well—making, as he put it, "the moral force of Christendom . . . felt in the conduct of nations." Nevertheless, Dulles was a man of some intellectual prowess, and nothing of the sort could be said for anyone else in the upper echelons. Eisenhower's measure of expertise in any field was that of success, usually financial success. Especially in the early days, it was a businessman's administration—to a degree that bred misgivings even in the mind of the first Senator Robert Taft of Ohio, who made no bones about being a spokesman for business but said, when he heard of the first appointments, "I don't know of any reasons why success in business should mean success in public service. . . . Anyone who thinks he can just transfer business methods to government is going to have to learn that it isn't so." Eisenhower's appointments were uninspired and uninspiring; one cannot think of any major office holder whose example might have led any young man or young woman to feel that public life might be a high calling. On the White House staff, there were from time to time highly gifted younger men—but for the most part they lacked power and visibility.

Still and all, who in 1971 wouldn't exchange a trainload of mediocrities, incompetents and even pickpockets for a speedy end to the war in Vietnam and to the rancor and discord it has created? There was peace under Eisenhower, and the question of historical interest to those of us who survived the ensuing decade is whether this indisputable fact is to be ascribed to his stewardship or to luck or to some combination of both. I lean toward the combination theory, with perhaps a heavier emphasis on luck than others might care to make.

The opportunities for military involvement during his tenure were fully as numerous as those of the Kennedy, Johnson and Nixon years. In Asia, there were Korea, the Formosa Strait and Indochina; in Europe, Germany and Hungary; in the Middle East, Suez and Lebanon, and in our own hemisphere, Cuba. In some of these troubled areas, intervention was seriously contemplated; in others, it seemed out of the question from the start. In the Suez crisis of 1956, our policy from the onset was to stay out militarily; we made our disapproval so clear to the British and the French that we were not consulted in the planning stages. Nor was there ever much likelihood of our doing anything about Hungary, which erupted just after Suez in the closing days of the Presidential campaign; the Dulles line on Eastern Europe was always that we stood ready to help in the task of "liberation," but it was never much more than a line, and in moments of crisis behind the Iron Curtain—except when there was trouble in Berlin—we looked the other way. In 1958 in Lebanon, we did, at the request of its beleaguered President, land combat-ready Marine and Army units, but there was no combat and the troops spent their time girl-watching on the beaches they had stormed.

But elsewhere the risks were large. Even before his inauguration, Eisenhower went to Korea in search of peace, and in a matter of months a welcome (though far from satisfactory) settlement was made. Politically, in this country, the credit was all his, and if the whole truth is ever known—it will probably never be—it might turn out that he deserves it all. From what is currently known, his principal strategy seems to have been nuclear blackmail—a threat conveyed to our adversaries that if they dragged their feet much longer in the truce talks while pressing on with the war, this country would not consider itself bound to a reliance on conventional weapons. (Eisenhower was never opposed to the use of atomic weapons on moral grounds. He regarded them simply as explosives, suitable for some demolition jobs and not for others. His later assertions about general war's being "unthinkable" in the atomic age were based not on a moral judgment but a military one. He saw no point in a war no one would survive. But tactical "nukes" were another matter.) Maybe that did it, and maybe not. The truth could only come from the other side, and about all we now have on any other factor is Khrushchev's memory of Chou En-lai later explaining that the Chinese losses in Korea had become militarily insupportable. In any case, with all due respect for and gratitude to Eisenhower, one is compelled to wonder what would have happened—what could have happened—if the Communists had said that they weren't afraid of our bombs and intended to carry on with the war. Did he have a fallback position? If so, was it credible? Or did he, as seems so out of character, stake everything on a widely dangerous threat of holocaust? These are questions that await answers that may never come. We know only that the war was terminated the following summer.

In Formosa we have what is perhaps the clearest case of prudent management during the Eisenhower Presidency. The danger was that we would be suckered into at least an air and sea war against Communist China, which was, as it still is, insisting on the rightness of its claim to sovereignty over Formosa and all the islands between it and the mainland. Eisenhower was, in 1954 and 1955, under enormous pressure from his own military and diplomatic advisers, among them Dulles, from congressional Republicans and from many prominent Americans who had supported his candidacy (Henry Luce, for example) to give Chiang Kai-shek every form of assistance he asked for and to help in the defense of every rock in the Formosa Strait—not only to help keep the Generalissimo in his fortress but to aid in preparations for a return to the mainland by the Nationalist armies that had been driven out half a decade earlier. Eisenhower quite clearly had no taste for the entire enterprise. He knew that Chiang alone could never dislodge the Communists, no matter how much matériel we gave him, and he knew, too, that Mao Tse-tung's forces, no matter how many shells they lobbed at the close-in islands, were unequipped for an amphibious invasion of Formosa. So he jollied Chiang with hardware and money and high-level visitors, meanwhile protecting himself with a congressional resolution and a treaty that pledged direct military assistance to Chiang only if we—not he—determined that Peking's maneuvers in the Formosa Strait were unmistakably preparatory to an assault on Formosa itself.

Had Admiral Radford, then Chairman of the Joint Chiefs, been in control, he might have made that fateful determination a dozen times over. Eisenhower read the cables and studied the maps and found no occasion for involving those parts of the agreements that could have led to war. His methods were in certain ways dubious —there were questions about the unconstitutionality of the treaty and the resolution—but at least in the perspective of the present he found a way of averting a war that could have been far costlier than the one we have been in for most of the last decade. There can be little doubt that this was his will and his doing, for, as far as Communist China was concerned, he was the only "dove" in his administration.

Indochina—as always, it is the most complicated of matters. Eisenhower did not get involved militarily, but he may, by his patronage of his Secretary of State and by other words and acts, have made subsequent intervention all but unavoidable. It was Eisenhower who articulated the "domino theory" for Southeast Asia, and we know from his memoirs that on several occasions he seriously considered intervention and was deterred not primarily by political or moral considerations but by military and, to some extent, diplomatic ones. An obvious restraint was our lack of troops and weapons suitable for fighting the kind of war he quite correctly judged it to be. He gave thought to the use of nuclear weapons, and two carriers whose planes had nuclear bombs were in the Tonkin Gulf. But, as Earl Ravenal writes in *Foreign Affairs,* he "could not identify an appropriate enemy or target to fit the massive nuclear response [and] narrowly declined to intervene."

He considered using ground troops to aid the French but stipulated that under no circumstances would he go it alone—that is, without Asian and European allies. Dulles looked for suitable allies but found none. Had Eisenhower found either the appropriate targets for nuclear retaliation or willing partners in intervention, he might still have come up with an excuse for staying out, for nonintervention seemed almost always his preference; his distaste for war was general and a consistent factor in his reasoning. But it was indisputably under Eisenhower that we made heavy commitments to the powers that were and were to be in Saigon, and it was with Eisenhower's blessing that Dulles set up the Southeast Asia Treaty Organization, at once a political joke and a political disaster.

During his time, Eisenhower was not called upon to make good on any of Dulles's commitments in the region. I think it quite conceivable, however, that had he held office in the early sixties he might have found himself a prisoner of his own past and of then-current events and have followed pretty much the course of his successors. One advantage he had over his successors, though, was confidence in his own military judgment, and this might have saved him, us and the Vietnamese from the horrows that were soon to come.

Eisenhower's two terms fell between the two great Berlin crises—the one brought on by the blockade of the Western Sector in 1948 and the one brought on by the Berlin Wall 10 years ago. There was continuous tension over Germany throughout the fifties, but the dangers of war lessened as NATO grew in strength and as circumspection seemed increasingly to prevail in the Kremlin. These were the early days of the world of two nuclear superpowers, and the "balance of terror" would probably have held under any leadership save that of a madman. Though in Europe Dulles made a good many enemies for himself and for his government, his European diplomacy was always more traditional and more prudent, as witness the Austrian treaty, than his diplomacy elsewhere in the world, and it would, I think, be rather difficult to fault Eisenhower for his handling of American policy in Germany.

In his memoirs, Eisenhower wrote of the Bay of Pigs as a "fiasco" for which "indecision and untimely counterorders" were "apparently responsible." He did not elaborate. But whatever he meant by Kennedy's "indecision," the original conclusion that we should sponsor an invasion came out of the Eisenhower, not the Kennedy, administration. As he acknowledged, his military and intelligence people had, with his encouragement, armed and trained the forces in exile and, as we learned in the aftermath, completion of the scheme was urged on the new President by such holdovers as Allen Dulles of the C. I. A. and Gen. Lyman Lemnitzer, Chairman of the Joint Chiefs of Staff. Kennedy took responsibility for the bad show of which Eisenhower was the original producer. Eisenhower was lucky enough to be out of office when the rehearsals were over and the performers were ready for the opening. We can only conjecture as to whether he would have called off the whole business or gone about it in some other way. But he surely bears some responsibility for the policy and for the crucial failure of intelligence which led the executors of the policy to believe that the Cuban people would welcome the invaders as liberators and would take up arms to join them.

I have been somewhat surprised in thinking and writing about the Eisenhower years a decade later to discover that we know a good deal less about the Eisenhower administration than about most recent ones. The historians haven't got around to it yet, and the few memorists it produced haven't revealed very much except about themselves. Eisenhower's two large volumes were put together mainly with scissors and paste. Richard Nixon's *Six Crises* is all about Richard Nixon. Sherman Adams's *First-Hand Report* is not first-hand at all but second- and third-hand—dealing extensively with large events, such as Indochina and Formosa, about which he knew little and, despite his closeness to the President, was seldom if ever consulted. Robert Murphy's *Diplomat Among Warriors* is a stiff-necked but instructive work, only part of which bears on the Eisenhower period. Emmet Hughes's *Ordeal of Power* is a thoughtful, critical work, but Hughes's experience was limited to two brief tours in the White House as a speechwriter and political consultant. A few journalists—notably Robert J. Donovan in *Eisenhower: The Inside Story*—produced creditable works, more useful on the whole than the memoirs, but the literature by and large is thin.

"The President of the United States," Alfred Kazin wrote in reviewing the first volume of Eisenhower's memoirs, "had to look up the public record that most of us more or less knew in order to find out what happened during his administration." This, I think, comes close to the heart of the matter about Eisenhower. For eight years as President, he presided in the most literal dictionary sense—he occupied the seat of authority. But he exercised authority only when there was no other choice. He headed an administration but he rarely administered. In foreign affairs, he stepped in only on certain European questions and when, as Commander in Chief, he was required to make command decisions. In domestic affairs his temperament was in line with his economics—laissez faire. Whenever possible, he let the Government run itself—and it was possible a good part of the time.

Eisenhower never offered himself an an activist. He never pledged innovation or any sort of basic reform. One cannot quite contend that he was the product of a political "draft," but, at least as much as any chief executive in this century, he had the office thrust upon him. His style was well known to those who engineered his nomination and to those who elected and re-elected him. Whatever else may be said in dispraise, he did not betray his trust. He construed it rather narrowly, but in doing so he embodied a long tradition and a specifically Republican tradition.

His command decisions seem, in retrospect, to have been generally wise. He was clear about the hazards of intervention in Asia. However, he deputized Dulles to contract military alliances all over the place—confident, perhaps, that in crises he could prevail as he had in Korea. He deputized much to the other Dulles, Allen, too—and it was under him that the C.I.A. became a force in world affairs and undertook such missions as the overturn of Governments in Iran and Guatemala. Eisenhower was anything but an empire builder—he was by almost any definition an anti-imperialist—but it was while he presided that this country began, if not to acquire new buildings, to use its power in an imperial manner far beyond the Americas.

Domestically, he and we marked time. In the first few years, this was more or less defensible. The country might not have sustained him if he had tried to remake it. Once the Korean war was over and McCarthy's fangs had been drawn, complacency was the dominant American mood, and very few Americans were aware of the large structural faults in many of our institutions. In 1954, the Supreme Court ruled that if we were to be true to ourselves and our pretensions, racism had to be deinstitutionalized, but this was about the only blow to complacency until, in the second term, sputnik went aloft and made some Americans wonder about our educational system. With hindsight, we can see that practically all the problems that bedeviled us in the sixties had been worsening in the fifties. It can be said, to be sure, that nearly all of them predated the fifties by decades, even centuries, and that Eisenhower was no more to blame in such matters than most of his predecessors. And this is only just. He was not a cause of any of our present domestic disorders. Neither, though, did he perceive them or heed the prophets of his time—and there were several—who did perceive them.

What Eisenhower clearly lacked—and this was due as much to the education and experience that had been his lot as a servant of his country as to any deficiency of mind or spirit—was the kind of knowledge of the American condition he might have gained if his background had been in politics rather than in the military. He went through most of the fifties and on into the sixties with an image of this country formed in Kansas *circa* 1910. Nowhere is this so dismayingly clear as in the closing words of the second volume of his memoirs, which was published in a dreadful year for this country, 1965—after his successor had met violent death in Dallas, at a time when violence increasingly characterized our race relations, when the generation gap was widening alongside the credibility gap, when our sons were marching by the tens of thousands into the Vietnam quagmire. In that year, he could bring himself to this apostrophe:

"I have unshakable faith that the ideals and the way of life that Western civilization has cherished . . . will flourish everywhere to the infinite benefit of mankind . . . At home . . . our level of education constantly rises . . . Opportunity for the properly ambitious boy or girl increases daily. Prospects for the good life were never better, provided only that each continues to feel that he, himself, must earn and deserve these advantages.

"Imbued with sense and spirit we will select future leaders [who will] keep a firm, sure hand on the rudder of this splendid ship of state, guiding her through future generations to the great destiny for which she was created."

A good man? Of course. A "brilliant" man? Hardly. "A political genius"? If so, the evidence remains concealed. A good President? Better than average, perhaps, and very useful in his early years. But by and large not what the times required.

Part 5

The Presidency Today-
What Is The Power?

19
Commander In Chief

Eric Goldman   **THE PRESIDENT, THE PEOPLE, AND THE POWER TO MAKE WAR**

From *American Heritage*, Vol. 21, No. 3 (April 1970), 28–35. © 1970 American Heritage Publishing Co., Inc. Reprinted by permission from *American Heritage*.

THE Constitution of the United States declares in the plainest possible English: "The Congress shall have Power . . . To declare War." Yet in the last twenty years Americans have fought two major wars—in Korea and in Vietnam—without a congressional declaration of war. Apart from the question of who has the right to send the armed forces into serious combat action, Vietnam has been a glaring instance of momentous foreign policy carried out with only the most cursory control by Congress.

Naturally, many Americans opposed to the Vietnam war are crying outrage. Many others, for or against the war or somewhere in between, ask a worried question: What has happened to the traditional constitutional procedure whereby the President leads in international affairs but Congress has a potent check on him when the decision involves life and death for the nation's young men and sweeping consequences for the whole country? Is there no way to bring foreign policy back under greater popular control, by restoring the congressional role or through some other technique?

On the surface, the questions have clear-cut answers, most of which revolve around the contention that particular recent Presidents simply have refused to play by the constitutional rules. Yet in actuality the answers are entangled in complex considerations of just what the Founding Fathers did and did not write into the Constitution, how their decisions have been put into practice over two centuries, and whether the circumstances of warmaking have not changed so much that some of the basic old rules simply do not apply.

The wise and hardheaded men who assembled in 1787 to write a constitution for the United States were members of a generation that had just fought a bitter war against the British executive, King George III. They were sick of battles and their devastation and intensely concerned to circumscribe any decision for war. A gangling freshman congressman from Illinois, denouncing the Mexican-American War a half century later, stated the mood of most of the Founding Fathers as accurately as any historian can. Representative Abraham Lincoln wrote in 1848 that the Constitutional Convention gave the warmaking power to Congress because "kings had always been involving and impoverishing their people in wars, pretending generally, if not always, that the good of the people was the object. This, our Convention understood to be the most oppressive of all kingly oppressions; and they resolved to so frame the Constitution that *no one man* should hold the power of bringing this oppression upon us." (The italics are Lincoln's.)

So the Congress, not the President, was to decide war or peace. But the Founding Fathers lived in an era filled with violence between countries that was not formal war. The new nation would be at a sharp disadvantage if in the event of depredations against its commerce or maraudings on its land, its armed forces were immobilized until congressmen could gather from thirteen states in their horse-drawn vehicles. The Founding Fathers made one man who was on the scene, the President, commander in chief of the army and navy. The wording of the first draft of the Constitution gave Congress the exclusive power to "make" war. On te floor of the convention, "make" was changed to "declare," assigning the President the right to use the army and navy in order to meet specific emergencies while retaining for the House and Senate the power to decide full-scale war.

The Constitution has often been called a bundle of compromises, and so it was—not least between those who wanted a strong and those who wanted a weak Chief Executive. The Founding Fathers may have made the President the Commander in Chief, but they gave Congress the power of the purse in determining the size and nature of the armed forces. Until late in the convention, the right to make treaties was vested in the Senate alone. But there were obvious advantages in having one man initiate treaties, receive foreign ambassadors, name and instruct American ambassadors. The Chief Executive would do these things although he was to appoint ambassadors only with the approval of a Senate majority and make treaties with the "Advice and Consent" of two thirds of the Senate.

In foreign affairs, as in all areas, the Founding Fathers were notably spare in laying down specific dictates and in the language that they used to write the provisions. Yet they said enough to make it clear that they envisaged a foreign policy system in which the President would lead, but in collaboration with Congress, especially the Senate, and in which the Chief Executive would be subject to continuing scrutiny and formidable restraints whenever his activities touched that most serious aspect of foreign affairs, general war.

On August 22, 1789, President George Washington, sound Constitutionalist that he was, appeared with his Secretary of War in the Senate chamber to "advise" with the senators on a treaty with the southern Indians and to seek their "consent." The reading of the document began. The wasp-tempered Senator William Maclay, from the back country of Pennsylvania, was annoyed because the passing carriages made it difficult for him to hear the words; he and other senators, in the process of forming an agrarian political opposition to President Washington, were ready to be annoyed at anything that came from this administration with its "monarchical" tendencies. The President wanted an immediate vote, but the Maclay group called for time to study the documents connected with the treaty. George Washington, according to Maclay, "started up in a violent fret." Had he not brought along the Secretary of War precisely to answer any questions that might arise? President Washington calmed down, the delay was granted, the treaty was ratified. But Maclay wrote in his diary, "The President wishes to tread on the necks of the Senate. . . . This will not do with Americans." As for George Washington, he is said to have let it be known that "he would be damned if he ever went there again." He did not go there again for advice on a treaty, and neither did any other President.

The clash over this minor document was a preview of the coming years, when the collaboration between the Chief Executive and the Congress, in the case of treaties or other aspects of international affairs, proved prickly and at times violent. Inevitably, Presidents tended to feel that they had superior information and were acting only after mature consideration of the matter; congressmen were interfering out of impulse, ignorance, politics, or a yen to encroach on White House prerogatives. Inevitably, congressmen, considering themselves sound in judgment and closer to the popular will, tended to believe that Chief Executives were trying, as Senator Maclay had declared, to create situations in which "advices and consents [would be] ravished, in a degree, from us."

Before many decades it also became clear that while Congress might have the war power, a determined Chief Executive could put the House and the Senate in a position where they had little alternative except to vote war. The Democratic President elected in 1844, the unsmiling, tenacious James K. Polk, believed it was manifest destiny for America to expand. Texas had been formally annexed, but Mexico still considered it a rebellious province, and border disputes continued; California lay a luscious plum ready for the plucking from Mexico. President Polk kept trying to maneuver Mexico into acceptance of his ambitions, while he built a fervid public opinion behind expansionism. Finally the President ordered General Zachary Taylor into territory claimed by Mexico, and Mexican troops attacked American cavalry, killing or wounding sixteen.

On Sunday, May 10, 1846, President Polk went to church but, as he put it, "regretted" that he had to spend the Sabbath on a quite different matter—working out a war bill and a strategy for Congress. The measure provided an appropriation of ten million dollars and the calling up of fifty thousand volunteers. The disciplined Democratic majority in the House of Representatives limited debate to two hours, and only in the last minutes did the Polk leaders present a preamble to the bill that was a declaration of war. The House and the Senate included a strong anti-war faction. But now all members were in the position where they either voted for the whole measure or—with a good deal of public opinion near hysteria—voted against money and troops for General Taylor's forces. The House approved 174–14; the Senate, 40–2.

Those dogged fourteen Noes in the House included ex-President John Quincy Adams; and Representative Abraham Lincoln, just arrived in Washington, who would soon begin his sharpshooting against the war. Major intellectuals joined in the assault. Henry Thoreau spent a night in the Concord lockup for refusing to pay his poll tax in protest, and when his aunt paid the money, much to his annoyance, he went back to Walden Pond and wrote his famous essay "Civil Disobedience." The agitation went on, but within five months American troops were swinging along the plaza of Mexico City, gazing in awe and in triumph at the great baroque cathedral and the pink walls of the Halls of Montezuma, asserting by their mud-spattered presence that President Polk was about to achieve in abundance the territorial acquisitions he sought.

Half a century later the obverse of the coin was showing. Of all wars the United States has fought, none has come to be considered more pointless and reprehensible than the Spanish-American War, and that venture was the doing of Congress, driven on by public opinion. During the 1890s a rebellion in the Spanish colony of Cuba, brutally combatted by the Madrid government, caught up a mounting jingo sentiment in the United States. Before long the principal opponents of armed intervention were the American businessmen owning property in Cuba, who wanted things settled without dislocating their economic arrangements, and the two Presidents of the era, Grover Cleveland and William McKinley.

When Congress roared through a resolution

recognizing the "belligerency" of the Cuban rebels, President Cleveland denounced the move as an intrusion on the powers of the Chief Executive and privately remarked that if Congress declared war, he as Commander in Chief would refuse to mobilize the army. President McKinley tried, too; he undertook negotiations with Madrid to bring better treatment of the rebels. But the popular uproar, stoked by tabloid papers, kept increasing. William McKinley's face grew haggard from the pills he was taking to get to sleep; once he sat on a big crimson brocade lounge in the White House and burst into tears as he spoke of the way Congress was forcing the country into war. Finally, the President capitulated. He planned to run for re-election; besides, he was scarcely deaf to voices like that of the senator who thundered to Assistant Secretary of State William R. Day, "Day, by ———, don't your President know where the war-declaring power is lodged? Tell him by ———, that if he doesn't do something, Congress will exercise the power." President McKinley sat working on a war message as the Spanish government conceded major American demands—a concession made before the message actually reached the House and the Senate—and he added poignantly that he hoped Congress would give the Spanish terms "just and careful attention."

A war of territorial seizure maneuvered through by a determined President, an ugly war forced by public opinion and Congress, six wars or significant uses of the armed forces in a little more than a hundred years, more and more instances of acrid White House-Congress clashes in foreign affairs—during the late eighteenth and nineteenth centuries the constitutional system was hardly functioning with glowing results in international matters. Yet the wars or quasi-wars did not pile up long casualty lists; they did not slash through everyday living. The most disruptive conflict, the Civil War, was removed by its very nature from the usual questions of constitutional responsibility. Whatever the underlying reality, even the Mexican-American War was fought under an authorization overwhelmingly granted by Congress. If the wars created savage debates, they spread little bitter feeling that questions of life and death were too far removed from grass-roots control.

President Theodore Roosevelt has often been called "the first modern President," and he was that in many ways. In international affairs the world was taking on its twentieth-century form of great powers jockeying for global position, vast economic stakes overseas, and armed forces designed to strike swiftly. These trends inevitably centered more foreign policy power in the hands of the American President, who was far more able than the cumbersome Congress to operate in this kind of arena. The rambunctious Teddy Roosevelt, no man to turn away from power, responded by driving deep into the American system the doctrine that the Chief Executive is—to use his phrase—"the steward" of the nation, endowed under the Constitution with vast "inherent powers" to act in behalf of what he considers the good of the country.

Action accompanied doctrine. Did T.R. deem it to be in the national interest for the United States to have a canal across Central America so that the Navy could be moved quickly from one ocean to another, and was the Colombian government proving balky? In 1903 T.R. saw to it that Panamanian rebels set up an independent state covering the desired canal zone, and the new nation, to no one's surprise, gave him what he wanted. ("I took the Canal Zone," said President Theodore Roosevelt, "and let Congress debate.") Did T.R. arrive at the conclusion during the Russo-Japanese War of 1904–05 that the security of the United States was best served by a Japanese victory? In entire secrecy he informed Tokyo that, if needed, America would act as an ally, which could have proved a commitment for war. Did the triumphant Japanese then seem a bit too cocky? In 1907 T.R. ordered the entire American fleet on a razzle-dazzle trip around the world, loosing all kinds of diplomatic reverberations. Congressional opponents stirred, particularly those from eastern regions fearing the lack of naval protection, and they talked of denying the appropriations for the fleet movement. Very well, T.R. replied. He had enough money to send the ships to the Pacific Coast, and they could stay there.

It was all very much Teddy Roosevelt, and more than a little rococo. Yet this first modern President was also anticipating in a serious way the modern Presidential trend. Stirred on by changed conditions, he was moving through that broad arch erected by the Founding Fathers—between, on the one side, the clear power of the Chief Executive to lead in foreign affairs and to command the armed forces and, on the other side, the powers of Congress to do certain specific things.

As the twentieth century progressed and the enmeshments of the world grew tighter and more troublesome, Presidents probed still more vigorously the limits of the arch. This development was not only implicit in the circumstances; it was furthered by the difference between the vantage of the Chief Executive and the Congress. The President felt full blast the forces of modernity, which came crashing daily into his office. As the leader of the whole nation, he was heavily influenced by considerations of collective security, the moral position of the United States before international opinion, and the problems that tied in with the stability of the country's economy. Of course members of Congress knew these same concerns, but they were also subject to local, more inward-looking pressures. The House and the Senate continued to include strong blocs which represented the decades-old view that the business of America is America and which resented the persistent intrusion of the world. The abrasion between the two ends of Pennsylvania Avenue in matters of foreign policy sharpened. More and more, Presidents viewed Congress as the adversary and thought in terms of skirting around it or, if necessary, ignoring it.

This occurred at critical points on the road toward American participation in both World Wars I and II. During the European phase of World War I, Germany climaxed three years of friction with the United States by announcing unrestricted submarine warfare. President Wilson had long been troubled by considerations of the moral position of the United States with respect to the conflict, and the feeling of his responsibility to assert American rights on the high seas; now he could not overlook the fact that hundreds of ships, fearful of submarines, were clinging to port and great supplies of wheat and cotton were piling up, threatening to dislocate the nation's economic life. In February, 1917, President Wilson asked Congress for authority to arm merchantmen, an act that could scarcely fail to lead to war. The debate was stormy, and in the upper house eleven senators filibustered the measure to death. Thereupon the President announced that "a little group of willful men had rendered the great government of the United States helpless and contemptible" and ordered the merchantmen armed anyhow. War was declared in April.

After the eruption of the second European war in 1939 President Franklin Roosevelt was convinced that for the good of the United States it belonged at the side of the antifascist powers. Yet he faced tremendous anti-intervention sentiment, so amply reflected in Congress that as late as the summer of 1941, a year after the fall of France, the House extended the draft law by exactly one vote. Under the circumstances, F.D.R. undertook an extraordinary series of executive actions, which sought to hem in Japan economically and to help the nations fighting Nazi Germany. Weeks before Pearl Harbor these moves included an order that in effect meant convoying—despite a congressional ban on convoying—and an order to the Army, Air Force, and the Navy to shoot first at German and Italian vessels found in the western Atlantic, which amounted to *de facto* warfare.

By the time America was fighting in World War II, it was manifest that President Roosevelt had made war and was continuing to conduct foreign policy with only a defensive concern for congressional opinion. Plenty of angry comment was made about this, yet still the war-making power did not become a major national issue. In the case of both World War I and II, a semblance of congressional authority was preserved by the ultimate declarations of war voted by the House and Senate. Of more significance, the two wars were generally accepted by the public; they were led by widely popular Chief Executives; and if they brought serious problems to the society, they did not seem to tear it apart.

In June, 1950, President Harry Truman was visiting his Missouri home when he learned of the invasion of South Korea by North Korea. Flying back to Washington, he mulled over the news. This was plain aggression, the President told himself; aggression unchecked during the 1930's had led to World War II; he was not going to be party to another such tragedy. The next morning the reports were grim: South Korea appeared about to collapse. That night Harry Truman ordered American armed forces into the Korean fighting. Then the United Nations Security Council, on motion of the United States representative, "recommended" assistance to South Korea, and the President summoned congressional leaders, as he put it, "so that I might inform them on the events and decisions of the past few days." The Korean War was under way, grinding on for more than three years, costing the nation 33,629 battle deaths and 103,284 wounded. At no time did President Truman ask congressional authority for the war.

Behind this White House attitude were all the reasons that had been accumulating for decades. But other and profoundly important elements had also entered into the relationship between the Chief Executive and Congress in the conduct of foreign affairs. The simple fact was that the traditional concept of a President leading in foreign policy and then, if necessary, going to Congress for a declaration of war had become obsolete. Historically, war meant that a nation, using whatever weapons seemed feasible, attempted to conquer another country or to beat it into submission. In an era of Cold War, and after the development of nuclear weapons, armed conflicts were taking a different form. Small Communist nations, unofficially backed by large ones, were probing remote areas. The United States was replying not by war in the conventional sense but by what was being called "limited war"—limited in the use of weapons because nuclear power was ruled out and limited in objective, which was not to crush the enemy but to stop him from spreading Communism and to discourage similar efforts in the future.

All the while, the relationship of war to the home front was altering. By the 1950's the United States was so complex a society and Washington so overweening a force that a declaration of war had immense impact. This was partly psychological, but it also involved fundamental workaday facts. Over the decades, by laws and even more by precedents, a declaration of war had come to confer on the President sweeping powers over the entire national life, particularly in the sensitive area of economic affairs. Fighting a limited war, President Truman wanted to limit its home effects, and the opposition to them which could be so easily aroused.

So President Harry Truman went on fighting the Korean War on the authority of President Harry Truman. At times he spoke of the "authorization" or "summons" resulting from the action of the U.N. Security Council; the references were not taken too seriously. The war took calamitous turns. It exacerbated American social problems that were already serious. The very idea of "limited war"—"fighting a war with one hand tied behind you," as people said—ground on the nerves of a nation accustomed to striding in for the knockout. Public opinion, which at first strongly favored the Korean intervention, swung against it and to an extent that had not occurred during any previous conflict; by 1951 the Gallup poll reported a majority believing that the whole intervention was a mistake and favoring prompt withdrawal. Opposition leaders in Congress now were storming against "Truman's War," that "unconstitutional" war; and this time the attacks were building a feeling that something was definitely wrong with the war-making procedures of the United States.

After the Korean War, and as part of the mounting American concern over Communist expansionism, the United States stepped up negotiations with other nations for regional defense pacts. These agreements were impeccably constitutional; they were treaties, negotiated by the executive branch, then debated in the Senate and approved by a two-thirds vote. Yet they contained clauses that could be construed to give Presidents further leverage in foreign affairs. A typical pact was SEATO, negotiated in 1954 by the Eisenhower Secretary of State, John Foster Dulles. It bound the United States, in the event of "armed aggression" by a Communist nation in Southeast Asia, to "act to meet the common danger in accordance with its constitutional processes" and, in the case of other types of threats in the area, to "consult" on the measures to be adopted—whatever a President might take all that to mean, in whatever specific circumstances be found himself.

Simultaneously, an old procedure—a joint House-Senate congressional resolution concerning international affairs—was gathering fresh meaning. After the lambasting President Truman took during the Korean War, Presidents who contemplated moves that might result in war or quasi-war sought some form of mandate from the House and the Senate. They also wanted to gather bipartisan support behind their action or projected action and behind their general policy, and—of great importance in their minds—they sought to present a united front to warn off Communist or Communist-allied nations from adventurous plans.

The joint resolutions came in rapid succession: in 1955, when President Eisenhower thought he might use armed forces to protect Formosa from Red China; in 1957, when he was considering intervening in the Middle East to prevent strategic areas from falling under Soviet control; and in 1962, when President Kennedy was maneuvering to isolate Castro's Cuba. The joint resolutions varied in a number of ways. But they were alike in their general pattern of giving congressional approval to a specific action or contemplated action of the Chief Executive and to his broadly stated policy for a particular troubled area of the world.

During the Presidential campaign of 1964, the celebrated shots were fired in the Gulf of Tonkin by North Vietnamese gunboats against an American destroyer. A heated debate has broken out concerning just how honest President Lyndon Johnson was in reporting the total episode to the public and concerning the larger circumstances surrounding it. The relevant facts here are that the President believed that he should, by retaliating, discourage the North Vietnamese from any such further attacks; that as a politician running for office, he wanted to underline that he was as anti-Communist as his opponent, Barry Goldwater; that the South Vietnamese situation was disintegrating and he did not know what he might want to do about it in the coming months; that he was acutely aware of what had happened to his friend Harry Truman; and that he did not overlook the potentialities of the new type of regional pacts and joint resolutions.

President Johnson ordered a harsh retaliatory bombing of North Vietnamese patrol-boat bases. Then he summoned congressional leaders and told them he thought a joint resolution, like the Formosa and Middle East and Cuban resolutions, should be put through Congress swiftly. The document reached the House and Senate the next morning. It approved the bombing; spoke of America's "obligations" under SEATO to defend South Vietnam; declared that the United States was "prepared, as the President determines, to take all necessary steps, including the use of armed force," to assist any SEATO nation "in defense of its freedom"; and provided that the resolution remain in force until the Chief Executive declared it no longer necessary or the Congress repealed it by majority votes.

The House devoted most of its time to speeches approving the retaliatory bombing of the previous evening, and Representative Henry S. Reuss, from Milwaukee, said all that could be said on that subject. He was reminded, Reuss observed, of the story about the bartender who called the saloon owner on the intercom and asked, "Is Casey good for a drink?"

"Has he had it?"

"He has."

"He is."

The Senate spent more time on the general authorization granted by the resolution. Members rose to ask, Didn't the language mean that the Congress was empowering the President to take any steps he deemed wise, including waging war, in Southeast Asia? Senator J. William Fulbright, the floor leader for the resolution, and a number of other senators replied that President Johnson had stated that it was his policy not to use combat forces in Southeast Asia; the resolution simply backed this policy; it had to be broad and to be approved quickly to show the North Vietnamese how much the American people, without regard to party, were against armed Communist expansion in Southeast Asia. How many congressmen wanted to vote No on such a proposition, especially three months before an election? The debate on the Tonkin Resolution in the House took just forty minutes, and the tally was 416–0. The Senate, after only eight hours of discussion, approved 88–2.

As President Johnson went on escalating the Vietnam war, he brandished freely the foreign policy powers of the White House, including making executive agreements—some secret—that went well beyond the Truman moves and entangled the United States and Asian countries in ways the full purport of which is still not known. More than the Korean War, Vietnam distorted American society at a time when it was still less able to stand further dislocation. And as a large part of public opinion and of Congress turned against the involvement, the cries once again went up, against "Johnson's war," that "unconstitutional horror." But this time there was a difference.

Lyndon Johnson used to carry the difference around with him on a piece of paper crumpled in his pocket. When the subject of his authority for the war came up, he would pull out the slip containing the Tonkin Resolution and read from it. The two Eisenhower joint resolutions and the Kennedy one had concerned crises that went away, or at least seemed to; the problem treated in the Tonkin Resolution turned into a major war, and L.B.J. exploited the document fully, privately and publicly. On one private occasion, he took it out and read emphatically the resolution's reference to American "obligations" under SEATO. With still more stress, hand clapping on knee, he repeated the phrases that the United States was "prepared, *as the President determines,* to take *all* necessary steps." Lyndon Johnson demanded to know, Did Congress limit its authorization in *any* way? Embittered by the opposition to the war and the personal attacks on him, he continued in a deliberately provocative allusion to nuclear bombs, which he had no intention of using: Did Congress limit at all even *what kind* of weapons he could use? . . .

The new regional pacts and even more the

joint resolutions—inaugurated with the best of intentions to meet contemporary circumstances—had given the Chief Executive still more war power, and done it in a manner that came close to caricaturing the intent of the Founding Fathers. For they were nothing less than a means by which Congress, with all the whereases of constitutional procedure, duly voted itself into impotence.

In 1967 President Johnson's Under Secretary of State, Nicholas deB. Katzenbach, appeared before the Senate Foreign Relations Committee. His remarks, reflecting the L.B.J. mood, came close to saying that the Chief Executive has the right to do anything he considers best in international matters without regard to Congress. Midway in the testimony a committee member, Senator Eugene J. McCarthy, got up and walked out muttering, "There is only one thing to do—take it to the country." This reaction was a factor in projecting McCarthy into his anti-war presidential candidacy. It was a reaction that was being felt throughout the country—combining discontent with the war and what it was doing to the nation with the charge that President Johnson was manipulating and bulldozing the American people through a war they did not want to fight.

Inevitably, a flood of proposals have come, some for amendments to the Constitution, others for congressional action. Almost all seek to return to Congress—and thus, presumably, closer to "the people"—greater participation in foreign affairs, with the usual assumption that the Congress would be less likely to venture into unwise wars than the President. . . .

But serious doubts are provoked by any of these proposals. The nub of the situation is the power of the Chief Executive as Commander in Chief and those general or "inherent powers" that have come to cluster about the office of the Presidency. Is there really a way to restrict the powers of the Commander in Chief without possibly doing more harm than good in an era when one man's swiftly pressing the button may be necessary for some degree of national survival, or his prompt decision to use non-nuclear armed forces could be essential to achieving a purpose generally agreed upon by the country? Do the words exist that could inhibit "inherent powers" without simultaneously harassing the President, or blocking him, in taking actions that are widely considered necessary? Is this not particularly true in a period when his office is the one instrumentality than can make decisive moves in behalf of the national interest, whether that interest be expressed in domestic or foreign affairs—in orders to armed forces to strike abroad or to enforce federal laws at home, to affect importantly the deployment of economic and social resources inside the country or eight thousand miles away, or to assert at home or abroad the nation's bedrock values? Yet if the proposals do not cut back on any of these essentials, how effectively do they close off the routes by which Presidents have moved independently to war? . . .

Apart from the difficulty of controlling the President by new language, there is a still more troublesome question—whether, in fact, the Congress and "the people" are less likely than a Chief Executive to get the country into an unwise war. There is not only the glaring instance of the Spanish-American war; other examples, most notably the War of 1812, give pause. Then a rampant faction in Congress—a group with dreams of conquering Canada, who brought the phrase "war hawks" into the American language—helped mightily in pushing the United States into a conflict that was a credit neither to the good sense nor the conscience of the nation. Similarly, in the early, frightened Cold War days, President Truman was worried, and justly so, about a considerable congressional bloc that was restless to take on Russia.

Yet whatever must be said about the dangers or difficulties of restricting the Presidential power to make war, the fact remains that something is decidedly wrong with the process as it has emerged. It *is* a travesty of democracy to have so vital a decision so completely in the hands of one man. As Benjamin Franklin observed during the Constitutional Convention, the nation can never be sure "what sort" of human being will end up in the White House; some might be overly ambitious or "fond of war." The country can also never be certain—no matter how able and peace-minded the Chief Executive—that he will not be led into an unfortunate decision by his dogmas or his limitations. Lyndon Johnson, to use a striking instance, was a Chief Executive of high abilities in a number of respects; he had a strong personal urge to be a peace President and well-seasoned political reasons for avoiding the travail of war. Yet he escalated the Vietnam intervention relentlessly, lashed ahead by old-style certitudes and an inadequate understanding of the forces at work in Asia.

Ideally, what is needed is the creation in modern terms of a system something like the one envisaged by the Founding Fathers, in which the President would have his powers as Commander in Chief and would lead in foreign policy while being guided and checked to some degree by Congress. Toward that end, no good purpose is served by continuing the practice of congressional joint resolutions in international affairs. Either the resolution must say so little that it does not significantly present a bipartisan front to the enemy, or it must be so sweeping that it hands the Chief Executive a blank check.

Beyond this negative suggestion there are all those difficulties in conceiving of a single congressional move that would better the situation. Probably improvement will have to come not by the beguiling expedient of one action but by slower and more complex changes within the existing relationship. For this purpose it is essential to note that in every instance when the United States has gone through all the prescribed constitutional forms, with the President recommending war and the Congress "declaring" it, the House and the Senate have never really "declared war." Five consecutive times from the War of 1812 through World War II, what Congress actually did was to recognize an existing state of war, allegedly caused by other nations. This was not simply the result of the natural desire to make the enemy appear the cause of the fighting. More importantly, it reflected the facts that by the time Congress considered a declaration of war, a long train of actions had made combat involvement inevitable or next to inevitable and that, in most instances, the actions had been taken by the White House.

The problem of increasing the participation of Congress in foreign policy therefore involves less the matter of a declaration of war than a continuing role for the legislative branch in the decisions that lead to large-scale military intervention. Thinking along these lines, it is useless to assume that the built-in tension between the White House and the Hill can be removed. Yet changes could be made that would increase the degree of genuine collaboration.

All modern Presidents have called in congressmen to "consult" concerning major foreign policy moves. The vital point is the nature of the "consulting." Is it a session in which the Chief Executive really listens to his guests, or is it one in which he is simply informing them of what he proposes to do or has done or, asking their advice, receives it merely with a politeness calculated to grease relations with the Hill? The Presidential attitude takes shape from many things, but in no minor degree from the type of men with whom he is talking. And outstanding congressmen can not only influence Presidents; they can rouse opinion in their own chambers and in the nation as a whole, which is certain to have its effects in the White House.

In his *Memoirs* President Truman touched upon the kind of congressional leaders with whom he was dealing during the Korean War.

At times bitingly, he indicated how little he thought of the ability of a number of them to rise above narrow-gauged partisanship, of their knowledgeability in world affairs, even of their willingness to observe discretion when the Chief Executive revealed to them information that was necessary for understanding but seriously affected national security.

Truman, a former senator, knew his Congress only too well. For years students of American government have been pointing to the deplorable effects of the seniority system in Congress, and nowhere has it operated more lamentably than in placing men on that critical body for international matters, the Senate Committee on Foreign Relations. In the early twentieth century, when the White House was enormously aggrandizing its power over foreign policy, a number of the senators who were the chairmen or the ranking minority figures on the committee were close to the clownish in their inappropriateness. Since the advent of nuclear weapons, which brought the gravest of issues before the committee, the chairman and first minority senator have at times been able, informed, and dedicated. Yet to run down the list of the number-one and number-two figures since 1945, not to speak of the total makeup of the body, is to come upon some men whose lack of qualifications is staggering.

The problem is not simply one of bringing to the Foreign Relations Committee senators who will command, and justly command, the ear of the President and the country. There is the further consideration of whether they will insist upon equipping themselves with the kind of staff that permits them to operate with knowledge and force. One of the basic reasons for the overweening supremacy of the White House in international affairs has been its machinery for accumulating facts and its capacity to withhold or distort information and to project its interpretations of events. There is no reason why a Congress that took seriously its role, and was backed by the public in its assertiveness, could not establish information machinery that would enable it to fight the battle of Pennsylvania Avenue on more equal terms.

The potential of such congressional action has been strikingly demonstrated in recent years. During the Vietnam debate in the L.B.J. days, the Senate Foreign Relations Committee, headed by the sharp-minded J. William Fulbright and more or less adequately staffed, began to operate like a countervailing power in international matters. Lyndon Johnson may have come to detest William Fulbright, but he read carefully every word the senator said. The committee launched hearings that were a prime factor in building congressional and public opinion against the war and in ultimately changing Johnson policies. Fulbright has apologized for the "perfunctory" attention his committee gave to the Tonkin Resolution in the early days, and the remark is of more than personal significance. It is an open question whether the United States would have ended up fighting in Vietnam if the Senate Foreign Relations Committee had been vigilant, continuously informed, and articulate during the years from 1954 when the essential shape of affairs in Southeast Asia was developing.

The slow and intricate process of building a realistic base for congressional participation in international affairs—will the American people press for it? A natural aftermath of war is the urge to forget about its horrors, including the way that the country got into them. Yet Vietnam has been a shock to millions and to groups containing many influential figures, and certainly the foreseeable trend of events will keep ever present the possibility of large-scale United States combat involvement. Perhaps the present high feelings about Vietnam will carry over sufficiently to create a congressional stance that will give the American people some degree of responsible surveillance over the disposition abroad of their lives, their fortunes, and their sacred honor.

20 Chief Diplomat

Saul K. Padover   **VIRTUALLY A DICTATOR IN INTERNATIONAL AFFAIRS**

From *Commonweal*, Vol. 88, No. 18 (August 9, 1968), 521–525. © 1968 Commonweal Publishing Co., Inc.

"They talk about the power of the President," Harry Truman once complained, "how I can just push a button to get things done. Why, I spend most of my time kissing somebody's ass." And a similarly thwarted Lyndon B. Johnson exclaimed: "Power? The only power I've got is nuclear—and I can't use that."

But not so international affairs. The concentration of foreign-policy power in the White House, especially in the last three or four decades, has been of such a nature that the customary constitutional and political checks have been made largely ineffective. For all practical purposes, the President is virtually a dictator in international affairs. His decisions are paramount and unrivalled. He occupies the field of decision and action by himself. He shares his authority and prerogative with no other person or group. The irony is that the President uses his preponderant authority legally, *within* the constitutional framework, but is not bound by normally prescriptive constraints.

This development would have appalled the Founding Fathers. It is informative to recall that the framers of the Constitution, in their Convention of 1787, were deeply concerned with the question of Presidential power and were worried that the Chief Executive might become autocratic. They had in their minds the European models all of whom they considered bad—including George III of England and the Stadtholder of Holland. Jefferson, who was not present at the Constitutional Convention, expressed a widely held American opinion of contemporary European Executives (monarchs whom he regarded as mostly fools or knaves panoplied in autocratic power), when, speaking of the "book of kings," he exclaimed fervently: "from all of whom the Lord deliver us. . . ."

In creating the Presidency, the framers of the Constitution were confronted by the age-old dilemma of those who appreciate the need for power and at the same time fear its use. "Make him too weak," said Gouverneur Morris, "—the legislature will usurp his power. Make him too strong—he will usurp the legislature."

On this issue, the debates in the Constitutional Convention are illuminating. One distinguished member, Roger Sherman of Connecticut, proposed that the Executive be chosen by Congress and be entirely accountable to it, because, he said: "an independence of the Executive over the Supreme Legislature was . . . the very essence of tyranny." Pierce Butler of South Carolina, expressing a dread of Executive power which, he said, "in all countries . . . is in constant increase," warned: "Gentlemen seem to think we had nothing to apprehend from an abuse of the Executive power. But why might not a Catiline or a Cromwell arise in this country as well as in others?"

The wise and aged (he was 81) Benjamin Franklin thought so too. Keeping George Washington in mind, Franklin said that the first Chief Executive "will be a good one," but what about his successors? "Nobody," he reminded his fellow-delegates, "knows what sort may come afterwards. The Executive will be increasing here, as elsewhere, till it ends in a monarchy." In those days, it should be remembered, "monarchy" had the connotation of "tyranny" or "absolutism."

The long and intermittent debates over the Presidency, which extended over a period of about 14 weeks, ended in a compromise. Thus the President was empowered to appoint "ambassadors, other public ministers and consuls," but each nomination was required to have the "advice and consent of the Senate." The President was made Commander in Chief of the armed forces of the United States, including the State militias in wartime, but had no authority to initiate war. The power "to declare war" was granted to Congress. It is interesting to note that during the constitution debates an early version stated that Congress shall have power "to make war." In subsequent years it was suggested that this changed phrasing *implied* that while Congress was empowered to "declare" war, it was left to the President to "make" it. The framers of the Constitution, however, did not seem to think so. Without defining the meaning of "war," they made specific enumerations of areas connected with all things military where Congress has exclusive authority. Article I, Section 8, of the Constitution provides that the "Congress shall have power. . . .

"To raise and support armies. . . .

"To provide and maintain a navy.

"To make rules for the government and regulation of the land and naval forces.

"To provide for calling forth the militia. . . .

"To provide for organizing, arming and disciplining the militia. . . .

"To exercise exclusive . . . authority over all places purchased for the erection of forts, magazines, arsenals, dock-yards, and other needful buildings. . . ."

In regard to the crucial problem of treaties—declared in the Constitution to be the "supreme law of the land"—the framers were equally wary about granting the Chief Executive extensive authority. This was particularly true in connection with peace treaties. Some of the delegates to the Constitutional Convention felt that the making of treaties of peace was a matter of such moment that it should be the prerogative of the Senate in cases where the President could not be trusted to end a war.

James Madison suggested that two-thirds of the Senate should have the power to make peace treaties, without Presidential concurrence. His reason for the proposal reveals the prevailing distrust of too much executive power. Madison shrewdly argued that a wartime President would, of necessity, be in such a commanding position that he might be reluctant to terminate a conflict that had clothed him with so much authority and special eminence. In Madison's words, a President "would necessarily derive so much power and importance from a state of war that he might be tempted, if authorized [i.e. Constitutionally allowed], to impede a treaty of peace." In a compromise solution, the framers of the Constitution granted the President power "to make treaties," but with a specific reservation—"provided two-thirds of the Senators present concur."

Even so, the framers were not altogether at ease about Presidential power. The congressional checks which they built into the Constitution did not allay their fear of some overbearing or corrupt Chief Executive in the future. They added a further safeguard—that of impeachment. As a guarantee for the "good behavior of the Executive," to quote North Carolina's William R. Davie, the framers thought it essential that the President (as well as the Vice President and other high officials) be made liable to impeachment, that is, legally tried (by the Senate sitting as a court) for certain stated causes. If found guilty, by two-thirds of the Senators present, he should be removed from office and then be subject "to indictment, trial, judgment and punishment, according to law." Benjamin Franklin added a wry note to the discussion on impeachment. He said that the provision was necessary to get rid of an "obnoxious Executive," because without it there would be "recourse . . . to assassination." Such an act, he felt was too drastic, since it would not only deprive the President of his life but also of "the opportunity of vindicating his character." Impeachment would give the Executive a chance of defending himself in a fair trial.

As the constitutionally created Diplomatic Chief and Army Chief, the President has occupied a unique position in the Federal system, enjoying—and using—special powers not granted to any other person or political body. In practice, if not necessarily in theory (although there is some constitutional theory here too), the Executive, beginning with George Washington, soon found that his functions as Chief Diplomat and Commander had to be performed in an arena that was, more or less, exclusively his own. As early as March 7, 1800, John Marshall, then a member of Congress, said in a speech in the House of Representatives: "The President is the sole organ of the nation in its external relations, and its sole representative with foreign nations . . . The demand of a foreign nation can only be made on him. He possesses the whole executive power. He holds and directs the force of the nation. Of consequence, any act to be performed by the force of the nation is to be performed through him."

A similar position was taken by the Senate Committee on Foreign Relations on Feb. 15, 1816. In its report, the Committee confirmed Marshall's view when it stated: "The President is the constitutional representative of the United States with regard to foreign nations." It affirmed that only the President "must necessarily be most competent to determine" the whole process of international negotiation; and while "he is responsible to the Constitution," nevertheless, any interference by the Senate would only "impair the best security for the national safety."

Over the years, the President's position of primacy as Chief Diplomat—as treaty-negotiator and treaty-maker—has been established in practice and confirmed in law. The courts have not only upheld this power but have deepened and widened it in their interpretations. One Supreme Court decision (*Geofroy v. Riggs*, 1890) actually declared that the treaty-making power was virtually limitless in range and subject matter. The basic limit, according to that decision, was only that which the Constitution expressly prohibited. Otherwise, stated Justice Stephen J. Field in *Geofroy v. Riggs*: "The treaty power, as expressed in the Constitution, is . . . unlimited . . . It would not be contended that it extends so far as to authorize what the Constitution forbids . . . But with these exceptions, it is not perceived that there is any limit to the questions . . . touching any matter which is properly the subject of negotiation with a foreign country."

Furthermore, the courts have been wary about putting restraints on the executive's commanding prerogative in the realm of foreign affairs. They have taken the position that the judicial branch was neither constitutionally empowered nor administratively equipped to pass judgment in foreign policy matters, which they regarded as essentially political and not judicial. In the case of *Chicago and Southern Airlines v. Waterman Steamship Corp.* (1948), Justice Robert H. Jackson summarized the Supreme Court's opinion thus: "The President, both as Commander in Chief and as the nation's organ for foreign affairs, has available intelligence services whose reports are not and ought not to be published to the world. It would be intolerable that courts, without the relevant information, should review and perhaps nullify actions of the executive taken on information properly held secret . . . But even if the courts could require full disclosure, the very nature of executive decisions as to foreign policy is political, not judicial . . . They are decisions of a kind for which the judiciary has neither aptitude, facilities, nor responsibility."

Justice Jackson concluded that foreign policy decisions, being the domain of political (executive, primarily) power, were "not subject to judicial intrusion or inquiry."

As Presidential power in foreign affairs has grown and expanded, the originally designed constitutional checks upon it have undergone a slow process of erosion. To a large extent, this development has been due to the ambiguity of the constitutional provisions. In the 1967 Senate *Hearings on U.S. Commitments to Foreign Powers*, Senator J. William Fulbright, Chairman of the Senate's Foreign Relations Committee, frankly admitted that he was troubled by "the imprecision that exists in this field." Constitutionally, it is not even clear what a "war" is, or when it becomes one. Is chasing bandits across a foreign frontier "war" in the constitutional sense? Is occupation by marines of foreign ports and customs houses "war"? Is large-scale fighting against Communists in Asia a "war" or a "police action"?

In a Supreme Court decision of 1936—*United States v. Curtiss-Wright Export Corp.*—Presidential domination in the foreign affairs field was summed up in sweeping terms. Speaking for the Court's majority (7 to 2), Justice George Sutherland stated, *inter alia*: "Not only . . . is the federal power over external affairs in origin and essential character different from that over internal affairs, but participation in the exercise of the power is significantly limited. In this vast external realm, with its important, complicated, delicate, and manifold problems, the President alone has the power to speak or listen as a representative of the nation. He *makes* treaties with the advice and consent of the Senate; but he alone negotiates. Into the field of negotiation the Senate cannot intrude; and Congress itself is powerless to invade it. . . ."

Circumventing the Senate

Presidents have been able to circumvent senatorial treaty power through the device of executive agreements. Such agreements are of two types: those that require legislative implementation and those that are "pure," that is, require no congressional action. Unlike a treaty, an executive agreement does not require the approval of the Senate. Presidents can make such agreements, provided they do not infringe on the private rights of Americans, on any subject, ranging from recognition of foreign governments to barter deals. Among the better known executive agreements, one may mention: the destroyer-for-bases exchange with Great Britain in 1940; the Lend-Lease program in 1941; the Atlantic Charter agreement in 1941; and the Allied conferences of Yalta in 1944 and Potsdam in 1945, which involved postwar settlements. Executive agreements, arranged between the President or his agents and foreign nations, have the binding force of treaties, as the Supreme Court has held in decisions such as *United*

States v. Belmont (1937) and *United States v. Pink* (1942).

The number of treaties, requiring senatorial concurrence, has decreased steadily while executive agreements, requiring none, have risen steeply. By 1939, out of 2,000 engagements made by the United States with foreign countries, 1,182 were executive agreements. In 1936, there were 8 treaties, and 16 executive agreements. In 1944, there was one treaty, and 74 executive agreements.

The vast, practically limitless, powers enjoyed by the President nowadays is seen most strikingly in the field of war making. From the very beginning, the "Commander in Chief" clause of the Constitution, not being defined or specifically limited, has provided the executive with as much military authority as his personal discretion allowed. The main restraints have been the President's own character and political judgment. From the earliest days of the Republic to now, Presidents have sent armed forces into action—without congressional authorization or war declaration—for the ostensible purposes of protecting life and property abroad. These have been recognized as legitimate steps in the defense of the "national interest." There have been at least 125 such instances, perhaps more.

John Adams waged an undeclared, although limited, war against France between 1798 and 1800. Jefferson sent a flotilla against the Algerian (Barbary) pirates in 1801. Polk ordered troops against Mexico in 1846, and Wilson in 1916. Presidents have dispatched marines to Central America on numerous occasions. More recently, Truman sent forces to Korea in 1950 (opening a large-scale war), Eisenhower to Lebanon in 1958, and Johnson to the Dominican Republic in 1966.

All these military steps were taken at the President's discretion, by virtue of the power inherent in him as Commander in Chief, without formal declarations of war. Occasionally there have been congressional resolutions, such as the Tonkin Gulf Resolution of 1964, but these must be construed, as statements of support, not formal grants of power. A congressional resolution is in the nature of a politico-psychological tactic, to show the world that a certain Presidential step has national support or sometimes merely to nudge the executive. But a resolution as such adds little, if anything, to the President's inherent military prerogative.

Currently there is a claim in the Senate that the war in Vietnam is illegal because the Tonkin Gulf Resolution, which the President has used as his presumed authorization to initiate the bombing and to widen the conflict, was based on misleading information deliberately supplied by the Pentagon. The facts of the case may or may not be true. But even granting that the Senate was booby-trapped by the military agents of the executive, the argument is of dubious constitutional validity, although it may have great moral force. The truth is that the Commander in Chief does not actually need congressional resolutions. If and when he decides upon military action, he has a plenitude of authority and precedent behind him. He has, in fact, an awesome power in this field.

Is such power constitutional? The answer is that it is not patently unconstitutional. There is nothing in the Constitution that says that the President may not wage war abroad at his discretion. The Constitution merely states that only Congress can "declare" war. But it does not say that a war has to be "declared" before it can be waged.

Vietnam is the culmination of this long-accumulating executive power in the military domain. Where it differs from preceding Presidential commitments of armed forces abroad without war declaration is in scale—in numbers of troops committed, worldwide consequences, and soaring casualties. There is obviously a considerable difference between the three small frigates and one sloop of war that Jefferson dispatched against the Barbary pirates in 1801, and the current deployment in Vietnam. However, the principle of Presidential discretion in the use of force abroad remains the same.

We should remind ourselves that Vietnam is a Presidential war. It was initiated ("Americanized") with the bombing of 1964 and then steadily escalated and systematically conducted entirely by the President. The military heads and the chiefs of the Pentagon have acted, and legally may act, only at his orders. Whatever the reasons for the plunge into the Vietnam war there can be no question that the decision emanated from the executive and has been his responsibility ever since. There is, moreover, no legal way to stop him.

Thus the fears that James Madison expressed in 1787 have actually come to pass, although under altered circumstances and under a different guise.

With luck, the war in Vietnam—now widely agreed to have been an American blunder—may end without global catastrophe. But what about the future?

Once in office, any man, by virtue of the power now inherent in the Presidency, is in absolute control over the levers of the mightiest military machine in the world, with an atomic-weapon capability of destroying much of humanity at his finger tips. That is a chance that this nation, or mankind as a whole, cannot afford to accept indefinitely. . . .

The situation is not only perilous in itself but it is also at variance with the philosophy of American democracy, which, in its governmental aspect, is based on the principle of "checked" and "balanced" powers. When one of the three coordinate branches of the national government is increasingly preponderant and unchecked, the structure is thrown out of kilter and creates a festering crisis that endangers the whole political system.

What is needed is not to take power in foreign affairs away from the President—the national security obviously requires that he has it —but to put manageable restraints upon it. What the situation requires is a counter-force to keep the overwhelming power of the executive in acceptable balance. Only Congress can do that constitutionally.

If Congress, especially the Senate, is to restore its eroded powers and reassert its originally assigned role as partner and balancer in foreign affairs, it will have to do it, not through the futility of accusatory speeches or committee reports, but through concrete legislation and institutionalized procedures. In the process, it may well have to reorganize itself. A number of steps come to mind:

—Legislation putting specified limits on the size of forces committed to war abroad when there is no war declaration.

—Legislation requiring congressional authorization for any increase of forces under such circumstances.

—Legislation requiring the executive to consult the Congress before committing sizeable forces abroad.

—Legislation requiring a time limit on commitment of forces, subject to congressional extension, or rescission.

—Reorganization of the Foreign Relations and Military Affairs Committees to small and wieldy size, with members making it their full-time occupation.

—Setting up of joint House-Senate Committees on the basis of continuous operations.

—Enlarging the professional and research staffs of those Committees.

—Establishing a congressional intelligence service, not to compete with the gigantic apparatus available to the Executive (such as the CIA), but sufficiently equipped, trained and skilled to help the Congress evaluate properly the findings and recommendations of Presidential agencies.

These are, of course, merely indications of the kind of action required to strengthen Congress so that it could carry out properly its constitutionally-assigned role. It is clear that without some such steps, future Vietnams may not be avoidable, and Congress will continue to be a paper tiger.

21
Controlling The Budget

Louis Fischer   **HIDING BILLIONS FROM CONGRESS**

From *The Nation*, (November 15, 1971), 486–490. Reprinted by permission.

According to the Budget and Accounting Procedures Act of 1950, it is the policy of Congress that the accounting of the government provide "full disclosure of the results of financial operations, adequate financial information needed in the management of operations and the formulation and execution of the budget, and effective control over income, expenditures, funds, property, and other assets." Despite that general policy, it has been estimated that, in a budget for fiscal 1972 of $229.2 billion, secret funds may amount to $15 billion to $20 billion.

The financing of the war in Vietnam illustrates how billions can be spent for programs known to relatively few congressmen. In September 1966, President Johnson expressed his "deep admiration as well as that of the American people for the action recently taken by the Philippines to send a civic action group of 2,000 men to assist the Vietnamese in resisting agression and rebuilding their country." Other announcements from the White House created the impression that not only the Philippines but Thailand, South Korea, and other members of the "Free World Forces" had volunteered troops.

However, hearings held by the Symington subcommittee in 1969 and 1970 revealed that the United States had offered sizable subsidies to countries that involved themselves in Vietnam. It was learned that the Philippines had received river patrol craft, engineering equipment, a special overseas allowance for its soldiers sent to Vietnam, and additional equipment to strengthen Filipino forces at home. It cost the United States $38.8 million to send one Filipino construction battalion to Vietnam. Senator Fulbright said that as he saw it, "all we did was go over and hire their soldiers in order to support our then administration's view that so many people were in sympathy with our war in Vietnam."

The Philippine Government denied that U.S. contributions represented a subsidy or a fee in return for the sending of the construction battalion, but an investigation by the General Accounting Office confirmed that "*quid pro quo* assistance" had indeed been given. Moreover, there was evidence that the Johnson administration had increased other forms of military and economic aid to the Philippines in exchange for its commitment of a battalion to Vietnam.

The Symington subcommittee also uncovered an agreement that the Johnson administration had made with the Royal Thai Government, back in 1967, to cover any additional costs connected with the sending of Thai soldiers to Vietnam. The State Department estimated that U.S. support to Thai forces—including payment of overseas allowances—came to approximately $200 million. A number of other expenses were also involved, such as modernization of Thai forces and the development of an antiaircraft Hawk battery in Thailand. The Foreign Ministry of Thailand denied that the United States had offered payments to induce Thailand to send armed forces to Vietnam, but GAO investigators revealed that U.S. funds had been used for such purposes as the training of Thai troops, payment of overseas allowances, and payment of separation bonuses to Thai soldiers who had served in Vietnam. An interim GAO report estimated that the U.S. Government had invested "probably more than $260 million in equipment, allowances, subsistence, construction, military sales concessions, and other support to the Thais for their contribution under the Free World Military Assistance program to Vietnam."

U.S. subsidies were used once again to facilitate the sending of South Korean forces to Vietnam. Assistance included equipment to modernize Korean forces at home, equipment and all additional costs to cover the deployment of Korean troops in Vietnam, additional loans from the Agency for International Development, and increased ammunition and communications facilities in Korea. To assure that the dispatch of men to Vietnam would not weaken the defensive capabilities of the Republic of Korea, the Johnson administration agreed to finance the training of forces to replace those deployed in Vietnam and to improve South Korea's antiinfiltration capability. From fiscal 1965 to fiscal 1970, Korea's military presence in Vietnam was estimated to have cost the United States $927.5 million.

The legal basis for this assistance to free world forces in Vietnam derives from authorization and appropriation statutes of 1966. Funds were made available to support Vietnamese "and other free world forces in Vietnam, and related costs . . . on such terms and conditions as the Secretary of Defense may determine." In 1967, assistance was broadened to include local forces in Laos and Thailand. Reports on such expenditures were submitted only to the Armed Services and Appropriations Committees of each house. One would not know from the general language of the statutes what type of financial arrangement the administration might enter into, or with what country. Even staff people who had access to the reports said that they did not know the nature and dimension of financing the free world forces until hearings were held by the Symington subcommittee.

Legislation in 1969 and 1970 tightened up the language of the statutes somewhat by placing a ceiling on the funds that could be given to free world forces. Standards were also established for payments of overseas allowances. The "ceiling" of $2.5 billion exceeded the amounts spent in previous years, and did not constitute much of a restriction. The fiscal 1970 appropriation bill for the Defense Department included a proviso stating that nothing in the Act should be construed as authorizing the use of funds "to support Vietnamese or other free world forces in actions designed to provide military support and assistance" to the governments of Cambodia and Laos. The force of that restriction was diluted by another provision which declared that nothing in the Act should be construed "to prohibit support of actions required to insure the safe and orderly withdrawal or disengagement of U.S. Forces from Southeast Asia, or to aid in the release of Americans held as prisoners of war." On February 8, 1971, after the United States had granted support to South Vietnam's intervention in Laos, the State Department justified the U.S. support partly on the ground that it "will protect American lives."

Presidential spending discretion has been used in the last two years to spread the costs of the Vietnamese war to Cambodia and Laos. It was by exercising his transfer authority that President Nixon could extend financial assistance to Cambodia after his intervention there in the spring of 1970. At the end of the year, he appealed to Congress for $255 million in military and economic assistance for Cambodia. Of that amount, $100 million was to restore funds which the President had *already* diverted to Cambodia from other programs. Under Section 610 of the Foreign Assistance Act, the President may transfer up to 10 percent of the funds of one program to another, provided that the second program is not increased by more than 20 percent. Taking advantage of that authority, the Nixon administration borrowed $40 million from aid programs originally scheduled for Greece, Turkey and Taiwan; took another $50 million from funds that had been assigned largely to Vietnam; and diverted still other funds until a total of $108.9 million in military assistance had been given, or committed, to Cambodia.

In the waning days of the 91st Congress, legislators attempted to place two restrictions on Presidential actions in Cambodia. The Special Foreign Assistance Act of 1971 barred the use of funds to finance the introduction of U.S. ground troops into Cambodia, or to provide U.S. advisers to Cambodian forces in Cambodia. But in its bombing operations in Cambodia, and in its subsequent "incursion" into Laos, the administration interpeted air power in such broad terms as to circumvent much of the legislative restrictions. When helicopter gun ships can patrol at treetop level, the distinction between "air power" and "ground troops" begins to disappear.

The Special Foreign Assistance Act of 1971 also stipulated that military and economic assistance to Cambodia "shall not be construed as a commitment by the United States to Cambodia for its defense." This amounted to whistling in the dark, for it is clear that a commitment has nonetheless been made. As Secretary Rogers explained to the Senate Foreign Relations Committee, on December 10, 1970: "I think it is true that when we ask for military assistance and economic assistance for Cambodia we do certainly take on some obligation for some continuity." In an interview with Henry Bradsher of the Washington *Evening Star*, the Cambodian Foreign Minister said that he felt there was an unwritten treaty between the two countries: "I am convinced that there really is a moral obligation of the United States to help. We are confident that the United States will continue to help us."

The extent of this support was indicated in October 1971, when the Senate debated an amendment to the Foreign Assistance Act which would limit the total authorization to Cambodia to $200 million. The administration opposed the restriction, contending that it would threaten the capacity of the Cambodian government to defend itself. John N. Irwin III, Acting Secretary of State, offered Senator Fulbright this appraisal in a letter dated October 13, 1971: "We believe that with continued United States assistance at the levels requested by the administration, the Cambodians with some external logistics and maintenance support will continue to make progress in defending their country from foreign invasion."

Thus our commitment is twofold: continued U.S. assistance and "some external logistics and maintenance support." Contemporary regulations on unauthorized commitments are explicit. The U.S. Code contains the following admonition: "No officer or employee of the United States shall make or authorize an obligation under any appropriation or fund in excess of the amount available therein; nor shall any such officer or employee involve the government in any contract or other obligation, for the payment of money for any purpose, in advance of appropriations made for such purpose, unless such contract or obligation is authorized by law" [31 USC 665(a)]. Despite that rigorous language, the administration can present Congress with a *fait accompli* and in effect compel it to appropriate the necessary funds.

Covert financing has also been used to support, through the CIA, such diverse activities as military operations in Laos and the broadcasting of U.S. information to Eastern Europe and Russia. The CIA can do this because of extraordinary authority over the transfer and application of funds. Section 10(b) of the Central Intelligence Act of 1949 provides that the sums made available to the CIA "may be expended without regard to the provisions of law and regulations relating to the expenditure of government funds. . . ." For objects of a confidential nature, such expenditures are accounted for solely on the certificate of the CIA director, with each certificate deemed a sufficient voucher for the amount certified. Section 6(a) of the Act authorizes the CIA to transfer to and receive from other government agencies "such sums as may be approved by the Bureau of the Budget" for the performance of any functions or activities authorized by the National Security Act of 1947. Other government agencies are authorized to transfer to or receive from the CIA such sums "without regard to any provisions of law limiting or prohibiting transfers between appropriations."

During February 1967 it was reported in the press that the CIA had been secretly subsidizing religious organizations, students groups, labor unions, universities, and private foundations. President Johnson appointed a three-member committee, headed by Under Secretary of State Katzenbach, to review the relationships between the CIA and private American voluntary organizations. On March 29, the committee reported that covert CIA assistance had been made available by the last four administrations, dating back to October 1951. The committee recommended that "No federal agency shall provide any covert financial assistance or support, direct or indirect, to any of the nation's educational or private voluntary organizations." President Johnson accepted the committee's statement of policy and directed all agencies of the government to implement it fully.

A footnote to the committee's report explained that its statement of policy did not entirely close the door to covert financing of private voluntary organizations. Exceptions might be necessary: "where the security of the nation may be at stake, it is impossible for this committee to state categorically now that there will never be a contingency in which overriding national security interests may require an exception—nor would it be credible to enunciate a policy which purported to do so."

The CIA continued to finance the broadcasting that had been conducted by Radio Free Europe to Eastern Europe and by Radio Liberty to Soviet Russia. The continuation could have been justified either on the ground of national security or by identifying RFE and RL as foreign-based institutions as distinct from "any of the nation's educational or private voluntary organizations." The latter had been the thrust of the Katzenbach report.

Senator Case, who sits on both the Appropriations and the Foreign Relations Committees, apparently had to rely on an article in *The Christian Science Monitor* to learn that the Administration had agreed to finance Thai troops in Laos. Further investigation by Senate staff members disclosed that the CIA was covertly financing 4,800 Thai troops fighting in northern Laos in support of the Laotian government. The cost of the operation was initially estimated at between $10 million to $30 million a year. A staff report prepared for the Senate

Foreign Relations Committee later disclosed that the CIA had spent at least $70 million in Laos during fiscal 1971.

In a letter to Secretary Rogers, Case asked whether the administration considered the financial support of Thai troops in Laos to be in accord with the Cooper-Church provisions in the 1970 Defense Appropriations Act, which banned the payment of mercenaries except to protect a safe and orderly American withdrawal from Southeast Asia or to aid in the release of United States prisoners. The State Department replied that "nothing is being done that is not within present legislative authority."

On the basis of a GAO report, Sen. Edward Kennedy charged that money appropriated for refugee programs, for public health, agriculture, economic and technical projects, and for the "Food for Peace" program, had been diverted to pay for CIA-directed paramilitary operations in Laos. During hearings, the Joint Economic Committee noted that nearly $700 million in Food for Peace funds has been channeled into military assistance programs. Since 1954, when Public Law 480 was enacted, $1.6 billion of funds generated by Food for Peace have been allocated to military assistance.

Statutory authority exists for this purpose, but few members of Congress were aware that Food for Peace was such a capacious vehicle for military assistance. Nor could they have gained that understanding by reading the budget, which describes Food for Peace in these terms: "The United States donates and sells agricultural commodities on favorable terms to friendly nations under the Agricultural Trade Development and Assistance Act (Public Law 480). This program combats hunger and malnutrition, promotes economic growth in developing nations, and develops and expands export markets for U.S. commodities."

Senator Proxmire castigated this use of rhetoric to conceal the nature of the Food for Peace program. "This seems to me," he said, "to be kind of an Orwellian perversion of the language; food for peace could be called food for war."

No one can determine from a present-day budget how much is spent for military assistance. For instance, the budget for fiscal 1972 estimates 1971 outlays for military assistance at $1.175 billion in Defense Department funds, plus an additional $504 million in supporting assistance. The total is apparently $1.679 billion. However, Senator Proxmire obtained from the Defense Department its estimates for the military assistance program and foreign military sales. The amount of military assistance for fiscal 1971 was as follows: (1) $3.226 billion in MAP, military assistance service funded and related programs; (2) $600 million in supporting assistance; (3) $7 million in additional public safety programs; (4) $143 million in Food for Peace funds for common defense purposes; and (5) $2.339 billion in military export sales. The total: $6.315 billion. . . .

The war in Southeast Asia has emphasized the fact that, although Congress still retains the power to appropriate money, it is fast losing control over how it is spent. The executive branch—through its ability to transfer funds, impound money, create unauthorized commitments, and engage in covert financing—now holds a substantial portion of the spending power. It does no good to bemoan that fact or complain of executive usurpation. Congress will have to legislate back into reality its traditional "power of the purse." In the steel seizure case of 1952, Justice Jackson reminded Congress of the maxim, "The tools belong to the man who can use them." His parting observation then is pertinent still: "We may say that power to legislate for emergencies belongs in the hands of Congress, but only Congress itself can prevent power from slipping through its fingers."

22
Keeping Tabs On The Public

Carl Cohen   **THE POISONOUS TREE**

From *The Nation*, (February 22, 1971), 231–232. Reprinted by permission.

Secret, electronic surveillance of private citizens by government agencies is a serious invasion of privacy and does irremediable damage to the decency of our civic life. How can it be stopped? One legal weapon against it, which can have important effect, is the refusal of the courts to use or to receive evidence in this unsavory way. Over the retention and strengthening of that weapon legal battle now rages.

Some background first. The Fourth Amendment of the U.S. Constitution lays it down that: "The right of the people to be secure in their persons, houses, papers, and effects, against unreasonable searches and seizures, shall not be violated, and no Warrants shall issue, but upon probable cause, supported by Oath or affirmation, and particularly describing the place to be searched, and the persons or things to be seized."

On this basis it is a long-standing principle of our courts that the government may not build its case against a defendant in a criminal action upon evidence obtained by unconstitutional methods. Even where that evidence, were it to be accepted, might clearly establish guilt, it must not be accepted, or even heard, because permitting any use of it is direct encouragement to law enforcers to gather such evidence in future cases. In applying this important exclusionary principle to search by wire tap, the U.S. Supreme Court also held in 1969 (*Alderman v. United States*) that the government must disclose to a defendant any record of conversations he participated in, or which occurred on his premises, which the government acquired by means of any illegal electronic surveillance.

But when is electronic surveillance legal and when illegal? The Omnibus Crime Control and Safe Streets Act of 1968, far less restrictive in this regard than it ought to be, does lay down strict conditions within which electronic surveillance may be carried out. Probable cause to believe that criminal activity is in progress must be sworn to before surveillance is undertaken, and a duly constituted court or magistrate must authorize specific surveillance and issue a warrant therefor. Unauthorized electronic surveillance by government officials is a serious crime.

But the Act also provides, unhappily, for exceptions to its own restrictions. By its own words the Act does not "limit the constitutional power of the President to take such measures as he deems necessary to protect the nation against actual or potential attack or other hostile acts of a foreign power, or to obtain foreign intelligence information deemed essential to the security of the United States, or to protect national security information against foreign intelligence activities. Nor shall anything contained in this chapter be deemed to limit the constitutional power of the President to take such measures as he deems necessary to protect the United States against the overthrow of the government by force or other unlawful means, or against any other clear and present danger to the structure or existence of the government. . . ."

Through this hole in the dike the Attorney General of the United States and his subordinates have surged, and the federal courts now face the difficult problem of restraining the zeal of law enforcers eager to tap the wires of anyone who might, by their lights, be deemed a threat to "national security." The threat, more deeply understood, is *from* the government—and the privacy of citizens is its victim.

The rub lies here. Who decides what is necessary for "national security"? The President, acting through the Attorney General, is authorized to conduct electronic surveillance without judicial warrant to protect the nation against the hostile acts of foreign powers. That is itself worrisome. But is the exception to be enlarged? Is wire tapping to be permitted, and its results received by the courts, in matters of alleged *internal* security?

The issue is not only theoretical. A case before the U.S. District Court, Eastern District of Michigan, presents the practical problem starkly. The defendants are charged with conspiring to injure government property, and one of them, Lawrence "Pun" Plamondon, is charged with the actual bombing of a CIA office building in Ann Arbor. Electronic surveillance of Mr. Plamondon's conversations has been conducted by the government, undertaken admittedly *without* the judicial authorization that the law requires. The sealed logs of these wire taps have been delivered to the court, and with them an affidavit from the Attorney General. This affidavit does not assert that at the time these wire taps were installed, law-enforcement agents had probable cause to believe that criminal activity was actually being plotted. (If such probable cause could have been shown—that, for example, the illegal overthrow of the government by violence was being planned—a proper warrant could surely have been obtained.) The affidavit argues, badly, that the Attorney General, as agent of the President, *may by himself authorize* electronic surveillance of "attempts of domestic organizations to attack and subvert the existing structure of the government." Therefore, he concludes, wire tapping in this case, although without judicial warrant or control, is yet legal.

It is to the enduring credit of the U.S. District Court, in the person of Judge Damon J. Keith, that this argument by the government has been flatly rejected. Keith's forceful and distinguished opinion affirms the constitutional right of citizens to be protected from such unauthorized electronic searches. He makes it clear that dissident domestic organizations may *not* be treated like unfriendly foreign powers.

Such an analogy, he points out "strikes at the very constitutional privileges and immunities that are inherent in United States citizenship. It is to be remembered that in our democracy all men are to receive equal and exact justice regardless of their political beliefs or persuasions. The executive branch of our government cannot be given the power or the opportunity to investigate and prosecute criminal violations under two different standards simply because an accused espouses views which are inconsistent with our present form of government."

Judge Keith adds his support to the well-reasoned argument of federal Judge Warren J. Ferguson, who ruled: "... in wholly domestic situations there is no national security exemption from the warrant requirement of the Fourth Amendment." If, therefore, in cases like this, the government conducts electronic surveillance without judicial warrant, all that it collects is collected in clear violation of the Fourth Amendment. Judge Keith and Judge Ferguson renew our confidence in the federal judiciary.

Having rejected the government's argument, what is to be done? Evidence got by wire tap is to be excluded, assuredly; but that is not by itself enough. Suppose, through the use of illegal wire taps, the government gets leads to further evidence about which it otherwise could not have known. That too in accord with an old Supreme Court ruling (*Silverthorn Lumber Co. v. U.S.*, 1920) must be wholly barred, as the "fruit of the poisonous tree." And how are defendants to be sure that all such illegitimate evidence is excluded unless they know the nature of the poison? Only by having *themselves* the right to examine the materials improperly acquired; in this way alone can they adequately protect themselves. Judge Keith therefore grants the pretrial motion of attorney William Kunstler: "This court hereby orders that the government make full disclosure to defendant Plamondon of his monitored conversations." Yet more. Government prosecutors must learn that by so conducting themselves they are not merely ineffective but also risk the security of an otherwise solid case. He concludes: "The court, in the exercise of its discretion, further orders that an evidentiary hearing to determine the existence of taint either in the indictment or in the evidence introduced at trial be conducted at the conclusion of the trial of this matter." Judge Keith courageously puts the Attorney General in his place.

This ruling, clearly designed to protect the privacy of all citizens, will be appealed by the government to the Sixth Circuit Court of Appeals in Cincinnati. The Michigan trial was delayed ... with the hope that a speedy review of this matter will be undertaken. Upon the outcome of that review, and probably its ultimate re-examination by the Supreme Court, rests much of the security of American citizens in their private lives.

23
Telling It Like He Says It Is

Hedrick Smith **WHEN THE PRESIDENT MEETS THE PRESS**

From *The Atlantic Monthly*, Vol. 226, No. 2 (August 1970), 65–67. Copyright © 1970 by The Atlantic Monthly Co., Boston, Mass. Reprinted by permission.

Something ought to be done to bring the Presidential news conference back to life. It has never been as lusty or exalted an instrument of democracy as its apologists and practitioners would have wished. But rarely has a news conference been as pallid or synthetic a ritual as the one held on May 8, 1971, the night the White House was girding for mass demonstrations against President Nixon's Cambodian decision and the killings at Kent State.

When the President strode into the subdued elegance of the East Room that evening to confront several hundred newsmen, it was a moment of high drama. The nation was in agony. The campuses were aflame. The stock market was plummeting. Secretary of the Interior Walter Hickel's letter of distress to President Nixon had exposed a split high within the administration. Members of Congress, angered at not having been consulted about sending U.S. troops into Cambodia, were rising to challenge or limit the President's warmaking powers. Within hours, the White House itself would face a siege of protesters.

Rarely has a news conference promised so much but, alas, produced so little. That session in the East Room was a pale shadow of the passion and trauma of the nation. It was as real-life as a minuet, as illuminating as a multiplication table. President Nixon held the assembled reporters at bay as easily as [Muhammad Ali] dabbling with a clutch of welterweights.

Vice President Agnew has raised the specter of a hostile press shading the news to suit its prejudices and unwilling to give the Nixon administration a fair shake. But many outsiders, on campus and elsewhere, worry about the opposite risk: that when the President actually meets the press, he finds it too deferential, too compliant, too harassed, or too disorganized to pose him a real challenge or to raise a serious and sustained critique. This is one reason why, in an age when all institutions are being questioned, the cream of the Washington press corps are viewed by many young skeptics as lapdogs rather than watchdogs of the government.

The favorite analogy among Washington reporters is that the Presidential news conference is the American counterpart to Parliamentary Question Time for the British Prime Minister and Cabinet. It is supposed to help fill a gap in the American Constitution, which made no provision for calling the Chief Executive before either Congress or the public to give some accounting of his administration between elections.

But the analogy with Parliament is false. Question Time in the British House of Commons is a much more rigorous and risky affair. The exchange, often bristling with barbs, takes place between two groups of equals, the Ins and Outs, the elected adversaries of a two-party system. An American Presidential news conference is an unequal contest from the start, for no newsman can stand toe-to-toe with the President in the way that the Opposition Leader can face the British Prime Minister.

Question Time also has a number of built-in procedures which help put the government on the spot. The inquiries are frequently very detailed and highly informed for they are as much a measure of the intelligence and ingenuity of the questioners as they are a test of the government's policies and its ability. Generally, they are submitted and printed in advance; but it is the supplementaries, the surprise follow-up questions, that add zing to Question Time and make it perilous for a clumsy minister. In a flash it can veer into gladiatorial combat, real rough-and-tumble debate. Another important difference is that Question Time is a regular affair, with an hour set aside four days a week. Cabinet ministers take it in rotation; the Prime Minister steps in only on the most crucial issues. The questions are grouped by subject and taken one at a time. This makes for continuity, in contrast to the frenetic, grab-bag, jack-in-the-box scramble of the televised quiz shows at the White House.

The American press cannot play the role of an elected parliamentary opposition and debate the President. But it would profit by following a number of techniques from Question Time. At the May 8 conference, for example, many of the questions were vague or timid, possibly conjured up in some haste during the final minutes before the show went live. The net effect was more a fusillade of spitballs at 50 paces than a searching examination of the President's mood and motives at a moment of national crisis. Nothing caught Mr. Nixon offguard or prodded him to acknowledge a shred of responsibility for the turmoil that was rolling over the nation. To wit: One reporter noted that some people were saying the United States was headed for revolution or repression and asked the President's view: true or false? Another invited Mr. Nixon to tell the public about the isolation of the Presidency. A third inquired whether the President thought the Vietnam war worthwhile. A fourth wanted to know if the President was prepared to pursue a political settlement in Paris with fervor. A fifth asked for "comment" on the Hickel letter.

Any of these might have served well enough for a White House dinner guest with hours to chat with the President. But in the hothouse tautness of a news conference, cut to fit the TV schedule (one minute to answer each question), each was an easy and open invitation for Mr. Nixon to speechify or filibuster as he chose.

In fairness, there were—and always are—cunning efforts to probe the President's policies and frame of mind, but he deflected them, and other reporters failed to pursue them. About halfway through, for example, one dark-haired young man a few rows back recalled that Mr. Nixon, in his Inaugural Address, had promised to bring Americans together, to move from an era of confrontation to an era of negotiation, and to bring peace in Vietnam. "During the past two weeks it seems that we are farther than ever from those goals," the reporter observed; how could the President account for this failure? Mr. Nixon, smooth as a cue ball and about as communicative, pointed proudly to the arms talk with the Soviet Union as evidence of serious and peaceful intent. A rush of jumping bodies spared him from having to go on and deal with Indochina or the troubled campuses, and no one later called Mr. Nixon back to this aching, unanswered question.

Another reporter asked the President why he had said on April 20 that Vietnamization was going so well that he could pull 150,000 American troops out of Vietnam, and yet just ten days later had to announce that Vietnamization was so seriously threatened that he was sending American forces into Cambodia. When Mr. Nixon replied that increased enemy action in Cambodia made the difference, no one asked him to explain precisely how and why. Given the enemy raids into Vietnam from sanctuaries in Cambodia for the past several years, how were the actions of the previous ten days suddenly so menacing to Americans in Vietnam— unless the Nixon administration was trying to save the Cambodian government or saw a military opening in Cambodia and decided to take advantage of it?

Some crucial questions were left unasked: Why hadn't Congress been consulted before the Cambodian assault? Had he usurped the war-making powers of Congress by sending American troops into a new country? And if not, did he recognize any restraint that the Constitution or Congress could impose on his powers as Commander in Chief? Since there had been no Cambodian request for American intervention, how did he answer the charge that it violated Cambodian neutrality or the United Nations Charter? Or, on the domestic side: What precautions had the administration taken to prevent another Kent State tragedy, say by restricting the use of live ammunition by the National Guard on campuses? And so on.

It is fashionable among Washington reporters to lament the decline of eloquence in the halls of Congress, to murmur that the coin of political debate has been cheapened. But evidently there has also been a decline in the calculated aggressiveness and perseverance of the press questioning the President. Few are the reporters who let fly blunt queries and then respectfully but firmly stand their ground before the President and their colleagues, demanding a responsive answer. It was not always thus. In November, 1962, several reporters closely hawked President Kennedy about the government's management of the news during the Cuban missile crisis. Three reporters pressed the President to relax administrative restrictions on the flow of news; finally one of them, Raymond P. Brandt of the St. Louis *Post-Dispatch*, persisted through five questions, forcing the President to explain how and when he would amend the news management policies. His tenacity produced a real dialogue.

An even more classic example of relentless group questioning came during the Eisenhower administration. President Eisenhower was called upon to explain Attorney General Herbert Brownell's charge that the late Harry Dexter White, appointed by President Truman to the International Monetary Fund, was a Communist spy, though a grand jury had previously refused to indict White on those charges. For almost the entire news conference—twenty questions—Mr. Eisenhower was pursued on this topic until, in the last two minutes, he asked to change the subject.

Many a White House regular has complained that the televised news conferences, initiated under Eisenhower and enshrined by Kennedy, are inevitably the President's show. Unquestionably the format favors him and handicaps the press. TV cameras draw an unwieldy crowd of several hundred reporters, and sheer numbers defeat the purpose of informative dialogue.

The crucial flaw is the failure of the press corps as a group to develop important lines of questioning. Most reporters recognize that it is the second or third question, like gang tackling in football, that is likely to get results. If the President is to be enticed or provoked into some meaningful revelation, it usually takes a collective effort. But the White House news conference is a series of virtuoso performances.

The system, as now operated, puts the squeeze on the reporter, and President Nixon has tightened the vise by holding conferences while many newspapers are going to press in the evening hours. Some reporters have only minutes to file their stories. They must not only take detailed notes on the President's exact words but mentally organize their stories during the waning minutes of the news conference. Little chance is left for them to spot the holes in the President's earlier comments and to raise new questions. (One way of coping with these conflicting pressures is for large news organizations to send several reporters to the proceedings—one to follow the exchange and ask the pertinent questions, and the others to take notes and write stories.)

Finally, no White House regular is entirely free of some conflict of interest. He normally depends on the White House staff for much of his everyday news. This leaves the President's aides in excellent position to discipline him, if they wish, were he to ask too many impertinent questions of the President. No reporter welcomes the prospect of provoking the President's anger or scorn on national TV, where a large part of the audience is quickly hostile to any questioner who puts the President on the spot. Moreover, the White House regulars themselves live so much within the President's orbit that they rarely mix with people outside Washington or get a direct and palpable feel of the public's passions.

None of these ailments is brand-new, and none is of President Nixon's making. But Mr. Nixon has compounded them by becoming the most inaccessible President since Herbert Hoover. This adds to the hectic superficiality of the few news conferences that he does hold because reporters feel they have so much ground to cover. Inevitably when time is limited, the verbal melee is more confusing than ever.

No two Presidents have handled the press in the same way, though over the past four decades a loose tradition has been established—Mr. Nixon is quietly breaking it—that the President meets the press at least once every two weeks. That was the interval adopted by Woodrow Wilson when he instituted news conferences with the White House reporters of his day. Franklin D. Roosevelt was the most accessible of all recent Presidents, a beguiling master of the press, whom he invited into his office for wide-ranging give-and-take sessions twice a week (998 sessions in just over twelve years). Harry Truman cut it to once every ten days or so (324 in eight years), and Presidents Eisenhower, Kennedy, and Johnson each saw the collective press roughly every two weeks.

By comparison President Nixon has met with the press less than once a month (sixteen times in his first seventeen months—ten times on TV, six times off-camera and only one of those for direct quotation).... This from a President who sniped in his [1968] campaign at Lyndon Johnson with the ringing pledge that he would run an open administration because, Mr. Nixon said, "The President cannot isolate himself from the great intellectual ferments of his time. On the contrary, he must consciously and deliberately place himself at their center."

Since the Cambodian venture, the President's isolation—his widely publicized penchant for going off with a yellow legal pad for solitary decision-making and speech-drafting—has become a matter of some concern. More news conferences are one answer. The press and public need, and by Mr. Nixon's own language are entitled to, a greater flow of give-and-take.

Some White House reporters have been pressing Mr. Nixon to hold regular, informal sessions, FDR-style, in his office. The President evidently feels more relaxed on these occasions, able to talk in greater depth, and the White House reporters find it easier to pursue questions in these smaller sessions. But there is no reason why the off-camera sessions cannot be vastly increased without cutting back on the televised news conferences that let the public view the President in the flesh.

Whether or not President Nixon does increase his press contacts, the basic responsibility for restoring the vigor of the White House news conference rests with the correspondents themselves. The rigor of the questioning itself is vital. Without sliding into malevolent heckling or the rasping cross-examination of a district attorney, newsmen can confront the President with more daring and tenacity than they have done recently.

Changes are also necessary in the format of the televised news conferences if they are to give us insights into the Nixon presidency. No reform is surefire, but the White House Correspondents Association might consider these steps: (1) limiting questions at certain crucial conferences to a single broad topic. This, for example, would have ruled out inquiries on the Middle East on May 8, leaving more time to plumb the Cambodian operation and its domestic repercussions; (2) alternatively, asking reporters to group all questions on the main topic of the day during the first half of the news conference, and leaving the remainder for any other kind of question; (3) establishing a firm tradition that each questioner can follow up his own inquiry at least once; (4) finding a new way to determine who gets the floor to replace the present jumping match. One approach would be for reporters to draw random-numbered slips as they enter the conference room and then ask questions in numerical order. Another approach is for the White House reporters to write out questions and submit them to a pool of four or five newsmen. This panel, basing itself on all questions received, could then engage in coordinated questioning of the President on one or two major topics in the first half of the conference, throwing open the final half to everyone else.

The hitch is that these suggestions cut into the Washington reporter's prized independence, the foundation stone of the present system. But chaos and superficiality are the price paid for that freedom. Some independence must be voluntarily surrendered if there is to be a more orderly and cunning pursuit of the President.

None of these reforms will guarantee candor, or newsworthy admission on the part of the President. But they will tax him where he is most vulnerable—in the need to honor his accountability to the nation.

24

The President And The Media

Nat Hentoff **A DEEPENING CHILL**

From *Commonweal*, Vol. 95, No. 21 (February 25, 1972), 486–488. © 1972 Commonweal Publishing Co., Inc.

A primary responsibility of dissenting journalists, I. F. Stone said a few years ago, is not to scare themselves into a state of paralysis. Terms like "repression," if routinely used as cheap rhetoric, will have slight effect on the citizenry at large while infecting the users with gradually immobilizing paranoia. Don't cry wolf, in short, until you see a specific set of sharp teeth.

Yet, in this fourth year of the Nixon Administration, an increasing number of print and broadcast journalists are decidedly and volubly apprehensive about the state of the First Amendment.

Many of them, moreover, represent the straight rather than the radical press. This past September, for instance, W. Bradford Wiley, chairman of the Association of American Publishers—a group more usually aroused by the rising price of newsprint—said, somewhat in shock, "It is a critical fact that we are now faced with defending the First Amendment. Nothing like this has happened since the days of Senator Joseph R. McCarthy."

And Richard Salant, the doughty head of CBS News, is greatly concerned by the possibilities of resultant self-censorship in the ranks of his paladins of the First Amendment. "I think it's something that's increasing," Salant emphasizes. "I think it's going to get worse and worse and worse and worse. I don't think we've seen the climax of it, and I don't think it's passing. The tendency is to say, 'Oh, well, this isn't the ideal one to fight, so let's let this one go.'"

It would appear that the wolf is indeed here. A recent Twentieth Century Fund report, *Press Freedom Under Pressure*, by an independent eleven-man task force of journalists, jurists, and lawyers, concludes that "press freedom might be more fragile than is widely assumed." In an editorial commenting on the report, *The New York Times*, not notably given to paranoia, expressed itself as being similarly troubled.

In an even more alarming American Civil Liberties Union survey, *The Engineering of Restraint: The Nixon Administration and the Press*, its author, Fred Powledge, claims that "the First Amendment is being lost, a little each day."

Taken together, the two reports underline many of the reasons for the growing anxiety within the fourth estate that this administration is not limiting itself to complaints about getting a "bad press" but is engaged in multi-pronged incursions intended to put and keep the press so on the defensive that it, rather than government, will be under continual, self-limiting scrutiny.

There has been, for one example, an unprecedented use of governmental subpoena power to try to get reporters and broadcast journalists to hand over raw files of information they have used to prepare a particular story. Or to appear in secret before a grand jury. In either case, the effect is "chilling" on the present or future confidential sources of these newsmen. In addition, as the Twentieth Century Fund report points out, "sometimes records of a newspaper or television network's telephone calls, disbursements, expense accounts, or other records can disclose the identity of a source as unerringly as the compelled testimony of a reporter. There have been instances in recent months in which prosecutors have attempted to subpoena such records."

Another way of closing off reporters from news sources, particularly sources among individuals and groups in opposition to the government, is to discredit the press by infiltrating it with secret police pretending to be reporters. (The main purpose of this not uncommon practice is to add more "information" to the swelling number of governmental dossiers on "persons of interest" to both the government and the press. But the long-term result is that dissenting activists, unsure of who the *real* reporter is, may decide to talk to no journalists at all, thereby further insulating themselves and making it easier for the government to deal with them without the press getting in the way by asking bothersome questions about civil liberties and due process.)

Entirely overt, of course, was the Nixon administration's attempt to censor the press by the use of prior restraint on the publication of the Pentagon Papers—the first such attempt by any administration in our history. Both the A.C.L.U. and the Twentieth Century Fund reports focus on the case, with the former especially noting how limited *The New York Times'* "victory" for the First Amendment actually was. Five of the nine Justices encouraged the government to believe that it could well punish those involved in the distribution and publication of the Pentagon Papers *after* they had appeared in print. Only the late Justice Black and Justice Douglas upheld the press' absolute right to freedom of expression.

Accordingly, grand juries in Boston and Los Angeles, directed by the Department of Justice's Internal Security Division, have subpoenaed not only Neil Sheehan, *The New York Times* journalist directly involved, but diverse friends and acquaintances of Daniel Ellsberg—including free-lance writers and scholars who also function as journalists. Most of the latter, critics of American foreign policy, depend on confidential sources inside government which may be no longer available to them as soon as they testify in secret before a grand jury.

Moreover, when Beacon Press decided to exercise *its* First Amendment rights by publishing the Senator Gravel edition of the Pentagon Papers, it was first visited by two Pentagon officials as a Pentagon spokesman in Washington said he knew of no legal action planned against Beacon Press "at this time." After the four volumes came out, the Boston grand jury issued a subpoena designed to give the FBI access to the bank records of Beacon Press and its parent organization, the Unitarian-Universalist Association. The grand jury is also trying to get Harold Webber, the editor of M.I.T. Press, to testify, even though he had only *considered* publishing the Senator Gravel edition.

While established newspapers and publishing houses are speculating on the First Amendment's ability to withstand a possible four more years of the President's loose construction of the Bill of Rights, the protean but chronically vulnerable underground press is under cruder and much more insistent siege. As the bimonthly, *Orpheus*, puts it, many of these papers "have been evicted from their offices and homes, harassed by the police, had their benefit parties raided, been bombed, burned, beaten, gypped, framed, and lost printer after printer."

Most of these assaults have not been widely publicized because the straight press, by and large, does not really believe full First Amendment freedoms apply to their scruffy juniors. *Press Freedom Under Pressure* notes: Of the numerous instances that were brought to the attention of the task force—instances in which elements of the underground press protested that they had been abused by the police—a majority were not mentioned in either the news or editorial columns of the established press. In those incidents that have developed into court cases, the underground press has been left largely to its own fragile devices by the more affluent elements of the media.

The First Amendment is indivisible, but some of those it is meant to protect do indeed consider themselves more worthy of its safeguards than others. Until recently, for another illustration, broadcast journalists' problems with overly inquisitive government have not greatly concerned established exemplars of freedom of information by means of print. Certain pieties have been duly expressed, but the underlying assumption seemed to be that radio and television journalists were of less fundamental importance to the health of the republic than those who could trace their form of communication back to Tom Paine and Benjamin Franklin.

By its often egregious attempts to intimidate broadcasters, however, the Nixon Administration has awakened a growing number of newspapers to a recognition of their common First Amendment interests with these post–18th-Century upstarts. When Daniel Schorr of CBS News, who had long refused to accept administration announcements at face value, was subjected to an FBI check—ostensibly to determine his qualifications for a mythical high administration post —editorial writers for *The New York Times* and the *Washington Post*, among others, were as indignant as if he were one of their own.

Similarly, a *frisson* of empathy was evident in a number of newspapers when the House Committee on Interstate and Foreign Commerce served a subpoena on Dr. Frank Stanton, president of CBS, directing him to submit "all film, workprints, out-takes, and sound-tape recordings, written scripts and/or transcripts utilized in whole or in part by CBS in connection with" *The Selling of the Pentagon.*

Dr. Stanton successfully resisted, but his "victory" for broadcasters was no more overwhelming than that of *The New York Times* in the Pentagon Papers case. As John J. O'Connor has observed in the *Times*, "The refusal of the House of Representatives to cite . . . Dr. Frank Stanton for contempt of Congress was carried in a vote of 226 to 181. More than 40 percent of the representatives, in other words, supported the contempt maneuver. (A preliminary vote left Dr. Stanton with a margin of only four votes.) And in the debate preceding the vote, the bitterness of many lawmakers—including some committed to support the CBS executive— about broadcast journalism offered ample evidence of government's ability to apply what has been called 'the chilling effect.' "

Being licensed and thereby all the more open to damage from hostile government, many television stations—as Fred Powledge discloses in the *Engineering of Restraint*—are well into self-censorship. A man responsible for deciding what goes on a local station's Six O'Clock News told Powledge: "It's a matter of deciding that a project you want to undertake, and that you would have undertaken before, just might not be worth the trouble to undertake now. It's the worst form of censorship, I think. It literally chills me when I think about it and see it, and I *have* been seeing it."

Public television, depending *directly* on Congress for most of its current financing—and on the administration for any chance of longterm financing—is becoming even more reluctant to chance the displeasure of government. The Corporation for Public Broadcasting's Public Broadcasting System, which co-ordinates and distributes non–local programming for most of the country's 205 public television stations, has sharply reduced its already limited number of muckraking public affairs programs. Bill Greeley, *Variety's* knowledgeable chronicler of public television, says flatly that a program such as *The Selling of the Pentagon* would not now be shown on public TV.

A few local public television stations, in such normally contentious cities as New York and San Francisco, intermittently engage in controversial forays, but most of their viewers tend to be dissenters of one kind or another anyway. In much of the rest of the country—where exposure to divergent views is most needed, if only as an antidote to the insular local newspapers—public television stations are less and less likely to disturb anyone.

All in all, however, while a case can be made that "the First Amendment is being lost, a little each day," it is far from frozen in disuse. A considerable accomplishment of the Nixon administration has been its forceful reminder to the press, print and broadcast, that the natural relationship between it and government is that of adversaries. Not for many years has government so manifestly and aggressively revealed its contempt for the First Amendment.

It is doubtful, for instance, whether the *Washington Post* would have broken the venerable tradition of accepting off-the-record "backgrounders" from administration officials if the hostility between the press and the Nixon administration had not become so marked. This past December, Benjamin Bradlee, executive editor of the *Post*, announced his intention "to get this newspaper once and for all out of the business of distributing the party line of any official of any government without identifying that official and that government."

The *Post*, in effect, has declared its independence of government on a larger scale than ever before. It may come to pass during Nixon's second term that more of the press may be intimidated into blandness but there will be further, increasingly abrasive declarations of independence by those willing to take the risk of finding out how free they are to fulfill "the people's right to know." And the risks could be formidable as Neil Sheehan of *The New York Times* may discover if he is indicted by the Boston grand jury.

As for the present deepening chill between government and the press, it's likely that so far, apprehension is more widespread than stiffening resistance. But to be afraid, you do have to be awake. And in that sense, the Nixon administration has been of great use to the press. It has jolted us all into an awareness that faith in the First Amendment is not nearly enough to make it work.

25
Executive Privilege

Sam J. Ervin, Jr.   **SECRECY IN A FREE SOCIETY**

From *The Nation*, (November 8, 1971), 454–457. Reprinted by permission.

I am alarmed, as are my colleagues in the Congress, by the increasing frequency with which the executive branch withholds from Congress information vital to its legislative functions. Congress' decision-making role cannot be denied, but by the invocation of "executive privilege," the President, in effect, excludes the legislature from meaningful participation in that process. This dangerously expanding trend toward government by secrecy negates the constitutional principle of "accountability" as envisioned by the founding fathers, and does violence to the principle of separation of powers upon which our system of government is based.

The term "executive privilege," as currently used, most commonly refers to a situation in which the executive branch refuses to divulge information requested by the Congress. It is a term employed more often by members of the legislative branch and by scholars than by the members of the executive branch who willfully withhold information. As I use the term, it refers to the executive branch's denial of any kind of information to any person, be he a member of the Congress or of the taxpaying public. . . .

At issue in any consideration of executive privilege are three conflicting principles: the alleged power of the President to withhold information, the disclosure of which he feels would impede the performance of his constitutional responsibilities; the power of the legislative branch to obtain information in order to legislate wisely and effectively, and the basic right of the taxpaying public to know what its government is doing.

These opposing principles have clashed in almost every administration since the legislative branch undertook an investigation of the St. Clair Expedition during George Washington's first term as President. Without questioning the propriety of the investigation, President Washington asserted:

> First, that the House was an inquest, and therefore might institute inquiries. Second, that it might call for papers generally. Third, that the Executive ought to com-

municate such papers as the public good would permit and ought to refuse those, the disclosure of which would injure the public: consequently were to exercise a discretion. Fourth, that neither the committee nor House had a right to call on the Head of a Department, who and whose papers were under the President alone; but that the committee should instruct their chairman to move the House to address the President.

In spite of his contention that the executive possessed the discretionary power—or duty—to refuse to communicate any information "the disclosure of which would injure the public," all of the St. Clair documents were turned over to the Congress.

There is ample precedent for the view that Congress has the power to institute inquiries and exact evidence. "The power to legislate carries with it by implication ample authority to obtain information needed in the rightful exercise of that power and to employ compulsory process for the purpose...."

Although the Constitution is silent with regard to the existence of executive privilege, its exercise is now asserted to be an inherent power of the President. Its constitutional basis allegedly derives from the duty imposed upon the President under Article II S.3 to see that the laws are faithfully executed. The President claims the power on the ground that he must have it in order to provide the executive branch with the autonomy needed to discharge its duties properly. Inasmuch as "the President alone and unaided could not execute the laws . . .," but requires the "assistance of subordinates"—*Myers* v. *U.S.* 272 U.S. 117 (1926)—the alleged authority to exercise executive privilege has been extended in practice to the entire executive branch.

In theory, the release of information from the executive branch is governed in part by Executive Order No. 10501, issued by President Eisenhower, and amended by him in Executive Order No. 10816, and by President Kennedy's Executive Order No. 10964. These orders establish a system of security classifications for information on defense matters whose release might injure or embarrass our national defense or our relations with foreign nations. Such orders are not authority to assert executive privilege; they simply forbid or restrict disclosure of classified material.

President Kennedy attempted to end the practice of delegating to employees of the executive branch the authority to claim executive privilege. In a letter to the House Foreign Operations and Government Subcommittee in 1962, he stated that the basic policy of his administration would be that "Executive privilege can be invoked only by the President and will not be used without specific Presidential approval." Presidents Johnson and Nixon reaffirmed this policy. Thus, theoretically, procedures instituted in the executive branch would place with the President the ultimate decision and responsibility for the exercise of executive privilege. However, throughout my years in the Senate, I have learned that there is a great discrepancy between theory and practice, a discrepancy demonstrated, among other ways, by Congress' continuing inability to obtain information from the executive branch.

The asserted doctrine of executive privilege has developed unrestrained. In the absence of any congressional statutory authority or constitutional grant of the power, the will of each succeeding President has been substituted for legislation in the field. A contest of political power between the President and Congress has superseded the proper administration of federal functions by the President under the restraints that would be provided by effective legislative oversight. Nor have the courts given any definite guidance on the issue, although the *Reynolds* 345 U.S. 1 (1953) and *Curtiss-Wright* 299 U.S.

304 (1936) cases do contain some dicta relating to the problem.

The assertion of executive privilege, or the power to withhold information, written and spoken, from Congress and the public under the assumed "inherent executive power," must I think be viewed in the context of the slowly but steadily increasing power of the executive—a development that has been duly noted by numerous political and legal scholars. This increased power has enabled the executive branch to make crucial decisions without answering to any system of formal "accountability" for the exercise of such powers beyond the Presidential election every four years. Because the President has been able to act through executive orders without the inconvenience and restraints of congressional authorization or delegation of power, the principle of the separation of governmental powers has been seriously eroded.

In all candor, we in the legislative branch must confess that the shifting of power to the executive branch has resulted from our failure to assert our own constitutional powers. Other than issue sporadic complaints, members and committees of the Congress have done little to prevent the executive branch from withholding information when, in its sole discretion, it determined that secrecy was necessary—or politically desirable. Moreover, through the almost unlimited delegation of authority to the bureaucracy, Congress has actively encouraged the aggrandizement of executive power. The executive branch has access to information which the Congress cannot possibly match, and it has asserted the discretionary authority to employ that data in performing its myriad tasks. I fear that the steady increase of executive power has come close to creating a "government of men, not of laws."

The practice of executive privilege, it seems to me, clearly contravenes the basic principle that the free flow of ideas and information, and the open and full disclosure of the governing process, are essential to the operation of a free society. Throughout history, rulers have imposed secrecy on their actions in order to enslave the citizenry in bonds of ignorance. By contrast, a government whose actions are completely visible to all of its citizens best protects the freedoms embodied in the Constitution.

Moreover, it is clear that the invocation of executive privilege is contrary to the spirit, if not the letter, of the Freedom of Information Act, which Congress passed with the express purpose of expanding to the fullest practical extent the full disclosure to the public of the actions of the government. While it provides for nine specific exceptions, it likewise specifies that none of those exceptions constitutes authority to withhold information from the Congress. Section (4)(c) of the Act explicitly states, "This section is not authority to withhold information from Congress."

It also can be argued with some cogency that the practice contravenes the philosophical thrust of the 1952 Supreme Court case of *Youngstown Sheet & Tube Co.* v. *Sawyers*, 343 U.S. 579, where the Court invalidated President Truman's seizure of the steel mills by executive order. The several majority opinions in that case indicate that Congress is a co-equal branch of the government, and that its prerogatives may not be usurped or impeded by actions of the executive.

Beyond the penchant for maintaining secrecy through the invocation of executive privilege, a more generalized attempt is made to withhold information through the classification system, the infirmities of which were so clearly reflected in the recent furor over the Pentagon Papers, and in the general failure or refusal to disclose data which are of potential interest to the public. When the people do not know what their government is doing, those who govern are not accountable for their actions—and accountability is basic to the democratic system. By using devices of secrecy, the government attains the power to "manage" the news and through it to manipulate public opinion. Such power is not consonant with a nation of free men. Thus the exercise of the assumed power of executive privilege is of basic importance to our governmental system, and the ramifications of a growing policy of governmental secrecy is extremely dangerous to our liberty.

The Senate Judiciary Subcommittee on Separation of Powers, of which I am chairman, was mindful of these dangers when it initiated its study on the subject, and recently held hearings on executive privilege. It found that the nation's history contains many examples of congressional demands for information that have been countered with the invocation of executive privilege or some other bureaucratic excuse for failing to reply. These practices include delaying tactics which continue for so long that the information, when submitted, is no longer pertinent, and the placing of security classifications upon information that is supplied, thereby preventing any meaningful use of the data. Such practices reflect a certain contempt for congressional requests for information and an apparent disdain for the right of the American people to be informed fully about the operations of their government.

As chairman of another subcommittee—the Senate Judiciary Subcommittee on Constitutional Rights—I have for some time attempted to obtain information pertinent to a study of Army surveillance and data bank programs which infringe on the privacy and First Amendment rights of citizens. While some of my requests for information and for the appearance of witnesses have been granted, the most important have been denied for the following stated reasons:

> . . . we are precluded by consistent executive branch policy from releasing to the public. (*J. Fred Buzhardt, General Counsel, Department of Defense*)
>
> Inappropriate to authorize the release of these documents. (*Melvin Laird, Secretary of Defense*)
>
> This information is solely for your use in conducting your inquiry. (*R. Kenly Webster, Acting General Counsel, Department of Army*)
>
> The records . . . cannot be obtained without an inordinate expenditure of time and effort. (*R. Kenly Webster, Acting General Counsel, Department of Army*)
>
> No useful purpose would be served by a public report on the materials. . . . (*J. Fred Buzhardt, General Counsel, Department of Defense*)
>
> I do not believe it appropriate that the general officers in question appear before your subcommittee, but that any "desired testimony" . . . should be furnished by *my* designated representative. (*Emphasis added.*) (*Melvin Laird, Secretary of Defense*)

Implicit in these rebuffs to me and the subcommittee is the assumption of these officers of the executive branch that they are entitled to dictate what may appropriately be investigated and the scope of any such "appropriate investigation."

In action, our system of government is not one of strictly separated powers, but a government based upon the concept of separate but balanced powers, divided along functional lines. For obvious reasons, such a system could not and does not operate in strict conformity to the underlying principle.

The Founding Fathers fully understood that governmental responsibility must be shared in order to make the whole fabric of government viable. Yet they knew that each branch must maintain a basic respect for the duties and prerogatives of the other branches and that such divisions are mandatory in order to avoid the undue accretion of power in any one branch of the federal government. As Madison observed in the *Federalist No. 48*, "After discriminating, therefore, in theory, the several classes of power, as they may in their nature be legislative, executive, or judiciary, the next and most difficult task is to provide some practical security for each...."

However overlapping the functions of the three branches may be, and however imprecisely the system may seem to work, the doctrine of separation of powers itself is based upon good and sound grounds and the ends it was designed to serve 200 years ago are at least as important today. Legislative remedies being considered by the Subcommittee on Separation of Powers would afford the legislative and executive branches an opportunity to seek together some common ground that would more clearly define the powers, duties, and prerogatives of the two branches in this sensitive area. We must remember at all times the cooperation between the Congress and the executive is essential, if the government is to operate efficiently. That pressing requirement makes it mandatory that we seek and find an amicable settlement to the problems involved in the use of executive privilege to prevent Congress and the American people from knowing the details of executive actions. In paraphrase of Woodrow Wilson, warfare between the legislative and the executive branches can be fatal.

26
Making Military Policy

Stuart Symington   **THE SECRET WAR IN LAOS**

From an article by Senator Stuart Symington in *The New York Times Magazine*, August 9, 1970. © 1970–1971 by The New York Times Company. Reprinted by permission.

Executive secrecy surrounding the conduct of our foreign policy and its associated military operations is, I am convinced, endangering not only the welfare and prosperity of the United States but also, and most significantly, the national security.

This is a conclusion I have reached slowly, reluctantly, and from the unique vantage point of having been a Pentagon official and now being the only member of either branch of Congress to sit on both the Foreign Relations and Armed Services Committees.

The practice of either editing or wholly withholding military information from Congress and the public is not new; the present administration is no better or worse than its predecessors. In recent years, the need for immediate reaction to a possible nuclear attack has made it necessary to transfer more authority to the executive branch, but this additional authority has apparently been carried over into the conventional military and foreign policy field. As a result, key foreign policy activities have not been properly debated in Congress, for we simply have not known enough to play our traditional and constitutional role in the formulation of foreign policy and the direction of the country.

A particularly heavy veil of secrecy has been drawn over one especially important and dangerous aspect of the foreign military policy field: the production and deployment overseas of United States nuclear weapons. While some secrecy in the nuclear field is justified, much of it is a carry-over from the past and deserves the most searching review within the government as well as more public disclosure and debate.

No one seriously concerned about the future can deny that our current worldwide military posture could be interpreted by a possible enemy—including the other superpower—as unnecessarily threatening, and in any case belying any real interest on our part for achieving, through the current SALT talks, a permanent peace by means of an agreement about the control of nuclear arms.

It seemed to me axiomatic that the American public should know and understand as fully as possible the implications of our current worldwide military deployment and the foreign policy commitments which this deployment presumably enforces. Yet the public in this country often knows less than much of the rest of the world....

My personal feelings of alarm began to stir in 1963, with the defense budget mounting toward $80–billion, and keen awareness based on personal experience that high cost and duplication are characteristic of our enormous military presence abroad. (Today we have overseas more than 1,000,000 men in some 384 facilities and 3,000 minor installations, along with 300,000 at sea.) At best, an examination of this vast military position could point up waste and inefficiency; at worst, it presents—because of its high dollar cost and its direct relations to issues of war and peace—a serious present danger to the continued vitality of our free and democratic institutions.

It was against this background that the Senate Foreign Relations Committee decided to undertake a study of just what this nation's foreign policy commitments are. Senator Fulbright asked me to serve as head of the new sub-committee and we began work in February 1969.

Seventeen months of investigating confirmed our already deep concern about executive branch secrecy surrounding much of our foreign policy and the military undertakings incident to those policies; secrecy which has now developed to a point where military activities often first create and then dominate foreign policy responses.

I do not refer to the concealment of military details which could aid the enemy, nor to the publication of the precise terms of negotiations or specific agreements which could frustrate their successful consummation. I do refer, however, to the continuing failure to reveal, explain, or justify the true dimensions of our activities abroad, dimensions which are far better known by our adversaries than by the American public —and in some cases, by the American Congress....

Publicity, I know, may be occasionally inconvenient to those who supervise the functioning of a bureaucracy. The "system" works more smoothly if unexposed to questioning. But public disclosure is a truly vital safeguard against government adoption of positions and policies of unknown and potentially dangerous implications. And when it comes to issues which involve actual survival (even more than mere prosperity and the question of whether so much of our money should be spent for military rather than domestic social needs), there is obvious need for more careful examination.

Beyond any pragmatic concept is the philosophical. If this government is one truly based upon the consent of the governed; if it is to function as the people's servant rather than their master, a proper measure of accurate information is essential for the people to determine whether their government is wise and right in its response to their needs.

Today's danger resulting from increased secrecy with respect to foreign military policy and programs exists at two levels: information denied the public and information denied . . . Congress. . . .

As illustration, let us look briefly at the deep and costly American involvement in the secret war of northern Laos.

Hearings on that country, which were held by our sub-committee, last October, gave members a fairly comprehensive view of just what has been going on for years in that part of Southeast Asia.

As shown by the transcripts, finally released six months after the hearings, the United States has been, and is, participating heavily in a secret war that has cost many American lives and billions of dollars. It is a war conducted far away from any Vietnam interdiction effort along the Ho Chi Minh Trail of southern Laos.

From a modest 1962 role as a supplier of

equipment to the government of Prince Souvanna Phouma, the United States has now become involved in fighting on a broad scale. Under the veil of what was officially termed "armed reconnaissance," American fighter bombers, as far back as 1964, began to attack Communist ground targets and troops—and therefore inevitably civilians—in northern Laos; and American air effort in that area has grown continuously since that time.

This air support took quantum leaps during the various bombing pauses over North Vietnam, reaching a peak after the 1968 executive order to cease all raids over that latter country.

For over five years, this secret American war has been going on in northern Laos; but until recently, the only reports on United States activities in that distant land were from representatives of the press who went to the scene. Some of these press stories contained much accurate detail; but almost without exception their accounts have understandably contained mistakes. . . .

During the years 1964–69, as the clandestine American role in Laos grew steadily, executive branch discussions and presentations to Congress were extremely limited; in some cases they were actually misleading.

An illustration of the latter is the testimony in January, 1968, of William H. Sullivan—the United States Ambassador to Laos at the time—before the Senate Foreign Relations Committee. The Ambassador told the committee, "We do not have a military training and advisory organization in Laos . . . We don't have advisers with them (the Laotians). However, some of these probably have been trained in Thailand under American supervision, though we don't have people with them. We don't have a military advisory group there."

When later asked whether Air America—the C.I.A. supported airline—was engaged in bombing, Ambassador Sullivan replied, "No, sir . . . They carry equipment for our AID program . . . But they are not engaged in combat operations. There are no Americans who fly Laotian planes." When asked whether the Royal Laotian Air Force was doing any fighting, he responded, "They are doing all the fighting."

This testimony was completely misleading. Nowhere did Ambassador Sullivan acknowledge the significant role of the United States Air Force, which for years has been bombing and napalming Laotians in northern Laos, actually closer to the border of Red China than to the Ho Chi Minh Trail. Even though I personally traveled all over Laos in 1966 and 1967, until these hearings in the fall of 1969 I never knew that United States pilots, flying out of Thailand, were bombing targets and napalming natives in that part of the country.

When confronted at our hearings with these earlier statements, Ambassador Sullivan, by then Deputy Assistant Secretary of State, stated the reason he had given this type of testimony was because he had not been asked any direct questions about American air operations in northern Laos. Senator Fulbright observed, "We do not know enough to ask you these questions unless you are willing to volunteer the information. There is no way for us to ask you questions about things we don't know you are doing."

The subcommittee finally heard testimony on all phases of Laos, including United States support of this war; but the American people are still being denied full information because of the continuing refusal of the executive branch to declassify portions of the transcript which, we think, should be in the public domain.

Also known throughout the Far East is the participation in said Laotian war by United States supported third country military forces; but the State Department to date has also refused to make public the extent of this participation.

Having achieved for the Congress during hearings last October a measure of disclosure about the situation in Laos, we turned our efforts to obtaining a release to the public of all testimony which would [not] help a possible enemy.

After more than six months of discussion with numerous officials of both the Defense and State Departments, during which period the President himself issued a statement containing some of the facts of United States involvement in Laos, the subcommittee finally obtained approval and then released what we considered to be a meaningful transcript of its hearings on this subject. Following this publicity, none of the negative results which the State Department had predicted as reasons for nondisclosure did in fact occur.

The implications of secrecy raised in connection with the war in Laos are more far-ranging than this particular episode. As example, the secrecy of the Laotian operation raises the fundamental constitutional question of the President's right to wage war without either a declaration from Congress or, as in the case of these United States military operations in northern Laos, even an authorization from Congress.

As a result of an arrangement between the United States Ambassador in Laos and the head of the Laotian Government, the bombing of northern Laos actually began in 1964. Funds for this operation, which involved the sending of American combat planes from Thailand to hit targets and people in the north, were obtained from the Defense Appropriation Act without any public discussion or specific authorization. Thus the executive branch, under a veil of strict secrecy, was not only permitted to wage an unauthorized war, but also to set a precedent for undertaking similar activities in other countries with which the United States has no formal treaty.

A corollary to this constitutional question is a specific foreign policy question also raised by this Laotian example: namely, does the executive branch have the right to make an agreement with a foreign government which would involve the use of American military forces, either air or ground, when part of that agreement includes a stipulation that the United States would not disclose such activities?

Also of grave concern is the fact that this secrecy concerning United States activities in northern Laos permitted the Administration to escalate heavily the fighting in that area while it was deescalating, with much public fanfare, the war in South Vietnam. As a result, the American people were misled as to the over-all role of the United States in Southeast Asia; whereas the enemy—fully aware of the stepped-up United States bombing—received quite a different impression with respect to the actual intentions of our Government.

This secrecy also prevented any objective review by the Congress of our policy with respect to Laos. Only after a closed session of the Senate, in which some details of the heavily stepped-up bombing were first disclosed to the members, did the Congress finally take action by adopting an amendment which prohibited the sending of ground combat troops into that country. The vote on the amendment was 73 to 17.

As for the future, if the precedent of Laos secrecy had gone unchallenged, the President, in effect, would have been able to assume authority to undertake secret military operations in any country he desired, disregarding the necessity of having, through treaty arrangement, either the authorization or even the prior consent of the Congress. Moreover, if in the same manner the executive branch in the future chooses to deny Congress the opportunity to approve or disapprove such major foreign policy decisions, then at the same time it would be denying the right of the people in a democracy to have a voice in policies which involve the overriding issues of war and peace. . . .

27
Appointing The Judges

Elizabeth Drew   **THE NIXON COURT**

From *The Atlantic Monthly*, Vol. 230, No. 5 (November 1972), 6 ff. Copyright © 1972 by The Atlantic Monthly Co., Boston, Mass. Reprinted by permission.

Nothing Richard Nixon does, if he is reelected for four more years, is likely to be more important than the appointments he makes to the Supreme Court. Barring unforeseeable domestic or international upheavals, no other actions he might take would have as profound and lasting consequences. The impact of Supreme Court justices outlasts that of the administration which appoints them. Unlike the President or members of Congress, they are not subject to electoral approval, but serve until death or retirement. Their rulings are, by the nature of the judicial process, less susceptible to change than are the laws of the Congress or the administrative actions of the executive branch. The very purpose of the Court is to act as a counter to immediate popular will and pressures. It was designed so as not to be accountable to the people at any given time. It was intended to serve as a check on the actions of the legislative and the executive branches.

The Supreme Court has already undergone a sea change as a result of the four appointments that President Nixon made to it in his first term. Because of the advanced age and poor health of several of the current nine justices, it is possible that as many as four more could be named to the Court over the next four years.

There can be little question concerning the nature of the appointments that Mr. Nixon would make. He has fulfilled his campaign pledge of 1968 that his nominees to the Court would share a conservative philosophy, and he has promised that if he is reelected, this policy will be continued. Whatever skepticism is due campaign promises in general, there is no reason to doubt Mr. Nixon's word on this particular subject.

It is risky to speculate about how Supreme Court justices might rule on any given question. Nevertheless, the consistency of Mr. Nixon's appointees has been such that some hypotheses can be made about the consequences of his having the opportunity to name more. For example, it is reasonable to speculate that if Mr. Nixon had made one more appointment during his first term, the death penalty would have been retained. The present Court, with the addition of one Nixon appointee, might have suppressed the Pentagon Papers. Moreover, the Court was closely divided on many other major issues.

Mr. Nixon describes the effect he wants to have on the Court as strengthening the "peace forces as against the criminal forces." The direction of the Warren Court toward broadening the rights of the accused has been reversed, and some of the previous Court's decisions have been substantially modified. But Mr. Nixon's appointments have also had important effects in affirming the power of the government over individuals, as well as its investigative powers. The new Court restricted the scope of the remedies for minorities seeking their civil rights. It has also begun to take a more circumspect approach to government regulation of business.

One of the most striking things about the Court is the frequency with which the Nixon appointees—Chief Justice Warren E. Burger, and Justices Harry A. Blackmun, William H. Rehnquist, and Lewis F. Powell, Jr.—have voted together. According to the *Harvard Law Review*, of the seventy cases in which all nine justices participated, the Nixon appointees voted together in fifty-three. Moreover, in unusual unanimity for four justices, they joined in one opinion in forty-five of those fifty-three. Blackmun voted so often with Burger, his old friend from Minnesota, that Court reporters dubbed the pair the "Minnesota twins." So fundamentally has the ideological balance of the Court changed, that Justice Potter Stewart, generally regarded as a "conservative" on the Warren Court, is now one of the "liberals" on the Burger Court, frequently aligned with Justices William O. Douglas, Thurgood Marshall, and William J. Brennan, Jr. Byron White, a Kennedy appointee and no liberal, was often in the position of casting the "swing" vote. And this change came about amidst great turbulence surrounding the Supreme Court.

It all began, it is worth recalling, when Lyndon Johnson decided to dispatch Justice Arthur Goldberg to the United Nations and to replace Goldberg on the Court with the President's close friend, Abe Fortas. When, in June, 1968, Chief Justice Earl Warren notified President Johnson that he wished to retire, the President decided to promote Justice Fortas to Chief Justice and name Homer Thornberry to Fortas' seat. Thornberry, also a friend of Johnson's, a federal court judge and former congressman, is one of the nearly forgotten footnotes of the recent stormy history of the Court. The proposed Fortas elevation became suspended amidst crossfire stirred by Fortas' own record and activities while on the Court, his relationship with the President, Lyndon Johnson's sinking prestige, and election-year politics.

Fortas was expected to continue to lead the Court in the ideological direction of Warren. At the same time, Richard Nixon was running for the Presidency, and the Warren Court was one of his issues. "I believe in a strict interpretation of the Supreme Court's functions," Mr. Nixon said in the course of the campaign. "In a sense this means I believe we need a Court which looks upon its function as being that of interpretation, rather than of breaking through into new areas that are really the prerogative of the Congress of the United States." The implication was that Nixon appointees would take a less expansive view of the role of the Court in the areas of crime and race. Nixon suggested that the decision to replace the Chief Justice should await the outcome of the presidential election. A combination of Southern Democratic and Republican opposition forced the withdrawal of Fortas' nomination to be Chief Justice. Fortas remained an associate justice, and Warren postponed his retirement until after the election. So much for Homer Thornberry.

Shortly after Richard Nixon's election to the presidency in 1968, *Life* magazine's disclosure that Fortas had, while on the Court, accepted a fee from Louis Wolfson's foundation led to

Fortas' resignation from the Court. . . . Shortly afterward, President Nixon named Warren Burger to replace Earl Warren. His first nominee to replace Fortas was Clement Haynsworth. Upon his rejection by the Senate, the President nominated G. Harold Carswell; and upon *his* rejection by the Senate, Burger's old friend Harry Blackmun was nominated.

In September, 1971, Justices Hugo Black and John Marshall Harlan, both ill, resigned from the Court. The Nixon Administration floated the names of several people, of whom it was seriously considering four: Congressman Richard Poff, Republican of Virginia, a conservative, who had practiced law for only four years; Senator Robert Byrd, Democrat of West Virginia, a former member of the Ku Klux Klan, who hadn't practiced law at all; Mildred Lillie, a controversial California state judge; and Herschel Friday, a bond lawyer who had represented the Little Rock, Arkansas, school board in its efforts to resist school desegregation. But all four were shot down by the American Bar Association and others in the legal profession. The Administration announced that the ABA would not be consulted in the future. The President finally settled upon Lewis Powell, a respected Virginia attorney, and William Rehnquist, a bright and very conservative official of the Justice Department. (All of this had its effect on the human beings who were at the time on the Court. Nina Totenberg of the *National Observer,* who has a fine eye for such things, reported during the uproar over the President's putative nominations: "The Supreme Court Justices reacted too. Justice Harlan, often described as the Court's conservative conscience, was so outraged that he seriously considered writing the President a letter of protest from his hospital bed. The seven active Justices were extremely perturbed. Even the more conservative Justices began wondering aloud whether the President was trying to 'denigrate the Court.' One liberal Justice read some of Judge Lillie's opinions that night, and promptly got drunk.")

The concept of judicial conservatism cuts two ways. Judicial conservatives do not consider the courts proper instruments for expanding social, political, and individual rights, as the Warren Court did; but neither are true judicial conservatives quick to strike down previous court decisions. There is thus a potential internal conflict, one that presents itself on questions of overturning prior liberal decisions.

The Burger Court's solution to this dilemma in dealing with two of the most controversial Warren Court decisions (*Miranda* and *Wade*) has been not to overturn them explicitly but to limit their scope. It is often some time before the practical effect of many court decisions, including these, can be determined. But some constitutional lawyers believe that the Warren decisions remain in form only, their substance largely negated. The Burger Court may have found a way, in other words, of overturning decisions without overturning them.

In *Miranda* v. *Arizona,* the Warren Court had held that no statement made by an arrested suspect could be used against him in court unless he had been told of his rights to remain silent and to have a lawyer. In 1971, the Burger Court ruled that such confessions could be used to contradict the testimony of an accused person who takes the stand in his own defense. This leaves a defendant who has confessed without having been advised of his rights the option of not testifying in court. It is widely agreed among lawyers that juries often suspect that a defendant who does not speak in his own behalf is hiding something.

In *Wade,* the Warren Court had held that suspects had a right to counsel at police lineups. The Burger Court restricted this protection, holding that it applied only after indictments had been made. Since most lineups occur before indictment, this decision, in the view of several court observers, effectively negated

Wade while claiming to uphold it. The Nixon appointees showed more inclination than did their predecessors to excuse as a "harmless error" a violation of a constitutional guarantee in the course of a prosecution. When the Supreme Court signals a change of attitude of this sort, lower court judges take note.

The Court also held that state juries need not be unanimous in order for a defendant to be found guilty. This would reduce the burden on prosecutors, and diminish the number of trials that end with hung juries. Unanimous jury verdicts have always been required in federal trials. The Warren Court and its predecessors had held in a number of decisions that the Bill of Rights applied no less to the states than it did to the federal government. The result of the Burger Court's ruling was that the right to a unanimous verdict of guilty did not apply to those being tried in state courts. Four of the justices also said that they did not believe that there was a constitutional right to unanimity in state or federal courts. (This view was taken by three of four Nixon appointees—Powell excepted—and White.) The addition of one more justice who shares this view could also eliminate the requirement of unanimous verdicts in federal trials.

There are now pending before the Supreme Court some cases that could have still greater impact on the legal protections of the accused. One would circumscribe the opportunities for those who had been convicted in state courts to turn to the federal courts (habeas corpus) on the grounds that their constitutional rights had been denied. Another has to do with the concept that illegally obtained evidence cannot be used in trials. This "exclusionary rule" has been in effect for over fifty years. It is described, depending upon one's point of view, as "policing the police" or "handcuffing the police." There is a case before the Court that would narrow its scope; and Burger, in a highly unusual action for a justice, has urged the Congress to write legislation which would practically eliminate the rule. The Justice Department and the new Director of the FBI, L. Patrick Gray, are also urging that the exclusionary rule be relaxed. If it is, through either legislative or judicial action, this would be a major turnabout in the area of criminal law.

Not all of the decisions of the Burger Court have come down against the accused. It expanded the right to free counsel to cover lesser crimes, and strengthened the rights of prisoners and the criminally insane. And it abolished the death penalty, 5-4.

In most instances where the Burger Court considered broad questions of the power of the government over individuals, it ruled in favor of the government. The major exception was its rejection of the Nixon Administration's assertion of the right, without having to seek a court order, to wiretap those it suspects of domestic subversion. The vote on the wiretapping decision was 8-0. (Rehnquist, having been an official of the Justice Department which fashioned the policy, did not participate. He was not, however, always so punctilious.)

While the decision pleased civil libertarians, it did not give them cause for unrestrained rejoicing. It is widely believed among students of the Court that the justices were not really unanimous, that Burger and Blackmun went along with the majority when they found themselves on the losing side. Moreover, the decision did not say that the government could not wiretap those it suspected of domestic subversion; it said that the government could not do so without getting a permit from a judge. The government does not ordinarily have difficulty in finding judges who can be persuaded to accede to such requests.

The Justice Department's contention that internal security matters are too complicated for judges was an affront to the judiciary. "If the threat is too subtle or complex for our senior law enforcement officers to convey its significance to a court," wrote Justice Powell for the majority, "one may question whether there is probable cause for surveillance." Moreover, wrote Powell, "the price of lawful public dissent must not be a dread of subjection to an unchecked surveillance power."

Yet one week later, the Court ruled that military surveillance could not be challenged by its civilian subjects simply on the grounds that it discouraged dissent. The Court held that the challengers would have to show that the surveillance had harmed them in some more concrete way. Justice Burger, writing for the majority, said that otherwise such challenges would make federal courts "virtually continuing monitors of the wisdom and soundness of executive action."

In other decisions, the Court affirmed and expanded the government's investigative powers. The Court held that the doctrine of congressional immunity did not protect Senator Mike Gravel, Democrat of Alaska, or his aides from having to tell a grand jury how they acquired and arranged for the publication of the Pentagon Papers. Justice White, writing for the majority, said that the senator's revelation of the Papers was not in connection with a legislative act, and therefore not immune. Some argue, nevertheless, that the decision opened the way for grand jury inquiries into the manner in which members of Congress come by information which the executive branch considers damaging to itself.

On the same day that it ruled on the Gravel case, the Court also held that journalists had no right under the First Amendment to refuse to provide grand juries with information given them in confidence or the names of confidential sources. In a dissent in which he was joined by Justices Brennan and Marshall, Justice Stewart said that the action of the Court "invites state and federal authorities to undermine the historic independence of the press by attempting to annex the journalistic profession as an investigative arm of the government." He wrote that the right to publish had to include the right to gather news and to maintain a confidential relationship between a reporter and his source.

But the dissenters did disagree over the extent to which the First Amendment protects journalists. Stewart outlined some circumstances under which a reporter might be subpoenaed; Justice Douglas, in a separate dissent, argued that a reporter "has an absolute right not to appear before a grand jury." (Justice Rehnquist participated in the decisions on newsmen's immunity, the Gravel case, and army surveillance, despite the fact that they involved policies he helped to fashion or defend while a Justice Department official. In all three cases, his vote broke a tie, providing a 5-4 decision. Rehnquist's involvement in these cases might be improper under a new ABA code adopted, as it happens, in the wake of the Fortas controversy. Some attorneys think that his action was in violation of the old code as well. The Court has been asked to rehear two of the cases on the grounds that Rehnquist should not have participated.)

In another decision, the Court narrowed the immunity from prosecution which must be granted a witness who is compelled to testify. Previously, it had been held that the constitutional right against self-incrimination required immunity from any prosecution for the crime which the testimony concerns. The Burger Court permitted prosecution, as long as the testimony or evidence derived from the testimony was not used. Critics of this decision argued that a prosecutor would find ways of using the testimony without appearing to do so.

The decision of the Court to permit publication of the Pentagon Papers was made in 1971, before Powell and Rehnquist joined the Court. It was . . . less than a total victory for the newspapers. . . . In the course of stating that publication could proceed, a majority of the justices indicated that there were circumstances under which they would approve government suppression of news. Moreover, since newspapers did, on the order of a lower court, suspend publication of the Pentagon Papers until the Supreme Court ruled, the precedent was established that the government could temporarily restrain publication of certain information by newspapers.

A Court decision that certain political pamphlets could not be distributed at shopping centers was attributed by some Court observers to the Court's increased sympathy for the interests of business. This decision was written by Powell and based on the concept of private property. Powell also wrote two other decisions in which the Court, as it very rarely has, ruled against the government in tax cases. The Court is now believed to be so closely divided on questions of antitrust and consumer rights and the powers of regulatory agencies that the addition of one more justice inclined to rule for business would bring about a historic turnaround in this area. It would, in the view of some, usher in an attitude on the part of the Court that has not been in evidence since the New Deal.

In the area of civil rights, the next appointment could be crucial. In June of this year, the four Nixon appointees dissented from a Court decision that a small Southern town, Emporia, Virginia, had violated the Constitution by establishing its own school district so as to avoid county-wide desegregation. The 5-4 decision was the first school desegregation case in which the Court divided in the eighteen years since it held state-enforced segregation of schools unconstitutional. In another decision, the Burger Court held that a private club, in this case a Moose lodge, is not obliged to desegregate simply because it holds a state liquor license. The Court held, by a 6-3 vote, that liquor licensing does not constitute the sort of state involvement with private conduct that imposes a constitutional duty not to discriminate. Some civil rights lawyers also believed that the licensing power was a tenuous basis for requiring desegregation.

The Court also limited the recourse, under the voting rights law, for blacks to challenge plans for reapportionment of Southern state legislatures. In earlier decisions, the Court had indicated that it was more reluctant than was the Warren Court to intervene in reapportionment cases. On the other hand, it has upheld legislation requiring equal employment opportunities.

It is difficult to foretell how the Court will proceed on the issue of busing. The issue will be before it as a result of lower court decisions, and, perhaps at a later time, as a result of legislation by the Congress. The Court upheld busing in a unanimous opinion written by Chief Justice Burger in 1971. However, Mr. Burger subsequently appended to a routine order—the sort that is usually handed down without comment—a statement giving his own view that the busing opinion should not be interpreted too broadly by lower courts. The Congress is considering antibusing legislation which would, among other things, reopen old court decisions. If it is enacted, it may well be upheld. The Burger Court appears less inclined than previous ones to overrule congressional legislation.

It is possible to read too much into the decisions of a single term, yet some important changes of outlook on the part of the Supreme Court already seem clear. These could be still more pronounced if additional justices are named who share the philosophy of the four most recent appointees. There would be exceptions, of course, but the Supreme Court might then be expected to take a series of positions that could have profound effects on our national life: While constitutional rights would be maintained in principle, the remedies available to individuals making claims under those rights might be narrowed or even denied. There might be greater reluctance to overturn the actions of either the executive branch or the Congress, even when they are responding to popular passions. At a time when popular passions are running high, the question could arise as to whatever happened to checks and balances.

28

An Awe-Inspiring Lifestyle

THE PRESIDENT'S PAY IS MANY THINGS

Reprinted from *U.S. News & World Report*, (January 27, 1969), 32–34.

The toughest public job in the world is also one of the richest.... And the salary is only the starting point. Many of the facilities and services available to the Chief Executive are priceless. The ... $200,000 a year salary is only the tip of the iceberg of the millions of dollars that go to America's Chief Executive....

It is estimated that a private citizen would need an annual income of close to 35 million dollars to live the way the President of the United States lives. This is based on the assumption that it would require that amount of income to generate take-home pay in excess of 10 million dollars annually.

In some ways, the services and facilities available to the President defy measurement in dollars and cents. For example, consider the Presidential residence, the White House: It has 132 rooms and it is set in an 18.3-acre estate in the heart of the District of Columbia. The grounds alone, according to Washington real estate experts, are worth about 75 million dollars. That is what comparable land in midtown Washington would cost if it were being purchased for high-rise apartments. As for the White House itself, the Department of the Interior estimates that the current value is "more than 50 million dollars." Real estate men call that estimate "conservative," insist the White House is literally priceless and could never be reproduced.

That is only the first item. To operate the White House, the President has an annual budget of $3,229,000. In addition, he has a "special projects" fund of 1.5 million dollars to be spent at his discretion. This fund finances such items as White House conferences, special reports, and study groups.

No effort or expense is spared to protect the President and his health. A staff of Secret Service agents and White House police is constantly on duty. This alone is a $2,503,000 item in the annual federal budget.

At Mr. Nixon's service, tuned up and waiting, are three Boeing 707 jet transports, lavishly fitted for Presidential travel. Those aircraft are valued at about 8 million dollars each. The White House "air force" also includes a fleet of

Lockheed Jetstar planes to transport important people to and from the nation's capital; a jet cargo plane to haul the President's armored car wherever he goes; and four or more helicopters for use as needed. The value of all the aircraft earmarked for White House use is estimated to be about 30 million dollars.

The President and First Lady are utterly free of housekeeping problems. A housekeeper sees that domestic operations run smoothly. Carpenters, plumbers, electricians, woodworkers, and painters—expensive and often hard to get for the average American—are full-time employes of the White House. They repair the ravages of tourists and time on a continuing basis. There are 34 of these workmen in all. Paying them and the domestic staff cost about $750,000 a year.

Also on the domestic staff are five maids, an assistant housekeeper, two laundresses, one seamstress, two storekeepers, one linen supervisor, two cooks, two chefs, one pantry assistant, two kitchen helpers, four doormen, and five housemen. The last-named take care of the heavy-cleaning duties.

The White House grounds are cared for by the National Park Service. That item alone cost about $200,000 in 1968.

The President's automobile fleet includes 20 black Mercurys, driven by Army chauffeurs, in addition to his specially built Lincoln and Cadillac models. These special cars are custom made and bulletproof. They are always driven by Secret Service men.

Generally speaking, automobiles are not purchased by the White House. They are leased at a nominal fee. The newest armored Lincoln sedan is to be leased by the White House at somewhere between $4,000 and $5,000 per year, it is reported. There are estimates that it cost the Ford Motor Company hundreds of thousands of dollars to build.

The Navy keeps a 92-foot yacht and a 60-foot cruiser ready for Presidential use. Their worth is estimated to be in the vicinity of $500,000.

Camp David, the hideaway in Maryland's Catoctin Mountains, is another fringe benefit. In President Franklin D. Roosevelt's day, it was known as "Shangri-La" and was furnished with odds and ends of surplus White House furniture. It became a luxurious resort and was renamed in the administration of President Dwight D. Eisenhower after his grandson, David Eisenhower. The verdict of real estate men today: "You couldn't touch anything to equal Camp David for $150,000."

Entertaining official guests is a demanding function of the Presidency. Mr. Nixon may call on his White House budget for such entertaining—or he may use State Department "representation" funds if the guest is a foreign dignitary.

The scope and variety of entertainment attractions available to the White House are unmatched anywhere in the world. Marine, Army, Navy, and Air Force bands play at White House functions—as do numerous dance orchestras and trios from the military services.

The White House kitchen is a gourmet's delight. The chefs and cooks are dedicated to preparing any dish the President desires—at any hour of the day or night.

First-run movies are always on hand at the White House projection room. Broadway and Hollywood stars feel flattered by an invitation for a "command performance" at the White House and vie with one another for this type of recognition.

A large library is kept up to date in the White House by the American publishing industry.

Within the White House grounds, facilities exist to offer the President and his friends a wide variety of exercise and recreation. There is an indoor swimming pool. A small gymnasium has the most modern conditioning equipment. There is a tennis court. There is a putting green. A masseur is available. So is a barber. And the President has his own personal photographer.

A single telephone call from the White House can set in immediate motion all the plans for a Presidential vacation—or a diplomatic confrontation—anywhere in the world.

Should the President or a member of the First Family become ill, there is the staff physician, plus free medical and hospital care in government hospitals.

Finally, Mr. Nixon can look forward to retirement pay of $25,000 a year plus a suite of offices to be maintained in the location of his choice when he leaves the Presidency.

President Nixon's salary of $200,000 nets him only $87,000 after federal income tax and the surtax are deducted. This, however, is scarcely relevant to the President's standard of living while in office. Putting it all together, you get this picture:

Salary: $200,000.
Expense allowance: $50,000.
Travel allowance: $40,000.
Special-projects fund: $1,500,000.
Over-all budget for the White House $3,229,000.
Secret Service and White House police: $2,503,000.
Maintenance of White House grounds by National Park Service: $200,000.
Upkeep of aircraft, ships and automobiles and pay of crews and chauffeurs: $1,000,000.
Automobiles (estimated leasing fees): $50,000. The total: $8,772,000.

In addition, the President has access to the White House estate, valued at 125 million dollars, to aircraft worth 30 million, Navy vessels appraised at $500,000 and Camp David, worth $150,000.

Those figures total $155,650,000.

Lumping together the money the President has to spend annually and the value of everything at his disposal make a grand total of $164,422,000.

And it all makes it a lot easier to endure the burdens of being President of the United States.

Copyright © 1969 by U.S. News & World Report, Inc.

The Power
And The Glory

As Chief Executive, the President is responsible for seeing that the bills he signs into law are "faithfully executed." He may have the help and advice of his aides and his Cabinet—but the ultimate responsibility for seeing that the government works is his, and his alone.

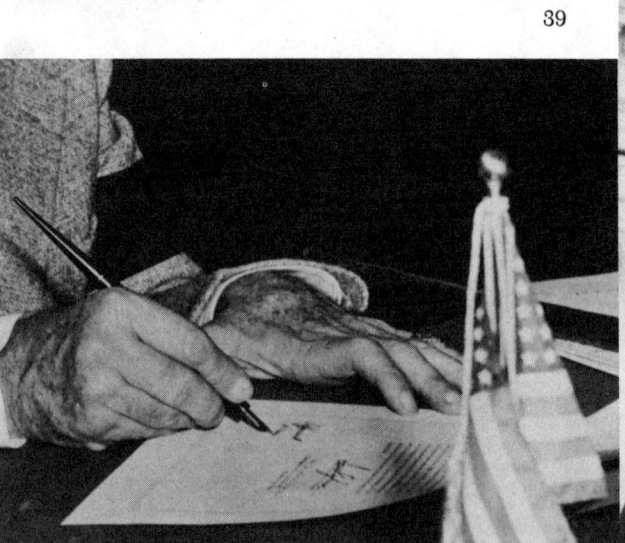

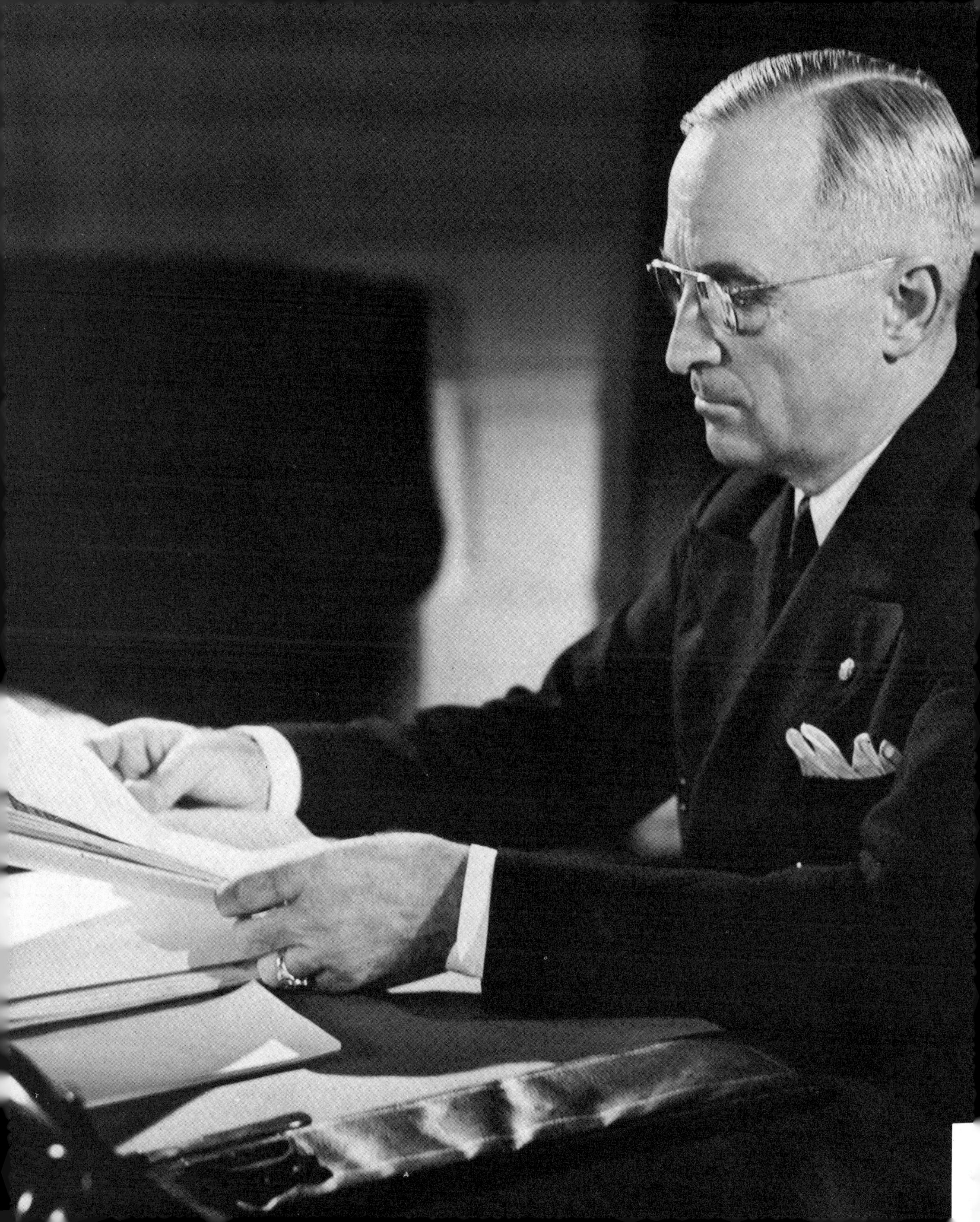

As commander in chief of the armed forces, the President has the power of life and death over us all.

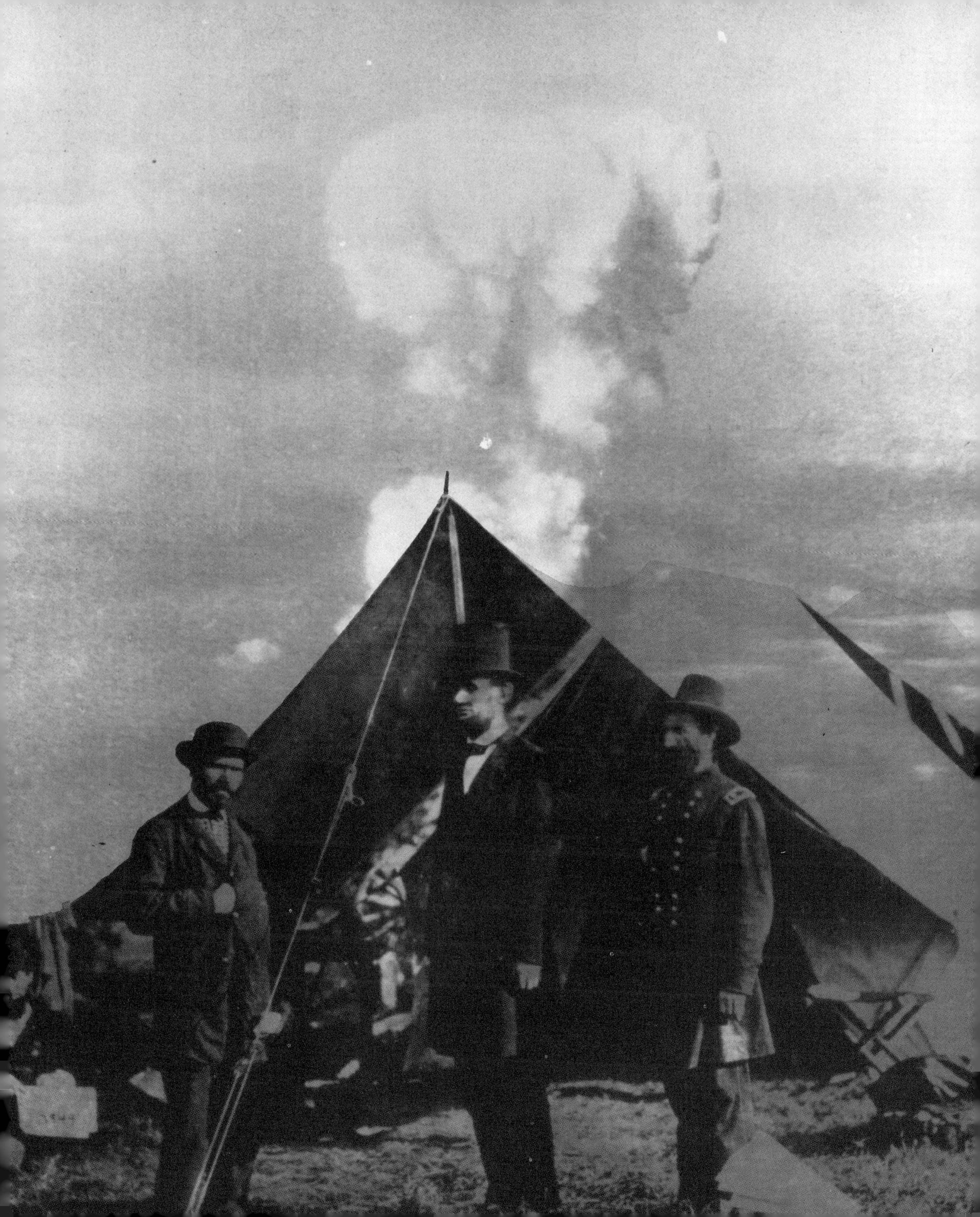

From Thomas Jefferson's war on the Barbary Pirates to Theodore Roosevelt's "big stick" diplomacy to Richard Nixon's overtures to the People's Republic of China, Presidents have often acted as this nation's Chief Diplomat—although nothing in the Constitution explicitly states they may do so.

THE WORLD'S CONSTABLE.

46

48

49

50

55

Pomp and ceremony is reserved for the President in his role as Chief of State—the embodiment of the nation; the President of all the people.

51

52

53

54

56

Political parties are not mentioned in the Constitution, but every President since Jefferson has been the leader of his party as well as leader of the nation.

fferson.
Washington.
Jackson.
OUR COUNTRY'S CHOICE
THOMAS A. HENDRICKS
NOMINEES

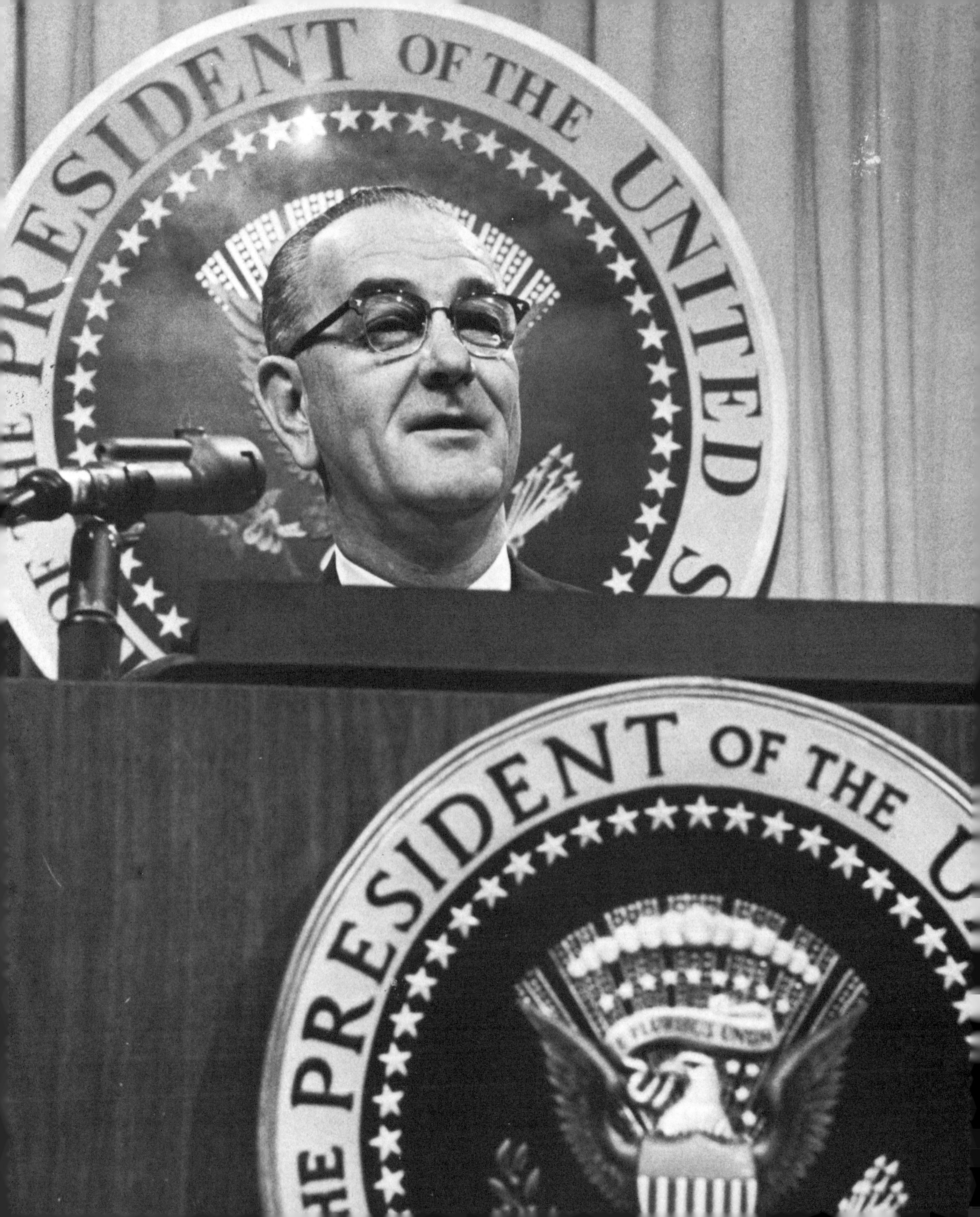
PRESIDENT OF THE UNITED
PRESIDENT OF THE

Radio, television, the press conference give the President a unique opportunity to mold public opinion—to win the nation to his point of view. The Presidency, in the words of Theodore Roosevelt, is a "bully pulpit."

According to the Constitution, the President "shall from time to time give to the Congress information of the state of the Union, and recommend to their consideration such measures as he shall judge necessary and expedient." Congress, of course, does not always agree; in which case the country's chief legislator can find the going rough indeed.

62

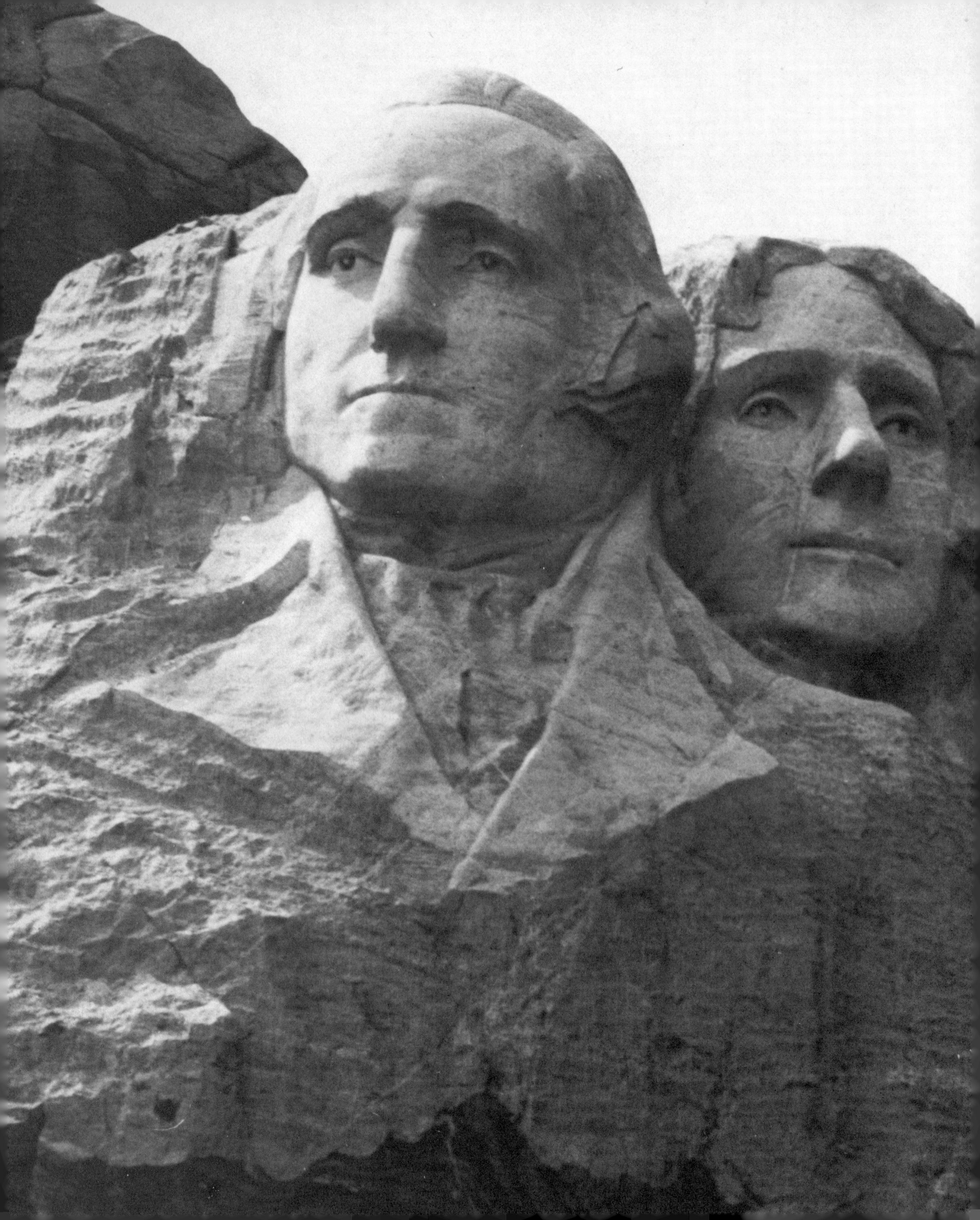

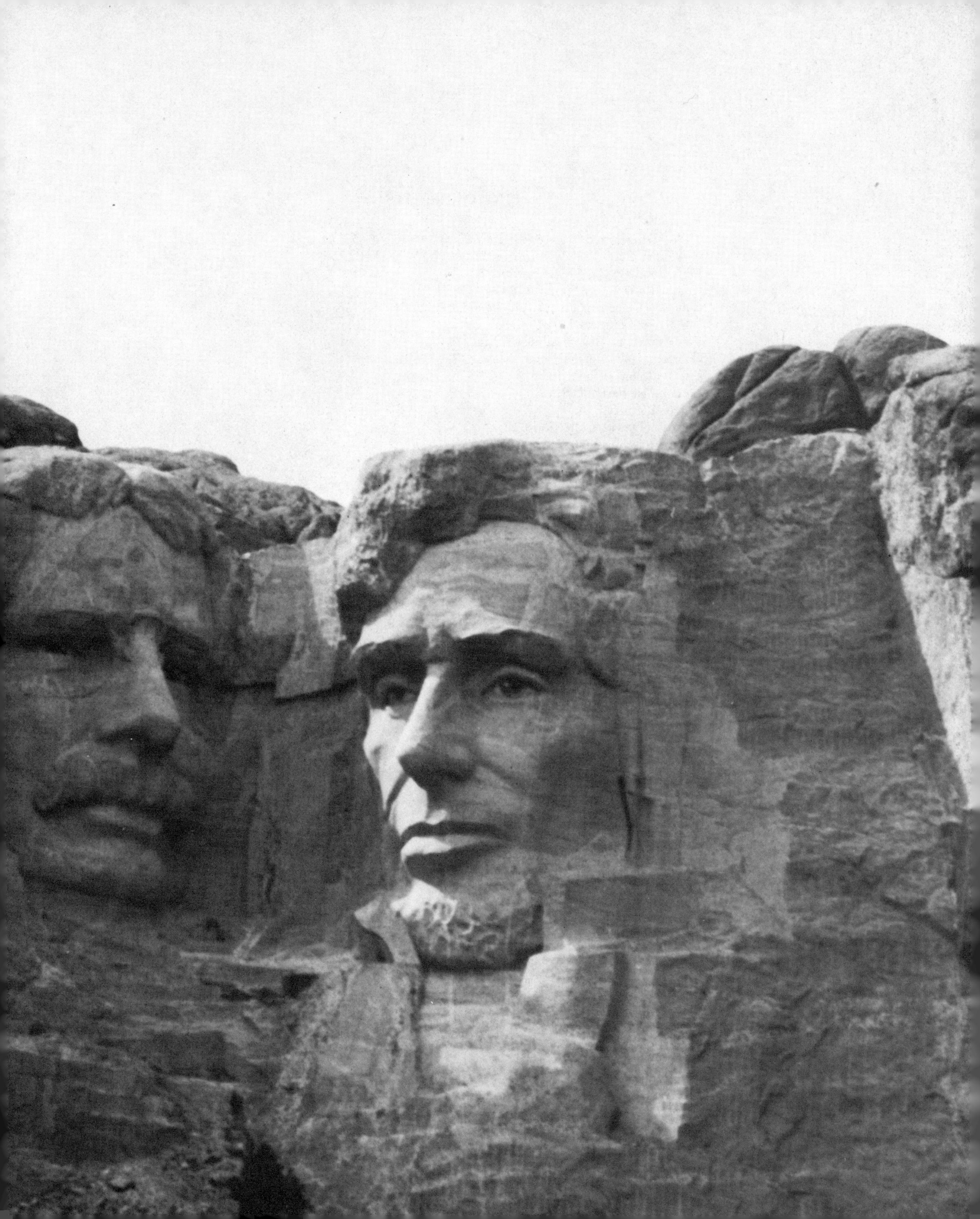

PHOTO CREDITS

Wide World Photos 10, 13, 21, 22, 23, 29, 30, 33, 46, 53, 61
New York Public Library 1, 3, 4, 15, 20, 39, 47, 51, 52, 55
John Goodwin 25, 27, 28, 42, 54, 59
United Press International 8, 38, 41, 58
Courtesy Lincoln National Life Foundation 17, 18, 24, 56
Library of Congress 11, 37, 43
Franklin D. Roosevelt Library 12, 44, 60
Courtesy Holt, Rinehart and Winston, Inc. 7, 19
The Bettman Archive 16
Communist Party, U.S.A. 26
Culver Pictures 35
J. Doyle Dewitt Collection 57
Harry Fleischman 32
Geofrey Gove 48
Rutherford B. Hayes Library 5
Minnesota Historical Society 36
National Park Service Photograph, Courtesy Harry S Truman Library 50
Painting by Gilbert Stuart, Courtesy of Pennsylvania Academy of Fine Arts 9
Theodore Roosevelt Association 45, 49
South Dakota Department of Highways 63
U.S. Army Photograph 6
U.S. Army Photograph, Courtesy Harry S Truman Library 40
U.S. Naval Photo Center, Courtesy Dwight D. Eisenhower Library 2
Courtesy George Wallace 34
Washington Star-News 31
Wesley Day Collection 62
White House Collection 14

Part 6
Presidents On The Presidency

29
The Stewardship Theory

Theodore Roosevelt **I DID GREATLY BROADEN THE USE OF EXECUTIVE POWER**

Excerpted from *The Autobiography of Theodore Roosevelt*, ed. by Wayne Andrews, (New York: Charles Scribner's Sons, 1958), 197–200.
Reprinted by permission of Charles Scribner's Sons. Copyright © 1958 Charles Scribner's Sons.

My view that every executive officer, and above all every executive officer in high position, was a steward of the people bound actively and affirmatively to do all he could for the people, and not to content himself with the negative merit of keeping his talents undamaged in a napkin. I declined to adopt the view that what was imperatively necessary for the nation could not be done by the President unless he could find some specific authorization to do it. My belief was that it was not only his right but his duty to do anything that the needs of the nation demanded unless such action was forbidden by the Constitution or by the laws. Under this interpretation of executive power I did and caused to be done many things not previously done by the President and the heads of the departments. I did not usurp power, but I did greatly broaden the use of executive power. In other words, I acted for the public welfare, I acted for the common well–being of all our people, whenever and in whatever manner was necessary, unless prevented by direct constitutional or legislative prohibition....

The course I followed, of regarding the Executive as subject only to the people, and, under the Constitution, bound to serve the people affirmatively in cases where the Constitution does not explicitly forbid him to render the service, was substantially the course followed by both Andrew Jackson and Abraham Lincoln. Other honorable and well-meaning Presidents, such as James Buchanan, took the opposite and, as it seems to me, narrowly legalistic view that the President is the servant of Congress rather than of the people, and can do nothing, no matter how necessary it be to act, unless the Constitution explictly commands the action. Most able lawyers who are past middle age take this view, and so do large numbers of well-meaning, respectable citizens. My successor in office took this, the Buchanan, view of the President's powers and duties.

For example, under my administration we found that one of the favorite methods adopted by the men desirous of stealing the public domain was to carry the decision of the secretary of the interior into court. By vigorously opposing such action, and only by so doing, we were able to carry out the policy of properly protecting the public domain. My successor not only took the opposite view, but recommended to Congress the passage of a bill which would have given the courts direct appellate power over the secretary of the interior in these land matters. . . . Fortunately, Congress declined to pass the bill. Its passage would have been a veritable calamity.

I acted on the theory that the President could at any time in his discretion withdraw from entry any of the public lands of the United States and reserve the same for forestry, for water-power sites, for irrigation, and other public purposes. Without such action it would have been impossible to stop the activity of the land-thieves. No one ventured to test its legality by lawsuit. My successor, however, himself questioned it, and referred the matter to Congress. Again Congress showed its wisdom by passing a law which gave the President the power which he had long exercised, and of which my successor had shorn himself.

Perhaps the sharp difference between what may be called the Lincoln-Jackson and the Buchanan-Taft schools, in their views of the power and duties of the President, may be best illustrated by comparing the attitude of my successor toward his Secretary of the Interior, Mr. Ballinger, when the latter was accused of gross misconduct in office, with my attitude toward my chiefs of department and other subordinate officers. More than once while I was President my officials were attacked by Congress, generally because these officials did their duty well and fearlessly. In every such case I stood by the official and refused to recognize the right of Congress to interfere with me excepting by impeachment or in other constitutional manner. On the other hand, wherever I found the officer unfit for his position, I promptly removed him, even although the most influential men in Congress fought for his retention. The Jackson-Lincoln view is that a President who is fit to do good work should be able to form his own judgment as to his own subordinates, and, above all, of the subordinates standing highest and in closest and most intimate touch with him. My secretaries and their subordinates were responsible to me, and I accepted the responsibility for all their deeds. As long as they were satisfactory to me I stood by them against every critic or assailant, within or without Congress; and as for getting Congress to make up my mind for me about them, the thought would have been inconceivable to me. My successor took the opposite, or Buchanan, view when he permitted and requested Congress to pass judgment on the charges made against Mr. Ballinger as an executive officer. These charges were made to the President; the President had the facts before him and could get at them at any time, and he alone had power to act if the charges were true. However, he permitted and requested Congress to investigate Mr. Ballinger. The party minority of the committee that investigated him, and one member of the majority, declared that the charges were well-founded and that Mr. Ballinger should be removed. The other members of the majority declared the charges ill-founded. The President abode by the view of the majority. Of course believers in the Jackson-Lincoln theory of the Presidency would not be content with this townmeeting majority and minority method of determining by another branch of the government what it seems the especial duty of the President himself to determine for himself in dealing with his own subordinate in his own department. . . .

30
The Progressive Tradition

Woodrow Wilson   **THE OFFICE WILL BE AS BIG AS THE MAN WHO OCCUPIES IT**

Excerpted from Woodrow Wilson, *Constitutional Government in the United States,* (New York: Columbia University Press, 1908), 73–79.

His is the vital place of action in the system, whether he accept it as such or not, and the office is the measure of the man,—of his wisdom as well as of his force. His veto abundantly equips him to stay the hand of Congress when he will. It is seldom possible to pass a measure over his veto, and no President has hesitated to use the veto when his own judgment of the public good was seriously at issue with that of the houses. The framers of the Constitution made in our President a more powerful, because a more isolated, king than the one they were imitating; and because the Constitution gave them their veto in such explicit terms, our Presidents have not hesitated to use it, even when it put their mere individual judgment against that of large majorities in both houses of Congress. And yet in the exercise of the power to suggest legislation, quite as explicitly conferred upon them by the Constitution, some of our Presidents have seemed to have a timid fear that they might offend some law of taste which had become a constitutional principle.

In one sense their messages to Congress have no more authority than the letters of any other citizen would have. Congress can heed or ignore them as it pleases; and there have been periods of our history when Presidential messages were utterly without practical significance, perfunctory documents which few persons except the editors of newspapers took the trouble to read. But if the President has personal force and cares to exercise it, there is this tremendous difference between his messages and the views of any other citizen, either outside Congress or in it: that the whole country reads them and feels that the writer speaks with an authority and a responsibility which the people themselves have given him. . . .

His office is a mere vantage ground from which he may be sure that effective words of advice and timely efforts at reform will gain telling momentum. He has the ear of the nation as of course, and a great person may use such an advantage greatly. If he use the opportunity, he may take his cabinet into partnership or not, as he pleases; and so its character may vary with his. Self-reliant men will regard their cabinets as executive councils; men less self-reliant or more prudent will regard them as also political councils, and will wish to call into them men who have earned the confidence of their party. The character of the cabinet may be made a nice index of the theory of the Presidential office, as well as of the President's theory of party government; but the one view is, so far as I can see, as constitutional as the other.

One of the greatest of the President's powers I have not yet spoken of at all: his control, which is very absolute, of the foreign relations of the nation. The initiative in foreign affairs, which the President possesses without any restriction whatever, is virtually the power to control them absolutely. The President cannot conclude a treaty with a foreign power without the consent of the Senate, but he may guide every step of diplomacy, and to guide diplomacy is to determine what treaties must be made, if the faith and prestige of the government are to be maintained. He need disclose no step of negotiation until it is complete, and when in any critical matter it is completed the government is virtually committed. Whatever its disinclination, the Senate may feel itself committed also. . . .

The President can never again be the mere domestic figure he has been throughout so large a part of our history. The nation has risen to the first rank in power and resources. The other nations of the world look askance upon her, half in envy, half in fear, and wonder with a deep anxiety what she will do with her vast strength. . . .

Our President must always, henceforth, be one of the great powers of the world, whether he act greatly and wisely or not, and the best statesmen we can produce will be needed to fill the office of Secretary of State. We have but begun to see the Presidential office in this light; but it is the light which will more and more beat upon it, and more and more determine its character and its effect upon the politics of the nation. We can never hide our President again as a mere domestic officer. We can never again see him the mere executive he was in the thirties and forties. He must stand always at the front of our affairs, and the office will be as big and as influential as the man who occupies it.

31
Pragmatism Raised To An Art

Franklin Delano Roosevelt **THIS NATION ASKS FOR ACTION AND ACTION NOW**

Excerpted from The First Inaugural Address, March 4, 1933.
The Presidents Speak, Davis Newton Lott, editor, (New York: Holt, Rinehart and Winston, 1969), 231–234. Copyright © 1961, 1969 by Davis Newton Lott.

I am certain that my fellow Americans expect that on my induction into the Presidency I will address them with a candor and a decision which the present situation of our Nation impels. This is preeminently the time to speak the truth, the whole truth, frankly and boldly. Nor need we shrink from honestly facing conditions in our country to-day. This great Nation will endure as it has endured, will revive and will prosper. So, first of all, let me assert my firm belief that the only thing we have to fear is fear itself—nameless, unreasoning, unjustified terror which paralyzes needed efforts to convert retreat into advance. In every dark hour of our national life a leadership of frankness and vigor has met with that understanding and support of the people themselves which is essential to victory. I am convinced that you will again give the support to leadership in these critical days....

This nation asks for action, and action now. Our greatest primary task is to put people to work. This is no unsolvable problem if we face it wisely and courageously. It can be accomplished in part by direct recruiting by the government itself, treating the task as we would treat the emergency of a war, but at the same time, through this employment, accomplishing greatly needed projects to stimulate and reorganize the use of our natural resources.

Hand in hand with this we must frankly recognize the overbalance of population in our industrial centers and, by engaging on a national scale in a redistribution, endeavor to provide a better use of the land for those best fitted for the land. The task can be helped by definite efforts to raise the values of agricultural products and with this the power to purchase the output of our cities. It can be helped by preventing realistically the tragedy of the growing loss through foreclosure of our small homes and our farms. It can be helped by insistence that the federal, state, and local governments act forthwith on the demand that their cost be drastically reduced. It can be helped by the unifying of relief activities which to-day are often scattered, uneconomical, and unequal. It can be helped by national planning for and supervision of all forms of transportation and of communications and other utilities which have a definitely public character. There are many ways in which it can be helped, but it can never be helped merely by talking about it. We must act and act quickly. . . .

If I read the temper of our people correctly, we now realize as we have never realized before our interdependence on each other; that we can not merely take but we must give as well; that if we are to go forward, we must move as a trained and loyal army willing to sacrifice for the good of a common discipline, because without such discipline no progress is made, no leadership becomes effective. We are, I know, ready and willing to submit our lives and property to such discipline, because it makes possible a leadership which aims at a larger good. This I propose to offer, pledging that the larger purposes will bind upon us all as a sacred obligation with a unity of duty hitherto evoked only in time of armed strife.

With this pledge taken, I assume unhesitatingly the leadership of this great army of our people dedicated to a disciplined attack upon our common problems.

Action in this image and to this end is feasible under the form of government which we have inherited from our ancestors. Our Constitution is so simple and practical that it is possible always to meet extraordinary needs by changes in emphasis and arrangement without loss of essential form. That is why our constitutional system has proved itself the most superbly enduring political mechanism the modern world has produced. It has met every stress of vast expansion of territory, of foreign wars, of bitter internal strife, of world relations.

It is to be hoped that the normal balance of executive and legislative authority may be wholly adequate to meet the unprecedented demand and need for undelayed action may call for temporary departure from that normal balance of public procedure.

I am prepared under my constitutional duty to recommend the measures that a stricken nation in the midst of a stricken world may require. These measures, or such other measures as the Congress may build out of its experience and wisdom, I shall seek, within my constitutional authority, to bring to speedy adoption.

But in the event that the Congress shall fail to take one of these two courses, and in the event that the national emergency is still critical, I shall not evade the clear course of duty that will then confront me. I shall ask the Congress for the one remaining instrument to meet the crisis—broad Executive power to wage a war against the emergency, as great as the power that would be given to me if we were in fact invaded by a foreign foe.

For the trust reposed in me I will return the courage and the devotion that befit the time. I can do no less.

We face the arduous days that lie before us in the warm courage of the national unity; with the clear consciousness of seeking old and precious moral values; with the clean satisfaction that comes from the stern performance of duty by old and young alike. We aim at the assurance of a rounded and permanent national life.

We do not distrust the future of essential democracy. The people of the United States have not failed. In their need they have registered a mandate that they want direct, vigorous action. They have asked for discipline and direction under leadership. They have made me the present instrument of their wishes. In the spirit of the gift I take it.

In this dedication of a Nation we humbly ask the blessing of God. May He protect each and every one of us. May He guide me in the days to come.

32
An Office Of International Importance

Harry S Truman

UPON ITS FUNCTIONING DEPENDS THE SURVIVAL OF THE FREE WORLD

President Truman delivered this speech at a Birthday Dinner in his honor on May 8, 1954. *The New York Times*, (May 9, 1954), 54.

... There's never been an office—an executive office—in all the history of the world with the responsibility and the power of the Presidency of the United States. That is the reason in this day and age that it must be run and respected as at no other time in the history of the world because it can mean the welfare of the world or its destruction.

When the founding fathers outlined the Presidency in Article II of the Constitution, they left a great many details out and vague. I think they relied on the experience of the nation to fill in the outlines. The office of chief executive has grown with the progress of this great republic. It has responded to the many demands that our complex society has made upon the government. It has given our nation a means of meeting our greatest emergencies. Today, it is one of the most important factors in our leadership of the free world.

Many diverse elements entered into the creation of the office, springing, as it did, from the parent idea of the separation of powers.

There was the firm conviction of such powerful and shrewd minds as that of John Adams that the greatest protection against unlimited power lay in an executive secured against the encroachment of the national assembly. Then there were the fears of those who suspected a plot to establish a monarchy on these shores. Others believed that the experience under the Confederation showed above all the need of stability through a strong central administration. Finally, there was the need for compromise among these and many other views.

The result was a compromise—a compromise which that shrewd observer, Alexis de Tocqueville, over 120 years ago, believed would not work. He thought that the Presidential office was too weak. The President, he thought, was at the mercy of Congress. The President could recommend, to be sure, he thought, but the President had no power and the Congress had the power. The Congress could disregard his recommendations, overrule his vetoes, reject his nominations. De Tocqueville thought that no man of parts, worthy of leadership, would accept such a feeble role.

This was not a foolish view and there was much in our early history which tended to bear it out. But there is a power in the course of events which plays its own part. In this case again, Jusice Holmes' epigram proved true. He said a page of history is worth a whole volume of logic. And as the pages of history were written they unfolded powers in the Presidency not explicitly found in Article II of the Constitution.

In the first place, the President became the leader of a political party. The party under his leadership had to be dominant enough to put him in office. This political party leadership was the last thing the Constitution contemplated. The President's election was not intended to be mixed up in the hurly-burly of partisan politics.

I wish some of those old gentlemen could come back and see how it worked. The people were to choose wise and respected men who would meet in calm seclusion and choose a President and the runner-up would be Vice President.

All of this went by the board—though most of the original language remains in the Constitution. Out of the struggle and tumult of the political arena a new and different President emerged—the man who led a political party to victory and retained in his hands the power of party leadership. That is, he retained it, like the sword Excalibur, if he could wrest it from the scabbard and wield it.

Another development was connected with the first. As the President came to be elected by the whole people, he became responsible to the whole people. I used to say the only lobbyist the whole people had in Washington was the President of the United States. Our whole people looked to him for leadership, and not confined within the limits of a written document. Every hope and every fear of his fellow citizens, almost every aspect of their welfare and activity, falls within the scope of his concern—indeed, it falls within the scope of his duty. Only one who has held that office can really appreciate that. It is the President's responsibility to look at all questions from the point of view of the whole people. His written and spoken word commands national and often international attention.

These powers which are not explicitly written into the Constitution are the powers which no President can pass on to his successor. They go only to him who can take and use them. However, it is these powers, quite as much as those enumerated in Article II of the Constitution, which make the Presidential system unique and which give the papers of Presidents their peculiarly revealing importance.

For it is through the use of these great powers that leadership arises, events are molded, and administrations take on their character. Their use can make a Jefferson or a Lincoln administration; their non–use can make a Buchanan or a Grant administration.

Moreover, a study of these aspects of our governmental and political history will save us from self-righteousness—from taking a holier-than-thou attitude toward other nations. For, brilliant and enduring as were the minds of the architects of our Constitution, they did not devise a foolproof system to protect us against the disaster of a weak government—that is, a government unable to face and resolve—one way or another—pressing national problems. Indeed, in some respects, the separation of powers requires stronger executive leadership than does the parliamentary and cabinet system.

As Justice Brandeis used to say, the separation of powers was not devised to promote efficiency in government. In fact, it was devised to prevent one form of deficiency—absolutism or dictatorship. By making the Congress separate and independent in the exercise of its powers, a certain amount of political conflict was built into the Constitution. For the price of independence is eternal vigilance and a good deal of struggle.

And this is not a bad thing—on the contrary, it is a good thing for the preservation of the liberty of the people—if it does not become conflict just for its own sake.

I've always said that the President who didn't have a fight with the Congress wasn't any good anyhow. And that's no reflection on the Congress. They are always looking after their rights. You needn't doubt that.

Having been in these two branches of government, legislative and executive, I think I am expressing a considered and impartial opinion in saying that the powers of the President are much more difficult to exercise and to preserve from encroachment than those of the Congress. In part, this comes from the difficulty of the problems of our time, and from the fact that upon the President falls the responsibility of obtaining action, timely and adequate, to meet the nation's needs. Whatever the Constitution says, he is held responsible for any disaster which may come.

And so a successful administration is one of strong presidential leadership. Weak leadership —or no leadership—produces failure and often disaster.

This does not come from the inherent incapacity of the people of the nation. It is inherent in the legislative government where there is no executive strong and stable enough to rally the people to a sustained effort of will and prepared to use its power of party control to the fullest extent.

Today, also, one of the great responsibilities and opportunities of the President is to lead and inspire public opinion. The words of a President carry great weight. His acts carry even more weight.

All of us remember the words of Franklin D. Roosevelt in his first inaugural address which did so much to rally the spirit of the nation struggling through the depths of a depression. He said "the only thing we have to fear is fear itself." Those words, however, would have had little effect if President Roosevelt had not backed them up by action. Following that speech, President Roosevelt plunged into a vigorous course, striking at the depression on all fronts. He backed his words by his action, and words and action restored the faith of the nation in its government and in its form of government, too. . . .

Today the tasks of leadership falling upon the President spring not only from our national problems but from those of the whole world. Today that leadership will determine whether our Government will function effectively, and upon its functioning depends the survival of each of us and also on that depends the survival of the free world. . . .

33
Organization In The Presidency

Dwight D. Eisenhower

EXECUTIVE ABILITY IS A VITAL ATTRIBUTE OF THE PRESIDENCY

Excerpted from an article by Dwight D. Eisenhower in *The Reader's Digest,* (November 1968), 49–55. Reprinted with permission from *The Reader's Digest.* Copyright 1968 by Dwight D. Eisenhower.

In the late afternoon of January 22, 1953—my first full day at the President's desk—my old friend Gen. Omar Bradley, then chairman of the Joint Chiefs of Staff, phoned me. For years we had been "Ike" and "Brad" to each other. But now, in the course of our conversation, he addressed me as "Mr. President."

Somehow this little incident rocked me back on my heels. Naturally, I knew all about Presidential protocol, but I suppose I had never quite realized the isolation that the job forces upon a man.

I couple this with another seemingly small circumstance that also put me on notice at once that the Presidency is something apart. During my first few hours in the Oval Room, a White House aide showed me a large push button concealed in the kneehole of my desk. If I were to touch the button with my knee, Secret Service guards appear instantly.

Doubtless every new President has experiences which quickly teach him that he has undertaken a lonely job. After these two episodes, I understood with deep impact that now, except for my immediate family, I would in a sense be alone—far more so than when I commanded the Allied forces in Europe. I have always liked people, and it was hard to surrender the easy camaraderie of the old days. Nor was it easy to accept the fact that I would always be under guard, that all movements must be planned, that I could never go anywhere unattended.

But these, after all, are minor frustrations, to which one grows accustomed. The American people respect the Presidency, and want the office to be conducted with dignity and with as much personal safety for the incumbent as can be devised—and it is right that they should.

Far more important than protocol or any other outward trappings of the office are certain inner qualities that any President must have to be effective. On several occasions I have said publicly that there are four prime requisites of the Presidency: Character, Ability, Responsibility, Experience. These need no explanation. But, on a more specific level, there are also many identifiable qualities, moods, characteristics, and attitudes that contribute to the success or defeat of a President. It is some of these human characteristics that I wish to discuss.

One of the most important necessities of the Presidency is vision—the ability to look far into the future and see the needs of the nation. Coupled with this is the courage to implement this vision with the necessary hard decisions, despite almost sure criticism—often actual vilification—from the press, the opposition party, and even from within the incumbent's own party....

There are certain deeply personal characteristics that any President needs to cope with the pressures and the buffeting of the job. One of these is a working balance between humility and vanity. I have been amused to read occasionally that I was a "humble President," while just as often I have been called an autocrat or a martinet. Every human being, and certainly a President, needs a certain amount of personal pride, but he shouldn't be so proud that he cannot change his mind or admit his mistakes. Nor can any President achieve his objectives if he permits others to walk roughshod over him.

Lincoln's humility was one of his storied qualities, but he also demonstrated over and over that he had iron in his soul. On the other hand, although Woodrow Wilson was surely a great President, I have always felt that his unbending pride kept him from being even greater. George Washington was, I think, the ideal in this respect. He possessed pride and dignity, but he was also considerate of others, consulted constantly with his subordinates, unfailingly weighed their advice.

As part of this working balance in a man's nature, a sense of humor can be a great help—particularly a sense of humor about himself. William Howard Taft joked about his own corpulence, and people loved it; it took nothing from his inherent dignity. Lincoln eased tense moments with bawdy stories, and often poked fun at himself—and history honors him for this human quality. A sense of humor is part of the art of leadership, of getting along with people, of getting things done.

On the other hand, I found that getting things done sometimes required other weapons from the Presidential arsenal—persuasion, cajolery, even a little head-thumping here and there—to say nothing of a personal streak of obstinacy which on occasion fires my boilers.

It is an essential quality of leadership to be able to inspire people. I have often thought how fortunate it was that the two great Allies of World War II were led by two men, Winston Churchill and Franklin D. Roosevelt, who had that ability and used it masterfully....

Executive ability, whose cornerstone is a talent for good organization and skill in selecting and using subordinates, certainly is a vital attribute of the Presidency. Any Chief Executive who tries to do everything himself, as some Presidents have, is in trouble. He will work himself into a state of exhaustion and frustration, and drive everyone around him half crazy....

In my own administration, we developed a fine working team of highly competent people. We had efficient organization and good staff work. Some writers have said that I conducted the Presidency largely through staff decisions. This, of course, is nonsense. Naturally, I consulted constantly with my staff, and I valued their opinions. But staff work doesn't mean that you take a vote of your subordinates and then abide by the majority opinion. On important matters, in the end, you alone must decide. As a military leader I had learned this hard lesson. Many times, during my two terms, my decisions ran contrary to the majority opinion of my advisers....

There is a strange theory among some pundits that smooth organization in the White House indicates that nothing is happening, whereas ferment and disorder are proof of progress. I recall that we had plenty of crises during my administration, but we were able to handle them without turning double handsprings—and usually without unnecessary public flap. In my opinion, a table-pounding executive is ridiculous.

With good executive organization in the White House and the departments, I do not think the heavy burdens of the Presidency need become intolerable. Nor do I believe that a plural Presidency, which has sometimes been suggested, is necessary or would work. In our kind of government, divided authority surely would result only in confusion and frustration.

Finally, I believe deeply that every occupant of the White House, whether he be conservative, liberal or middle-of-the-road, has one profound duty to the nation: to exert moral leadership. The President of the United States should stand, visible and uncompromising, for what is right and decent—in government, in the business community, in the private lives of the citizens. For decency is one of the main pillars of a sound civilization. An immoral nation invites its own ruin.

34
The Vital Center

John F. Kennedy — **THE PEOPLE DEMAND A VIGOROUS PROPONENT OF THE NATIONAL INTEREST**

> John Kennedy delivered this speech during the 1960 Presidential campaign. *The New York Times*, (January 15, 1960), 1.

The history of this nation—its brightest and its bleakest pages—has been written largely in terms of the different views our Presidents have had of the Presidency itself. This history ought to tell us that the American people in 1960 have an imperative right to know what any man bidding for the Presidency thinks about the place he is bidding for—whether he is aware of and willing to use the powerful resources of that office—whether his model will be Taft or Roosevelt—Wilson or Harding....

But the question is what do the times—and the people—demand for the next four years in the White House?

They demand a vigorous proponent of the national interest—not a passive broker for conflicting private interests. They demand a man capable of acting as the commander in chief of the grand alliance, not merely a bookkeeper who feels that his work is done when the numbers on the balance sheet come out even. They demand that he be the head of a responsible party, not rise so far above politics as to be invisible—a man who will formulate and fight for legislative policies, not be a casual bystander to the legislative process.

Today a restricted concept of the Presidency is not enough. For beneath today's surface gloss of peace and prosperity are increasingly dangerous, unsolved, long-postponed problems—problems that will inevitably explode to the surface during the next four years of the next Administration—the growing missile gap, the rise of Communist China, the despair of the underdeveloped nations, the explosive situations in Berlin and in the Formosa Straits, the deterioration of NATO, the lack of an arms control agreement, and all the domestic problems of our farms, cities, and schools....

In the decade that lies ahead—in the challenging, revolutionary Sixties—the American Presidency will demand more than ringing manifestoes issued from the rear of the battle. It will demand that the President place himself in the very thick of the fight, that he care passionately about the fate of the people he leads, that he be willing to serve them at the risk of incurring their momentary displeasure.

Whatever the political affiliation of our next President, whatever his views may be on all the issues and problems that rush in upon us, he must above all be the Chief Executive in every sense of the word. He must be prepared to exercise the fullest powers of his office—all that are specified and some that are not. He must master complex problems as well as receive one-page memoranda. He must originate action as well as study groups. He must reopen the channels of communication between the world of thought and the seat of power.

Ulysses Grant considered the President "a purely administrative officer." If he administered the government departments efficiently, delegated his functions smoothly, and performed his ceremonies of state with decorum and grace, no more was to be expected of him. But that is not the place the Presidency was meant to have in American life. The President is alone, at the top —the loneliest job there is, as Harry Truman has said. If there is destructive dissension among the services, he alone can step in and straighten it out—instead of waiting for unanimity. If administrative agencies are not carrying out their mandate—if a brushfire threatens some part of the globe—he alone can act, without waiting for the Congress. If his farm program fails, he alone deserves the blame, not his Secretary of Agriculture.

"The President is at liberty, both in law and conscience, to be as big a man as he can." So wrote Professor Woodrow Wilson. But President Woodrow Wilson discovered that to be a big man in the White House inevitably brings cries of dictatorship. So did Lincoln and Jackson and the two Roosevelts. And so may the next occupant of that office, if he is the man the times demand. But how much better it would be, in the turbulent Sixties, to have a Roosevelt or a Wilson than to have another James Buchanan, cringing in the White House, afraid to move.

Nor can we afford a Chief Executive who is praised primarily for what he did not do, the disasters he prevented, the bills he vetoed—a President wishing his subordinates would produce more missiles or build more schools. We will need instead what the Constitution envisioned: a Chief Executive who is the vital center of action in our whole scheme of government.

This includes the legislative process as well. The President cannot afford—for the sake of the office as well as the nation—to be another Warren G. Harding, described by one backer as a man who "would, when elected, sign whatever bill the Senate sent him—and not send bills for the Senate to pass." Rather he must know when to lead the Congress, when to consult it, and when he should act alone. Having served fourteen years in the legislative branch, I would not look with favor upon its domination by the executive. Under our government of "power as the rival of power," to use Hamilton's phrase, Congress must not surrender its responsibilities. But neither should it dominate. However large its share in the formulation of domestic programs, it is the President alone who must make the major decisions of our foreign policy.

That is what the Constitution wisely commands. And even domestically, the President must initiate policies and devise laws to meet the needs of the nation. And he must be prepared to use all the resources of his office to insure the enactment of that legislation—even when conflict is the result. . . .

But in the coming years, we will need a real fighting mood in the White House—a man who will not retreat in the face of pressure from his congressional leaders—who will not let down those supporting his views on the floor. Divided government over the past six years has only been further confused by this lack of legislative leadership. To restore it next year will help restore purpose to both the Presidency and the Congress.

The facts of the matter are that legislative leadership is not possible without party leadership, in the most political sense. . . . No President, it seems to me, can escape politics. He has not only been chosen by the nation—he has been chosen by his party. And if he insists that he is "President of all the people" and should, therefore, offend none of them—if he blurs the issues and differences between the parties—if he neglects the party machinery and avoids his party's leadership—then he has not only weakened the political party as an instrument of the democratic process—he has dealt a blow to the democratic process itself.

But the White House is not only the center of political leadership. It must be the center of moral leadership—a "bully pulpit," as Theodore Roosevelt described it. For only the President represents the national interest. And upon him alone converge all the needs and aspirations of all parts of the country, all departments of the government, all nations of the world. It is not enough merely to represent prevailing sentiment—to follow McKinley's practice, as described by Joe Cannon, of "keeping his ear so close to the ground he got it full of grasshoppers." We will need in the Sixties a President who is willing and able to summon his national constituency to its finest hour—to alert the people of our dangers and our opportunities—to demand of them the sacrifices that will be necessary. Despite the increasing evidence of a lost national purpose and a soft national will, F.D.R.'s words in his first inaugural still ring true: "In every dark hour of our national life, a leadership of frankness and vigor has met with that understanding and support of the people themselves which is essential to victory."

Roosevelt fulfilled the role of moral leadership. So did Wilson and Lincoln, Truman and Jackson and Teddy Roosevelt. They led the people as well as the government—they fought for great ideals as well as bills. And the time has come to demand that kind of leadership again. And so, as the vital campaign begins, let us discuss the issues the next President will face—but let us also discuss the powers and tools with which he must face them. For he must endow that office with extraordinary strength and vision. He must act in the image of Abraham Lincoln summoning his wartime cabinet to a meeting on the Emancipation Proclamation. That cabinet had been carefully chosen to please and reflect many elements in the country. But "I have gathered you together," Lincoln said, "to hear what I have written down. I do not wish your advice about the main matter—that I have determined for myself." And later when he went to sign it after several hours of exhausting handshaking that had left his arm weak, he said to those present: "If my name goes down in history, it will be for this act. My whole soul is in it. If my hand trembles when I sign this proclamation, all who examine the document hereafter will say: 'He hesitated.'" But Lincoln's hand did not tremble. He did not hesitate. He did not equivocate. For he was the President of the United States. It is in this spirit that we must go forth in the coming months and years.

35
A Vehicle For Reform

Lyndon B. Johnson **THE PRESIDENCY BELONGS TO ALL THE PEOPLE**

Reprinted from Robert S. Hirschfield, ed., *The Power of the Presidency* (New York: Atherton Press, Inc., 1968) 147–150. Copyright 1968 by Atherton Press, Inc. Reprinted by permission of the author and the Aldine Publishing Company.

[The Presidency] is a much tougher job from the inside than I thought it was from the outside.

I have watched it since Mr. Hoover's days, and I realize the responsibilities it carried, and the obligations of leadership that were there, and the decisions that had to be made, and the awesome responsibilities of the office.

But I must say that, when I started having to make those decisions and started hearing from the Congress, the Presidency looked a little different when you are in the Presidency than it did when you are in the Congress, and vice versa. . . .

Thomas Jefferson said the second office of the land was an honorable and easy one. The Presidency was a splendid misery. But I found great interest in serving both offices, and it carries terrific and tremendous and awesome responsibilities, but I am proud of this nation and I am so grateful that I could have an opportunity that I have had in America that I want to give my life seeing that the opportunity is perpetuated for others. . . .

One of the hardest tasks that a President faces is to keep the time scale of his decisions always in mind and to try to be the President of all the people.

He is not simply responsible to an immediate electorate, either. He knows over the long stretch of time how great can be the repercussions of all that he does or that he fails to do, and over that span of time the President always has to think of America as a continuing community.

He has to try to see how his decisions will affect not only today's citizens, but their children and their children's children unto the third and the fourth generation. He has to try to peer into the future, and he has to prepare for that future.

If the policies he advocates lack this dimension of depth and this dimension of staying power, he may gain this or that advantage in the short term, but he can set the country on a false course and profit today at the expense of all the world tomorrow. So it is this solemn and this most difficult responsibility, and it is always hard to interpret confidently the future patterns of the world.

There are always critics around imploring the President to stick to the facts and not to go crystal-gazing. Some of them tell me to try to keep my feet on the ground, if not my head in the sand.

But this is the point: The facts include today, the overwhelming, built-in, irresistible forces of change that have been unleashed by modern science and technology. And the very facts dissolve and regroup as we look into them.

To make no predictions is to be sure to be wrong. Whatever else is or is not that certain in our dynamic world, there is one thing that is very sure. Tomorrow will be drastically different from today. Yet it is in all of these tomorrows that we and our children and our children's children are going to be forced to live. We have to try to see that pattern and we have to try to prepare for it.

The President of this country, more than any other single man in the world, must grapple with the course of events and the directions of history. What he must try to do, try to do always, is to build for tomorrow in the immediacy of today.

For if we can, the President, and the Congress, and you leaders of the communities throughout the Nation, will have made their mark in history. Somehow we must ignite a fire in the breast of this land, a flaming spirit of adventure that soars beyond the ordinary and the contented, and really demands greatness from our society, and demands achievement from our government. . . .

The world is no longer the world that your fathers and mine once knew. Once it was dominated by the balance of power. Today, it is diffused and emergent. But though most of the world struggles fitfully to assert its own initiative, the people of the world look to this land for inspiration. Two-thirds of the teeming masses of humanity, most of them in their tender years under forty, are decreeing that they are not going to take it without food to sustain their body and a roof over their head.

And from our science and our technology, from our compassion and from our tolerance, from our unity and from our heritage, we stand uniquely on the threshold of a high adventure of leadership by example and by precept. "Not by might, nor by power, but by my spirit, saith the Lord." From our Jewish and Christian heritage, we draw the image of the God of all mankind, who will judge his children not by their prayers and by their pretensions, but by their mercy to the poor and their understanding of the weak.

We cannot cancel that strain and then claim to speak as a Christian society. To visit the widow and the fatherless in their affliction is still pure religion and undefiled. I tremble for this Nation. I tremble for our people if at the time of our greatest prosperity we turn our back on the moral obligations of our deepest faith. If the face we turn to this aspiring, laboring world is a face of indifference and contempt, it will rightly rise up and strike us down.

Believe me, God is not mocked. We reap as we sow. Our God is still a jealous God, jealous of his righteousness, jealous of his mercy, jealous for the last of the little ones who went unfed while the rich sat down to eat and rose up to play. And unless my administration profits the present and provides the foundation for a better life for all humanity, not just now but for generations to came, I shall have failed. . . .

I think I know some of the things that Americans want. They want their President to be a source of leadership and responsibility. They know that a President who strides forward to do the people's business is a bulwark against the decline and chaos in this country. They know that a President who is willing to move ahead, whose means are just, whose ends are democratic, can be the difference between national stagnation and national progress.

And the people want progress. They want to keep moving.

Americans know that the Presidency belongs to all the people. And they want the President to act and be President of all the people.

Something else is very clear. The source of the President's authority is the people. A President who refuses to go out among the people, who refuses to be judged by the people, who is unwilling to lay his case before the people, can never be President of all the people.

The people want to see their President in person. They want to hear firsthand what he believes. They want to decide if he can act for them.

And unless the President goes to the people, unless he visits and talks with them, unless he senses how they respond as he discusses issues with them, he cannot do the President's job. The voice of the people will be lost among the clamor of divisions and diversities, and the Presidency will not become a clear beacon of national purpose.

As long as I hold it, I will keep the office of President always close to all the people. I think I know what it is the people want, and I make that as a solemn pledge. . . .

The office of the Presidency is the only office in this land of all the people.

Whatever may be the personal wishes or the preferences of any man who holds it, a President of all the people can afford no thought of self. At no time and in no way and for no reason can a President allow the integrity or the responsibility or the freedom of the office ever to be compromised or diluted or destroyed, because when you destroy it, you destroy yourselves.

I hope and I pray that by not allowing the Presidency to be involved in division and deep partisanship I shall be able to pass on to my successor a stronger office, strong enough to guard and defend all the people against all the storms that the future may bring us.

36
In The Activist Tradition

Richard M. Nixon

THE DAYS OF A PASSIVE PRESIDENCY BELONG TO A SIMPLER PAST

Richard Nixon delivered this speech during the 1968 Presidential campaign. *Newsweek*, (September 30, 1968), 24–25. Copyright Newsweek, Inc. 1968. Reprinted by permission.

The days of a passive Presidency belong to a simpler past. Let me be very clear about this: the next President must take an activist view of his office. He must articulate the nation's values, define its goals and marshal its will . . .

The President is trusted, not to follow the fluctuations of public–opinion polls, but to bring his own best judgment to bear on the best ideas his administration can muster. There are occasions on which a President must take unpopular measures. But his responsibility does not stop there. The President has a duty to decide, but the people have a right to know why. The President has a responsibility to tell them—to lay out all the facts, and to explain not only why he chose as he did but also what it means for the future. Only through an open, candid dialogue with the people can a President maintain his trust and his leadership.

It's time we once again had an open administration . . . We should bring dissenters into policy discussions, not freeze them out; we should invite constructive criticism, not only because the critics have a right to be heard, but because they often have something worth hearing.

And this brings me to another, related point: the President cannot isolate himself from the great intellectual ferments of his time. On the contrary, he must consciously and deliberately place himself at their center. The lamps of enlightenment are lit by the spark of controversy; their flames can be snuffed out by the blanket of consensus.

This is one reason why I don't want a government of yes–men. It's why I do want a government drawn from the broadest possible base —an administration made up of Republicans, Democrats, and independents, and drawn from politics, from career government service, from universities, from business, from the professions —one including not only executives and administrators, but scholars and thinkers . . . .

Only if we have an administration broadly enough based philosophically to ensure a true ferment of ideas, and invite an interplay of the best minds in America, can we be sure of getting the best and most penetrating ideas . . . .

This I pledge, that in a Nixon Administration,

America's citizens will not have to break the law to be heard, they will not have to shout or resort to violence. We can restore peace only if we make government attentive to the quiet as well as the strident, and this I intend to do...

The President's chief function is to lead, not to administer; it is not to oversee every detail, but to put the right people in charge, to provide them with basic guidance and direction, and to let them do the job. This requires surrounding the President with men of stature, including young men, and giving them responsibilities commensurate with that stature. It requires a Cabinet made up of the ablest men in America, leaders in their own right and not merely by virtue of appointment—men who will command the public's respect and the President's attention by the power of their intellect and the force of their ideas.

Such men are not attracted to an administration in which all credit is gathered to the White House and blame parceled out to scapegoats, or in which high officials are asked to dance like puppets on a presidential string...

A President must tell the people what cannot be done immediately, as well as what can. Hope is fragile, and too easily shattered by the disappointment that follows on promises unkept and unkeepable. America needs charts of the possible, not excursions into the impossible...

What has to be done, has to be done by President and people together, or it won't be done at all.

In asking you to join this great effort, I am asking not that you give something to your country, but that you do something with your country; I am asking not for your gifts, but for your hands.

37
A Dissenting View

William Howard Taft   **THE EXECUTIVE POWER IS LIMITED**

Excerpted from William Howard Taft, *The President and His Powers* (New York: Columbia University Press, 1916), 139–145; 156–157.

The true view of the executive functions is, as I conceive it, that the President can exercise no power which cannot be fairly and reasonably traced to some specific grant of power or justly implied and included with such express grant as proper and necessary to its exercise. Such specific grant must be either in the Federal Constitution or in an act of Congress passed in pursuance thereof. There is no undefined residuum of power which he can exercise because it seems to him to be in the public interest. . . .

The grants of executive power are necessarily in general terms in order not to embarrass the Executive within the field of action plainly marked for him, but his jurisdiction must be justified and vindicated by affirmative constitutional or statutory provision, or it does not exist. There have not been wanting, however, eminent men in high public office holding a different view and who have insisted upon the necessity for an undefined residuum of executive power in the public interest. . . .

Mr. Roosevelt, in his "Notes for a Possible Autobiography" on the subject of "Executive Powers," says:

> The most important factor in getting the right spirit in my administration, next to insistence upon courage, honesty, and a genuine democracy of desire to serve the plain people, was my insistence upon the theory that the executive power was limited only by specific restrictions and prohibitions appearing in the Constitution or imposed by Congress under its constitutional powers. My view was that every executive officer and above all every executive officer in high position was a steward of the people bound actively and affirmatively to do all he could for the people and not content himself with the negative merit of keeping his talents undamaged in a napkin. I declined to adopt this view that what was imperatively necessary for the Nation could not be done by the President, unless he could find some specific authorization to do it. My belief was that

it was not only his right but his duty to do anything that the needs of the Nation demanded unless such action was forbidden by the Constitution or by the laws. Under this interpretation of executive power I did and caused to be done many things not previously done by the President and the heads of the departments. I did not usurp power but I did greatly broaden the use of executive power. In other words, I acted for the common well being of all our people whenever and in whatever measure was necessary, unless prevented by direct constitutional or legislative prohibition.

I may add that Mr. Roosevelt, by way of illustrating his meaning as to the defining usefulness of Presidents, divides the Presidents into two classes, and designates them as "Lincoln Presidents" and "Buchanan Presidents." In order more fully to illustrate his division of Presidents on their merits, he places himself in the Lincoln class of Presidents, and me in the Buchanan class....

My judgment is that the view of.... Mr. Roosevelt, ascribing an undefined residuum of power to the President is an unsafe doctrine and that it might lead under emergencies to results of an arbitrary character, doing irremediable injustice to private right. The mainspring of such a view is that the Executive is charged with responsibility for the welfare of all the people in a general way, that he is to play the part of a Universal Providence and set all things right, and that anything that in his judgment will help the people he ought to do, unless he is expressly forbidden not to do it. The wide field of action that this would give to the Executive one can hardly limit....

There is little danger to the public weal from the tyranny or reckless character of a President who is not sustained by the people. The absence of popular support will certainly in the course of two years withdraw from him the sympathetic action of at least one House of Congress, and by the control that that House has over appropriations, the executive arm can be paralyzed, unless he resorts to a coup d'état, which means impeachment, conviction and deposition. The only danger in the action of the Executive under the present limitations and lack of limitation of his powers is when his popularity is such that he can be sure of the support of the electorate and therefore of Congress, and when the majority in the legislative halls respond with alacrity and sycophancy to his will. This condition cannot probably be long continued. We have had Presidents who felt the public pulse with accuracy, who played their parts upon the political stage with histrionic genius and commanded the people almost as if they were an army and the President their Commander-in-Chief. Yet in all these cases, the good sense of the people has ultimately prevailed and no danger has been done to our political structure and the reign of law has continued. In such times when the executive power seems to be all prevailing, there have always been men in this free and intelligent people of ours, who apparently courting political humiliation and disaster have registered protest against this undue executive domination and this use of the executive power and popular support to perpetuate itself.

The cry of executive domination is often entirely unjustified, as when the President's commanding influence only grows out of a proper cohesion of a party and its recognition of the necessity for political leadership; but the fact that executive domination is regarded as a useful ground for attack upon a successful administration, even when there is no ground for it, is itself proof of the dependence we may properly place upon the sanity and clear perceptions of the people in avoiding its baneful effects when there is real danger. Even if a vicious precedent is set by the Executive, and injustice done, it does not have the same bad effect that an improper precedent of a court may have, for one President does not consider himself bound by the policies or constitutional views of his predecessors.

The Constitution does give the President wide discretion and great power, and it ought to do so. It calls from him activity and energy to see that within his proper sphere he does what his great responsibilities and opportunities require. He is no figurehead, and it is entirely proper that an energetic and active clear-sighted people, who, when they have work to do, wish it done well, should be willing to rely upon their judgment in selecting their Chief Agent, and having selected him, should entrust to him all the power needed to carry out their governmental purpose, great as it may be.

Part 7

The Presidency-
What Of The Future?

38
Striking A Balance

Arthur Schlesinger, Jr. **THE LIMITS AND EXCESSES OF PRESIDENTIAL POWER**

From *Saturday Review*, (May 3, 1969), 17–19. Copyright © 1969 by Saturday Review Inc. Used with permission.

The Presidency of Lyndon B. Johnson had its impact, of course, on the nation and on the world. It has also had a marked impact on thinking about the American Presidency itself. For it compelled American historians and political scientists to begin to question their traditional and rather uncritical acceptance of the virtues of a strong Presidency. After all, so far as the theory of Presidential power is concerned, Lyndon Johnson's leadership in connection with the war in Vietnam was an exemplary case of Presidential activism. It represented a splendid rejection of theory that the Presidency was an office of limited and enumerated powers—the Whig theory of the Presidency or, as Theodore Roosevelt liked to call it, the Buchanan–Taft theory. It represented a bold use of the spacious powers that strong Presidents such as TR, Woodrow Wilson, and Franklin Roosevelt had perceived in the Presidency and added to it.

Yet, many historians and political scientists—this writer included—who had previously been what Professor Edward S. Corwin had presciently termed in 1954 "high-flying prerogative men," found themselves deeply troubled fifteen years later by the way in which President Johnson was applying the thesis of a strong Presidency to Vietnam. Invoking honored doctrine, he sent half a million American fighting men halfway around the world to enter a war that seemed to bear no overpowering relation to the vital interests of the United States. Moreover, he did so without giving either Congress or the electorate any clear sense that they had been consulted about the decisions which had deepened the commitment and escalated the war. (To do President Johnson justice, probably a majority of both were in favor of escalation until 1968. To do Congress and the electorate justice, they might not have been had they received an accurate picture of what was going on in Vietnam.)

Moreover, the executive appeared to be swallowing up vital powers of decision as a matter not only of practice but of principle. When a former Attorney General, later an Under Secretary of State, told the Senate Foreign Relations Committee that the declaration of war, expressly reserved in the Constitution for Congress, had become "outmoded in the international arena," and that the SEATO agreement and the Gulf of Tonkin resolution were together the "functional equivalent" of a declaration of war, the Committee formally concluded that "the intent of the framers of the Constitution with respect to the exercise of the war power has been virtually nullified." President Johnson himself carried the supposed usurpation even further when he said at Omaha on June 30, 1966, "There are many, many who can recommend, advise, and sometimes a few of them consent. But there is only one that has been chosen by the American people to decide." Everett M. Dirksen added a senatorial—and Republican—blessing: "It is a rather interesting thing," he told the Senate on October 3, 1967, "I have run down many legal cases before the Supreme Court, [and] I have found as yet no delimitation on the powers of the Commander in Chief under the Constitution."

The Vietnam experience thus provided an unexpected demonstration that a strong Presidency might have its drawbacks. It consequently forced scholars to face a disturbing question: Had they promoted the cult of the strong Presidency simply because, up to 1965, strong Presidents had mostly been doing things which historians and political scientists had mostly wanted done? The spectacle of a strong President doing things they mostly did not want done suddenly stimulated many of us to take a fresh look at the old problem of Presidential power.

Then Senator Eugene McCarthy in the 1968 campaign gave powerful expression to this rising doubt about the virtues of a strong Presidency. "The New Politics," he said, "requires a different conception of the Presidency." He declared his opposition to "the sort of presidential power which extends itself in a personal way into every institution of government." He asked: "Has the integrity of Congress, of the Cabinet, and of the military been impinged upon by undue extension of the executive power?" The powers of the Presidency, he argued, should be decentralized. As against the idea of a strong Presidency on the Jackson–FDR model, Senator McCarthy offered instead a revival of the Whig theory of a passive Presidency, though he proposed to adapt his theory to progressive purposes. "This is a good country," he once said, "if the President will just let it be." The next President, he said, "should understand that this country does not so much need leadership.... He must be prepared to be a kind of channel." The President's duty is to "liberate individuals so that they may determine their own lives." In a variety of ways McCarthy made clear his fear of strong Presidential leadership and his faith in greater independence among the units of the national government and greater initiative in the localities. He was the first liberal this century to run *against* the Presidency.

This was one of his major differences with Robert F. Kennedy. Kennedy retained the more traditional liberal belief in a strong Presidency. He saw affirmative Presidential leadership as an indispensable means of welding disparate groups together into a common cause. He knew that Franklin Roosevelt, for example, had forged his coalition and held it together through precisely the sort of Presidential leadership McCarthy condemned. Roosevelt had been able to persuade the working classes of the Thirties to go along with him on issues outside their daily concern—such as foreign policy, civil liberties, and equal rights—not because they had more enlightened views on such issues than their counterparts have today, but because they had a confidence in Roosevelt founded in his leadership on the issues that *were* part of their daily concern and because, for this and other reasons, they trusted and loved him. I think that Kennedy supposed that today's white, low-income groups were similarly composed of decent, if confused, people, and that they could be similarly reclaimed for political rationality.

Kennedy saw a strong Presidency as essential not just to unite the country but to enable the country to meet its problems. Certainly President Johnson had abused his power in foreign affairs. But a general cutback in Presidential power, Kennedy feared, would only increase the nation's impotence in the face of deep and angry national division. He believed that as a country we were heading into perilous times, that the ties which had precariously bound Americans together were under almost intolerable strain, and that reducing Presidential authority could be a disastrous error when only a strong President could rally us to meet our most difficult and urgent internal issue: racial justice. The President, in Kennedy's view, had to be the active protector of the alienated groups, the tribune of the disinherited and the dispossessed; he had to be the active champion both of racial justice and of civil peace (and he could only be the second if he had demonstrated that he was the first); and, if any President renounced these obligations, the country might well break up.

McCarthy and Kennedy thus might agree that the Vietnam war revealed a dangerous concentration of power over war and peace in the hands of the man in the White House. But they disagreed in the conclusions they drew from this situation. McCarthy concluded that the situation demanded a general limitation of the Presidency, with all functions questioned and all powers reduced. Kennedy advocated a selective approach to the question of Presidential power. He feared that if the American people recoiled indiscriminately against abuses of Presidential authority in foreign affairs, they ran the risk of inviting a new period of weak Presidents—as in the dreary years from Taylor through Buchanan—at a time when only a strong President could serve as the center of action and purpose to hold the country together.

The problem of the future of the Presidency therefore resolves itself, in one of its aspects, into the question whether, if Presidential power is excessive, it is unitary and must be diminished across the board, or whether Presidential powers are separable—whether the President has too much power in foreign policy but conceivably not enough in domestic policy.

The argument is persuasive, it seems to me, that the problem of the American Presidency in domestic affairs is not that he has too much power but that he has too little. He does not have in internal matters, for example, the same constitutional authority he has in foreign policy. The Supreme Court in the Curtiss–Wright case spoke of "the very delicate, plenary, and exclusive power of the President as the sole organ of the federal government in the field of international relations," adding that this power is "in origin and essential character different from that over internal affairs." Nor can a President in domestic affairs so easily shield and enhance his authority by wrapping the flag around himself, invoking patriotism, and national unity, and claiming life-and-death crisis.

He is therefore much more at the mercy of Congress. From 1938 to 1968 a series of strong Democratic Presidents sought congressional approval for social programs which, had they been enacted, might have greatly alleviated some of the tensions presently convulsing our national community. But in these thirty years a coalition, predominantly rural, of Republicans and Southern Democrats in the House of Representatives blocked or whittled down most of the Presidential proposals—except for a period of two years, 1965–67, when, as a result of the Goldwater fiasco, enough Northern Democrats were elected to create a short-lived but effective liberal majority in the House. Where a parliamentary Prime Minister can be reasonably sure that anything he suggests will become law in short order, the President of the United States cannot even be sure that *his* proposals will get to the floor of Congress for debate and vote. And no executive in any other democratic state has so little control over national economic policy as the American President.

In recent years, a second factor has arisen to limit Presidential power: the growth of the executive bureaucracy. The expansion of governmental functions under the New Deal produced the modern bureaucracy—a development which the conservatives of the time, with their customary wisdom, regarded with consternation. The New Deal bureaucrats, in the demonology of the right, were the forerunners of radical revolution. Of course, as any sensible person should have expected, the government bureaucracy has turned out to be a conservatizing rather than a liberalizing force, at least against innovating Presidents. Its basic loyalty is to the established way of doing things, and, with age and size, it has acquired an independence which enables it to ignore or circumvent Presidential initiative.

The rise of the modern bureaucracy has divided the executive branch between the Presidential government and the permanent government. In this complex relationship, the Presidential government has preferences and policies backed by a presumed mandate from the electorate. But the permanent government has preferences and policies of its own. It has vested interests of its own in programs; it has alliances of its own with congressional committees, lobbies, and the press; it has its own particular, and not seldom powerful, constituencies. Also, it is around longer. We now have, in consequence, four branches of government. An activist President may have quite as much trouble with the federal bureaucracy as with the legislative or judicial branches.

A third limitation on the Presidency in domestic affairs is the fact that nearly every President, who has enlarged the power of the White House, has provoked a reaction toward a more restricted idea of the Presidency, even if the reaction never quite cuts Presidential power back to its earlier level. Thus Jackson and Polk were followed by a parade of weak Presidents. When Lincoln expanded Presidential power, Congress took out its frustrations by impeaching his successor and establishing a generation of congressional government. Theodore Roosevelt begot Taft; Wilson begot Harding; Franklin Roosevelt and Truman begot Eisenhower. FDR, in addition, was posthumously punished by the Twenty-second Amendment for the offense of having been elected President four times.

All these considerations make the President notably weaker in dealing with internal than with international problems. If this is so, the next question is whether it is possible to think up devices that would strengthen his hand in domestic matters and restrain his hand in foreign matters.

A number of such devices have been proposed. There would seem no convincing reason why, for example, the President and the congressional leadership should not agree that all significant Presidential proposals would go to the floor for debate and vote. This would not be a guarantee of enactment, but it would be a guarantee that proposals deemed vital to the nation by the President could no longer be filed away in committee and denied consideration by the whole. Such an arrangement, incidentally, would spare the Senate the perennial row over Rule XXII [cloture]. Similarly, there would seem to be no convincing reason why the President should not have the right of item veto; even the Confederate Constitution gave Jefferson Davis authority to "approve any appropriation and disapprove any other appropriation in the same bill." There would seem to be no reason why the President should not have the authority to adjust tax rates within a specified range in order to deal with economic fluctuations, or that he should not have greater discretion in reorganizing the executive branch or in moving funds from one program to another.

Congress resists such proposals out of conditioned institutional reflexes. It has the visceral fear that structural reform will transfer further power to the executive. Yet, the era of what Wilson called "congressional government" did not fade away at the end of the nineteenth century because of structural reform. It faded away for the simple reason that through so much of the twentieth century, Presidents have seemed right and Congress wrong on issues. The people, anxious to have necessary things done, welcomed Presidents who saw the necessity of doing these things—even if the Roosevelts and Wilson thereby increased the power of the Presidency at the expense of the power of Congress. So long as Congress falls behind Presidents in the perception of the needs of the nation, so long it may expect to lose ground in the war of attrition. And the only way that Congress will reclaim lost powers is by being right on issues when the executive is wrong—as the Senate Foreign Relations Committee proved in the case of Vietnam.

The best hope for Congress lies, not in withholding from the President powers which would benefit the nation, but in modernizing itself and thereby enabling it to compete with the Presidency on judgments of policy. The place to begin, of course, would be the seniority system. Contrary to congressional impression, this system was not handed down at Mount Sinai. Many state legislatures get along very well indeed without it. Its effect in Washington is to give disproportionate influence to men born in another century and shaped by small town or rural experience—hardly men qualified to deal with the problems of young people or of black people in an urban and industrial society.

Structural revisions of this sort would help both the President and the Congress to deal more intelligently with the accumulating troubles of our national community. Are there countervailing structural revisions on the international side which would prevent the President from running away with all initiative and decision in the conduct of foreign policy? This is the area which creates the real problem of Presidential power. For . . . acts in domestic policy are generally reversible; they are subject to revision and recall through democratic processes. But acts in foreign policy are often irreversible. President Kennedy used to say that domestic policy can only defeat us; foreign policy can kill us. Moreover, the nuclear age makes this quality of irreversibility more fateful than ever before. And foreign policy decisions very often are made in emergency contexts, real, imagined, or contrived, and this fact encourages the flow of power to the White House. It is possible through structural reform to secure for Congress, and the people, an authoritative and continuing voice in the basic decisions of war and peace?

The Senate Foreign Relations Committee thought hard about this question and came up, in 1967, with Senate Resolution 187. This resolution declared it as "the sense of the Senate" that American armed forces could not be committed to hostilities on foreign territory for any purpose other than to repel an attack on the United States or to protect American citizens or property without affirmative action by Congress specifically intended to give rise to such commitment." This or comparable resolutions must surely pass two tests: They must offer a plausible hope that 1) they will not tie the hands of the executive in a case of genuine national emergency; and 2) they will effectively prevent a step-by-step movement from marginal to major involvement.

These questions must be considered in specific situations; the answer one fears, is that SR 187 would probably have prevented President Roosevelt from taking his actions in 1941 in defense of American security, but that it would not have prevented President Johnson from pursuing his course of gradual military escalation in Vietnam. The reason for this is that Roosevelt would have found it difficult to put together a congressional majority for his North Atlantic policy, while, as the Gulf of Tonkin example showed, Johnson would have encountered little difficulty in getting congressional endorsement for his Vietnam policy before 1968.

[In 1969] the Committee came up with a broader resolution declaring it the sense of the Senate that "a national commitment by the United States to a foreign power necessarily and exclusively results from affirmative action taken by the executive and legislative branches of the United States Government through means of a treaty, convention, or other legislative instrumentality specifically designed to give effect to such a commitment." On the fact of it, this resolution would outlaw executive agreements.... If the principle behind the resolution had prevailed in 1940, Franklin Roosevelt could not have transferred the overage destroyers to Great Britain without seeking congressional approval. He most probably could not have obtained that approval; in any case, the debate would have been angry and protracted, leading to a filibuster as bitter as the one by which the "little group of willful men" blocked Wilson's policy of arming merchant vessels in 1917, and the subsequent history of the world might have been very different.

These examples suggest, I believe, the futility of trying to solve substantive problems by structural means. The probable result of efforts to limit Presidential power through institutional contrivance would be to introduce dangerous rigidities into our system of national decision which would stop Presidents from doing good as well as from doing harm, and which would ultimately cause more trouble than benefit.

The solution to the problem of excessive Presidential power in foreign affairs lies, I would conclude, in the political and educational realm. The fundamental strength of the Congress in this area springs from its capacity to raise issues and thereby to shape national opinion....

In particular, Congress is well placed to assail the myth with which every foreign office seeks to silence critics: that only those who see the top secret cables know enough to make intelligent judgments on questions of foreign policy. As one who has had the opportunity to read such cables at various times in my life, I can testify that 95 percent of the information essential for intelligent judgment is available to any careful reader of *The New York Times*. Indeed, the American government would have had a much wiser Vietnam policy had it relied more on the *Times*; the estimate of the situation supplied by newspapermen was consistently more accurate than that supplied by the succession of ambassadors and generals in their coded dispatches. Secrecy in diplomatic communication is mostly required to protect negotiating strategies, techniques of intelligence collection, details of weaponry, and gossip about personalities. One does not require full knowledge on such points to assess a political situation. The myth of inside information has always been used to prevent democratic control of foreign policy; if Congress derides that myth, it may embolden others to doubt the infallibility of Presidents and Secretaries of State.

But the responsibility rests even more heavily on the President than on the Congress. A President must, above all, be a man who acts not just because he is sure about the wisdom of a course of action, but because he is responsive to the democratic process. It is not enough for policies to be sound. In all but the most extreme cases, that soundness must be accompanied by explanation and tested by acceptance. The President must act on the principle of self-limitation and live within the discipline of consent. He must understand the legitimacy of challenges to his own authority and wisdom. He must cherish an inner skepticism about the anointment of office, and a constant awareness of what Whitman called "the never-ending audacity of elected persons." He must be especially skeptical about the unique value of information that arrives through official channels, and about self-serving bureaucratic versions of anything. He must be sensitive to the diversity of concern and conviction in a nation; he must be sensitive in advance to the verdict of history; he must always pay "a decent respect to the opinions of mankind."

No structural solutions can guarantee the choice of such Presidents, or can guarantee that, once chosen as open and modest men, they will remain so amid the intoxications of the office. Yet, surely the whole point of democracy is that it is not an automatic system. It involves risks, because risks are the means of growth. Rather than renounce the idea of an affirmative Presidency or surround the President with hampering restrictions, it would seem better to continue to regard Presidential leadership as the central instrument of American democracy, and to exercise scrupulous care in the choice of Presidents.

39

To Make The Office More Creative

James MacGregor Burns   **THE SHADOW PRESIDENCY**

From *The Nation,* (September 6, 1965), 115–118. Reprinted by permission.

People were freely predicting at the time of Lyndon Johnson's inaugural in January 1965, that the nation was headed for a modern era of good feelings. The President himself had said after his election that the country had reached a new "consensus on national purpose and policy." He was quite right—the nation had indeed reached a consensus over the goals of freedom and equality. But these are not the only problems that occupy men, and history warned that eras of apparent good feelings could conceal heats and ferments that would erupt in turbulence and strife years later.

And an unblinking look at the world and the nation in the mid-sixties disclosed a profusion of interlaced problems: . . . at home the problems of rapidly changing group and class and generational relationships, education, urban disorder, mounting crime rates, social anomie and alienation, automation, political apathy, along with the more old-fashioned issues such as transportation, farm subsidies, labor-management relations, tax reform, monopoly and administered prices, medical care; and abroad, nuclear proliferation, the continuing and in many areas deepening poverty of tens of millions, the population explosion, the disruption of old rural cultures and the flood of people into the restless cities, the fragmentation of Africa, the social unrest of Latin America, Communist expansion in Asia, along with the week-to-week "little" crises, any one of which could explode into a major one.

It is impossible . . . to predict in what forms these problems will emerge with the passage of time. One might speculate, though, that many of the most crucial domestic problems will revolve around certain old but still compelling value questions. Given the trends in the nation that one can predict with the greatest certainty —huge population increases in the urban and suburban areas, accelerated social mobility, a constantly enlarging and increasingly homogenized middle-class population, a decline in ethnic solidarity and variety—one might guess that once the old problems of equality and freedom have been subdued, sharper questions will emerge over the possibilities of individuality and privacy in a mass culture. If the past century has seen the early tension and later partial reconciliation of values of liberty and equality, we may be at the threshold of an age increasingly preoccupied with the relation of liberty and fraternity, of privacy and community, of the individual and the group. If in past years we have been concerned with mainly quantitative problems—the amount of goods and services produced and how they were distributed—we may be more occupied in the future with the quality of American life in a great, affluent, complacent, and perhaps mediocre society.

The quality of American life—this is not a new phrase nor a new political issue. It is older than Jefferson's dreams and as young as the Great Society. No one has defined the hope and the promise better than President Johnson. In May of 1964 he proclaimed at the University of Michigan:

> The Great Society is a place where every child can find knowledge to enrich his mind and enlarge his talents. It is a place where leisure is a welcome chance to build and reflect, not a feared cause of boredom and restlessness. It is a place where the city of man serves not only the needs of the body and the demands of commerce but the desire for beauty and the hunger for community.
>
> It is a place where man can renew contact with nature. It is a place which honors creation for its own sake and for what it adds to the understanding of the race. It is a place where men are more concerned with the quality of their goals than the quantity of their goods. But most of all, the Great Society is not a safe harbor, a resting place, a final objective, a finished work. It is a challenge constantly renewed, beckoning us toward a destiny where the meaning of our lives matches the marvelous products of our labor.

The crux of the problem is whether a system of Presidential government so perfectly adapted to, and so largely facilitative of, quantitative liberalism—that is, of the augmentation, and fairer distribution of goods—can redefine its purpose and shift its strategy in order to embrace new values with their implications for changes in means and instrumental goals. Such a shift calls for much more than making the White House into a show place of the arts, or awarding medals to heroes of culture, or bestowing Presidential recognition on private cultural enterprises. It means a concerted and sustained and expensive effort to impart values like those of Johnson to the barren lives of millions of Americans, middle class as well as deprived. It means diverting the kind of resources into cultural, recreational, and educational activities that we have in the past poured into economic recovery, or even into national defense. And such an effort might be controversial and even unpopular. Many Americans would oppose it and deride it; by its very nature such an effort would bring foolish blunders and mishaps that could be easily caricatured; and certain ventures—perhaps an effort to improve the quality of commercial radio and television —could precipitate clashes with powerful interests.

Above all, the shift from the pursuit of quantitative to qualitative goals would call for comprehensive, sustained, and broadly unified policies—in short, for planning. Effective planning is impossible except in the context of at least a rough ordering of values, instrumental goals and means. It will be as important to have clearly thought out, longrange priorities in this respect as it would be in planning increased productivity....

Presidential government is a superb planning institution. The President has the attention of the country, the administrative tools, the command of information, and the fiscal resources that are necessary for intelligent planning, and he is gaining the institutional power that will make such planning operational. Better than any other human instrumentality he can order the relations of his ends and means, alter existing institutions and procedures or create new ones, calculate the consequences of different policies, experiment with various methods, control the timing of action, anticipate the reactions of affected interests, and conciliate them or at least mediate among them. If, as Hubert Humphrey has said, we need not a planned society but a continuously planning society, the Presidency provides strong and versatile tools for that purpose.

Still, we must acknowledge that the Presidency has become an effective planning agency for reasons of chance as well as volition. In this century, the Presidency has been the center of the conflict between labor and capital and later between segregationists and civil rights forces; it has steeled its will and its ideology in the struggles against Nazi tyranny and Communist expansion. After a century of planless growth the Presidency found its place as a key part of the American system of ends and means. The question is whether Presidential government can detach itself enough from set ideas and existing institutions and old ways to embrace new goals.

To define new goals, to fashion new institutions to realize those goals, to avoid both utopianism and opportunism, to build popular support without improper manipulation, to allow for flexibility of means and redefinition of ends, and always to elevate purpose over technique—all this is the test of creative leadership. It will be the test of Presidential government in the years ahead.

To define leadership in this way is to see the importance of a number of proposals that have been made to strengthen the Presidency and hence to enable the President to reshape institutions and processes: four-year terms for representatives (to bring Presidential and congressional constituencies into closer correspondence); the granting of full power to the President to control executive department organization; finding means of attracting the highest talent to the executive department, especially to its major staff positions; efforts to bring into the policy-making process intellectuals with creative and innovative gifts; providing the President with greater discretionary power over fiscal policy, including the item veto and the granting of authority to change tax rates within certain limits; and above all, the further strengthening of the elected leadership of Congress so that it can act more quickly and comprehensively in harmony with the President.

But the greatest need of Presidential government does not lie in this kind of reform. We can expect many of these changes to take place in any event as the Presidency becomes increasingly institutionalized. Indeed, some are already taking place, in substance if not in form. Some of them at best will simply speed up transitions that already are under way—for example, greater Presidential control over fiscal policy.

The greatest need of the Presidency in the years to come will be an opposition that challenges Presidential values, Presidential methods, Presidential institutions, that is eager to take power and to present its own definition of the national purpose.

Of all the vital elements of American democratic government the national opposition is the most disorganized, fragmented, and ineffective. As a responsible opposition to the President, Congress is an almost total failure. Hostile senators and representatives bombard the White House from all directions. Typically they fail to advance alternative proposals and hence they do not provide the voters with an idea as to how the opposition would govern if it got the chance. The congressmen usually prefer to play the game of bargain and even resort to various forms of genteel blackmail with the President rather than criticize forthrightly and dramatically. No wonder that Presidents in recent years have been far more sensitive to criticism in the press than on Capitol Hill.

Good reasons exist for the debility of the opposition. In part it is a simple reflection of the power of Presidential government. "The aggrandizement of the President, especially by the electronic media," as V. O. Key, Jr., has said, "has made the dispersed minority leadership one of low public visibility." The main difficulty is the bifurcation of the opposition into the Presidential and congressional parties. Once the Presidential candidate—the Presidential party's leader—has made his strenuous campaign and lost, he then becomes "titular" leader of the whole party. This is a polite term for being shelved or even repudiated. For once the campaign is lost, the congressional party leaders try to assume the opposition role. They hold formal and visible positions from which to conduct the attack, while the titular leader usually has no formal position to fall back on. . . . But the congressional party cannot carry the burden of militant leadership, because of its own internal divisions, its separation between the House and the Senate, and its lack of institutional structure (as compared with the Shadow Cabinet in Great Britain. If the opposition party has lost the Presidency but still controls one or both branches of Congress, as in the case of the Democrats after 1956, it lacks the advantage of being completely in the opposition; it suffers from having a modicum of power and responsibility. If the opposition party lacks control of Congress as well as of the White House, it has a poor forum from which to appeal to the public and virtually no machinery to support a focused and sustained attack on the government.

The opposition's impotence becomes more serious as Presidential government becomes more powerful. No matter how benign a government may be, it will be tempted to manipulate public opinion, to try to dominate the flow of opinion, to cover up mistakes, and to cast doubt on the patriotism or at least the honesty of outside consensus, or claims to, the more tempted it may be to succumb to some of these tendencies. Above all a consensus government may become flabby and complacent and lose the cutting edge of energy, initiative, and innovation. The very tendencies toward excessive concern with technique that we noted above can cause a government to lose direction and momentum unless the opposition holds it to its promises and threatens to oust it from power.

The problem is especially acute in the United States because of the lack of well-organized and programmatic parties. This is less of a problem for the President because . . . he has built up his own Presidential party to provide him with an electoral footing and other political resources. The opposition Presidential party, lacking a President and having to make do with a titular leader, is not anchored in an organized mass following and a militant cadre. It must improvise—and that in turn encourages a similar opportunism and absence of direction in the Presidential establishment.

Another great need of the American Presidency is a potent and competitive shadow Presidency. At the very least, the opposition party should establish some kind of collective leadership . . . to give the Presidential party a strong voice. More than this, it should experiment with an annual or biennial convention or conference both to choose a top leader and to renovate its program. The failure of the opposition to take this primitive step is not due to any innate difficulty but mainly to the divergent constituencies and institutional jealousies of the Congressional party, which wants to dominate the opposition role even though it fills that role so feebly. Ideally there would be an annual convention, a dependable system for collecting adequate funds, a large national staff with regional and state units under it, an effective propaganda apparatus, and talented, articulate and highly visible leadership. Whatever the exact form, it is clear that the opposition party today has a rare opportunity to exercise Jeffersonian critics. The more that government represents a leadership—that is, to build a new political institution.

Even more important, the opposition party must display creative leadership in defining its own version of the national purpose. It is not for outsiders to lecture the opposition party as to the goals it might propose, but one must note the great opportunity that may lie before it. If Presidential government as shaped by liberals for egalitarian purposes cannot shift its own strategy toward qualitative goals, if Presidential government under Democratic Party leadership may be hobbled by its own successes, then the opposition could seize the initiative. . . .

INDEX

A

Abrahams, Albert, 132
Adams, John, 18, 19, 143, 145
   and undeclared war against France, 172
   veto power, use of, 61
Adams, John Quincy, 63, 143, 159
Adams, Sherman, 148, 152
Agency for International Development (AID), 175
Albert, Carl, 84
Alderman v. United States, 179
American Bar Association, and Court nominees, 202
American Civil Liberties Union (ACLU), 188
American fleet, and Russo-Japanese War, 160
Americans, attitudes of, toward U.S., 32
Anderson, Clinton, 126
Arrests, under Lincoln, 78
Arthur, Chester, 143–145
Articles of Confederation, 12
Assassination attempts, 27
Association of American Publishers, 187
Atlanta, Georgia, Nixon visit to (1972), 131
Attorney General, and electronic surveillance, 180

B

Bank of the United States, 68, 69
Barkley, Alben, 118
Bay of Pigs, 151
Beacon Press, 188
Benet, Stephen Vincent, 82
Black, Hugo, 202
Blackmun, Harry A., 201, 202
Blaine, James G., 85, 137
Booth, John Wilkes, 136
Boyle, William M. Jr., 124
Brandt, Raymond P., 184
Brennan Jr., William J., 201
Broadcasters, attempts to intimidate, 189

Brock, William, on Congress, 84
Broun, Heywood, 82
Brownell, Herbert, 184
Bryan, William Jennings, 122
Buchanan, James, 143–145, 229
Budget, 87
Budget, operating, of the White House, 206
Bureau of the Budget, 86
Bureaucracy, and the New Deal, 258
Burger, Warren E., 201, 202
Burns, James MacGregor, 262–266
Businessmen, American, and Cuba, 159
Butler, Pierce, 14, 169
Butt, Archie, 19, 20
Butz, Earl, 84
Byrd, Robert, 202

C

"Canal Ring, the," 138
Cannon, Joe, 243
Carlisle, John G., 85
Carswell, G., Harrold, 202
Censorship, and Lincoln, 78
Central Intelligence Agency (CIA), 177
Chamberlain, Daniel H., 139
Chapman, Oscar, 124
Chesapeake, 64
Chiang Kai-shek, 150
Chicago and Southern Airlines v. Waterman Steamship Corp. (1948), 171
Christian Science Monitor, 177
Civil Disobedience, 159
Civil War, the, 21
   Presidential power, use of during, 76
Clark, Blair, 115
Clark, Thomas, 127
Clay, Henry, 69, 85, 119
   and opposition to the President, 72
Cleveland, Grover, 143, 159
Cohen, Carl, 179–181

Colson, Charles, 130
Commissions, 4
Committee on Detail, 12
Communist expansionism, concern over, 163
Confederacy, the, 76
Congress of the United States, 58, 88
   and the declaration of war, 166
   and computers, need for, 88
   and electors, 4
   and Lyndon Johnson, 164
   leadership in, 88
   and the press, 89
   and re-election pressures, 89
   and the restoration of powers, 173
   seniority in, 88
Congressional Behavior, 87
Congressional committees, 88
Congressional Government, 29
Conkling, Roscoe, 140
Connally, John B., 131
Connelly, Matt, 124
Conscription, 75
Constitution, the:
   of New York (1777), 12
   of Massachusetts (1780), 12
   of Maryland (1776), 13
Constitution of the United States, the, 3
   Fourth Amendment of the, 179
   and Gouverneur Morris, 11
   and Presidential power, 157–159
Constitutional Convention of 1787, 59
Constitutional crisis, 83
Coolidge, Calvin, 143–145
   the Presidency, views on, 21
Cronkite, Walter, 146
Cuba, American businessmen in, 159
Cunliffe, Marcus, 24

D

Davie, William R., 170
Dawson, Donald, 124

268 INDEX

Democratic Convention of 1948 (Philadelphia), 117
Democrats for Nixon Committee, 131
Depew, Chauncey M., 20
Depression, the Great, 21, 22
de Tocqueville, Alexis, 235
  on Congress, 84
Dewey, John, 82
Diplomat Among Warriors, 152
Dirksen, Everett M., 256
Dole, Robert, 132
Donovan, Robert J., 128, 152
Douglas, William O., 201
Drew, Elizabeth, 200–205
Drew, G. F., 140
Drinan, Robert, on congressional seniority system, 89
Duane, W. J., 71
Dulles, Allen, 153
Dulles, John Foster, 148
  and the Cold War, 149

E

Eastland, James, 84
Ehrlichman, John, 130
Eisenhower: The Inside Story, 152
Eisenhower, Dwight, 124, 143–145, 146–153
  on Bay of Pigs, 151
  on Winston Churchill, 239
  on executive ability, 238
  on Franklin D. Roosevelt, 239
  and Formosa, 150
  and Indochina policy of, 147, 151
  and Interstate Highway program, 147
  on John F. Kennedy, 152
  and Korea, 150
  on Abraham Lincoln, 239
  and military involvement by the United States, 149
  as a national symbol of unity, 148
  and Senator Joe McCarthy, 147
  and St. Lawrence Seaway, 147
  on William H. Taft, 239
  and undeclared war, 172
  on George Washington, 239
  on Woodrow Wilson, 239
Ellsberg, Daniel, 188
Ervin, Sam J., Jr., 191–195
  on Congress, 84
Executive power, 18

F

Federal spending, 83
Federalist, The, 13, 14, 15
Federalist, No. 48, The, 195
Fenno, Richard, 87
Ferguson, Warren J., 181
Ferry, Thomas, 140
Field, Stephen J., 170
Fillmore, Millard, 143–145
Fireside Chats, 81
First-Hand Report, 152
Fischer, Louis, 174–176
Food for Peace program, 178
Ford, Henry Jones, 16
Foreign Affairs, 151
Foreign policy, 63, 64
  and the President, 160
Formosa, and Eisenhower, 150
Fortas, Abe, 201
Founding fathers, the, and distribution of power, 161
France, 64
Franklin, Benjamin, 169
  on the Presidency, 166
Freedom of expression, and the press, 188
Freedom of speech, 78
Friday, Herschel, 202
Fulbright, J. William, 164, 171
  and Lyndon B. Johnson, 167
Funds, impounding of, 87
  and Richard M. Nixon, 87
  and Thomas Jefferson, 87

G

Gans, Curt, 115
Gardner, John, 89
Garner, John Nance, 126
Geofroy v. Riggs (1890), 170

George III, King of England, 157
Goldberg, Arthur, 201
Goldman, Eric, 157–168
Goldwater, Barry M., 163
Grant, Ulysses S., 136, 143–145
"Grantism," 137
Gravel, Mike, 188, 204
Gray, L. Patrick, 203
Great Britain, 64
Greeley, William (Bill), 190
Greene, General Nathaniel, 58

H

Habeas Corpus Act of 1863, 77
Habeas corpus privilege, 75
Haldeman, H. R., 132
Hamilton, Alexander, 13, 60
  on senators' role, 85
Hampton, Wade, 139
Hanna, Mark, 19
Harding-Coolidge era, 21
Harding, Warren G., 121, 143–145
  the Presidency, views on, 21
  and declaration of Presidential moderation, 27
Harlan, John Marshall, 202
Harrison, Benjamin, 143–145
Harvard Law Review, on the Nixon Court, 201
Hayes, Rutherford B., 136, 137–140, 143–145
Hayes-Tilden election, Federal intervention in, 140
Haynsworth, Clement, 202
Henry, Patrick, 18
Hentoff, Nat, 187–190
Hickel, Walter, 182
Hofstadter, Richard, 81
Hoover, Herbert, 121, 143–145
  Memoirs, 22
Hopkins, Harry, 81
House of Representatives, Speaker of the, 29
House speakers, and the use of power, 85
Hughes, Emmet John, 17, 80, 152
Huitt, Ralph, 87
Hurley, General Patrick J., 126

I

Impeachment, 4
Indochina, and Eisenhower, 151
International Monetary Fund, 184
Interstate highway system, 147

J

Jackson, Andrew, 143–145, 229
   and Congress, 85
   election of, 68–74
   enemies of, 28
   attitude toward Whigs, 71
Jackson, Robert H., 171
Jay, John, 58
Jefferson, Thomas, 12, 14, 60, 143–145
   as a diplomat, 63
   and impounding of funds, 87
   inaugural address, first, 62
   subordinates, relations with, 67
   and undeclared war, 172
Jester, Beauford, 127
Johnson, Andrew, 143–145
Johnson, Lyndon B., 121, 143–145, 166, 168
   conduct of, 25, 86
   and Congress, 164
   and J. William Fulbright, 167
   describes the "Great Society," 263
   impact on the Presidency, 255
   and the Philippines, 174
   on the Presidency, 244–246
   and the Supreme Court, 201
   and television, 17
   and the Gulf of Tonkin, 163
   and undeclared war, 172
   on the vice presidency, 244
   and Vietnam War expansion, 166
Jones, Charles, 90
Journalists, dissenting, 187

K

Katzenbach, Nicholas deB., 165
Kazin, Alfred, 152
Keith, Damon J., 180
Kempton, Murray, 146
Kennedy, Edward M., 178
Kennedy, John F., 24, 28, 86, 121, 143–145
   assassination of, 24
   on "big man in the White House," 242
   Eisenhower on, 152
   on Ulysses Grant, 242
   on the Presidency (before election), 241–243
   on scope of Presidential powers, 242
Kennedy, Robert F., 256
Kent State University tragedy, 184
Kerr, Robert S., 127
Key, V. O. Jr., 165
Keynes, John Maynard, 23
Khrushchev, Nikita, 148
Kleber, Louis C., 136
Klein, Herbert G., 133
Korea, 157
   and Eisenhower, 150
Korea, South (see South Korea)
Korean War, 162
   and Harry S. Truman, 86
Krock, Arthur, 81
Ku Klux Klan, 202

L

Laird, Melvin R., 134
Landon, Alfred, 121
Laski, Harold J., 21, 82
Leadership, congressional, 88
   Presidential, 60
Lee, Robert E., 136
Leopard, 64
Lewis, Meriwether, 61
Lillie, Mildred, 202
Lincoln, Abraham, 78, 143–145, 229
   and Congress, 85
   and the Constitution of the United States, 75
   on constitutional power, 157, 158
   and the power of proclamation, 75
   as representative to the Congress, 159
   war power, view of, 75
Lippmann, Walter, 82
Locke, John, 73
Lomax, Louis, 114
Louisiana, 75
Louisiana Purchase, 63, 64
Lowell, Robert, 115
Loy, Myrna, 114
Luce, Henry, 150
Lynn, James T., 84

M

MacArthur, General Douglas, 147
Maclay, William, 158
MacNeil, Neil, 86
Macon, Nathaniel, 61
Madison, James, 11, 85, 143–145, 169, 173
Malek, Frederick, 134
Malone, Dumas, 60
Manifest destiny, doctrine of, 159
Mansfield, Mike, 83
Mao Tse-tung, 150
Maranell, Gary M., 142–145
Marshall, John, 32, 170
Marshall, Thurgood, 201
Maryland, Constitution of, 1776, 13
Mason, George, 12
Massachusetts, Constitution of, 1780, 12
Mathias, Charles, 86
McCarthy, Eugene J., 165, 256
McCarthy, Joe, 147
McCarthy, Michael, 112, 113
"McCarthy youth corps," 115
McCombs, W. J., 122
McCulloch v. *Maryland*, 69
McGovern, George, 130–135
McGovern Manual, 134
McGregor, Clark, 132
McKinley, William, 143–145, 159, 160
   and use of sleeping pills, 160
Memoirs (of Herbert Hoover), 22
Memoirs (of Harry S. Truman), 166
Mencken, H. L., 81

INDEX

Mexican-American War, 160
Mexico, and U.S. expansion, 159
Militia Act of 1862, 75
Miller, Emma G., 117
Mills, Wilbur, 89
Miranda v. *Arizona*, 202
Mitchell, John N., 132
M.I.T. Press, 188
Mondale, Walter, on Congress, 88
Monroe, James, 14, 18, 143–145
Morgan, William, 119
Morris, Gouverneur, and the final draft of the Constitution, 11
Mumford, Lewis, 82
Murphy, Robert, 152

N

National Guard, on college campuses, 184
National Observer, 202
Nevins, Allan, 80
New Deal, the, 80
 and bureaucracy, 258
New Jersey plan, the, 13
New York, Constitution of, 12
New York Herald-Tribune, 128
New York Tribune, 138
New York Times, The, 21, 81, 128, 138, 187, 188
Nicola, Colonel Lewis, 58
Niebuhr, Reinhold, 82
Nixon, administration of, 176
Nixon Agonistes, 146
Nixon, Richard, 83
 "attempts" to intimidate broadcasters, 200–205
 in Atlanta, Georgia (1972), 130
 and Cambodian decision, 182
 campaign of (1972), 130–135
 on Dwight D. Eisenhower, 148
 and inaccessibility, 185
 and impounding of funds, 87
 on the Presidency, 247–248
 and press conferences, 185
 and Nelson Rockefeller, 131
 and the Supreme Court, 200–205
 in Westchester County, N.Y. (1972), 131

North Atlantic Treaty Organization (NATO), 151
North Carolina, 12
North Vietnam, bombing of, 33
Notes on Virginia, 12

O

Omnibus Crime Control and Safe Streets Act of 1968, the, 179
O'Neil, Paul, 117
Ordeal of Power, 152
Orpheus, 189
Ostrogorski, Moisei, 123
Our Chief Magistrate and His Powers (1916), 26

P

Padover, Saul K., 168–173
Panama Canal Zone, 20
 and Theodore Roosevelt, 160
Parrington, Vernon, 19
Peale, Charles Willson, 66
Pentagon Papers, 86, 188, 201
 and *The New York Times*, 189
Philippines, the, 175
Pierce, Franklin, 14, 143–145
Place Bill of 1692, 14
"pocket veto," 83
Poff, Richard, 202
Political campaigns, 124–129
Political conventions, 117
 evolution of, 119
Polk, James K., 62, 143–145, 159
 and Mexico, 159
 and Manifest Destiny, 159
 and undeclared war with Mexico, 172
Poll tax, 159
Polsby, Nelson, 87
Powell, Lewis F., 201
Power, Presidential (see also Presidential power), 31, 32, 57, 58
 Civil War, during the, 77
 and foreign policy, 160
 growth of, 68–74

Powledge, Fred, 187, 189
Presidency, the,
 and the Constitution, 3
 Benjamin Franklin on, 166
 and inaccessibility, 185
 and international affairs, 168–173
 as a monarchy, 57–59
 and the power to make war, 157–168
 regalia of, 33
 shaping of, 11
 style of, 17, 18, 80, 82
President, the,
 automobile fleet of, 207
 as commander-in-chief, 4
 compensation of, 4, 207–208
 domestic staff of, 207
 and entertainment, 207
 and inaccessibility, 185
 as leader of a political party, 236
 medical care of, 208
 and the people, 236
 and the press, 182, 186
 rating of, 24, 143–145
 removal of, 4
 and secrecy, 33
 selection of, 3
 term of, 6
 vacation retreats of, 207
Presidential,
 aircraft, 206
 campaign (1972), 130–135
 election of 1876, 136
 spending discretion, 177
 status, 31, 32
Presidential power, 86 (see also Power),
 expansion of, 258
 and foreign policy, 160
 priorities, 88
Presidents, rating of the, 142–145
Press, the, and freedom of expression, 188
 and Congress, 89
Press Conferences,
 and Richard Nixon, 185
 and Franklin D. Roosevelt, 185
 and Harry Truman, 185
Press Freedom Under Pressure, 187, 189
Proxmire, William, 178
Public Broadcasting System, 190

Public Television, and funding by Congress, 190

Q

Quality of American life, 263

R

Randall, Samuel J., 85, 140
Randolph, Edmund, 11
Randolph, John, 61
Ravenal, Earl, 151
Rayburn, Sam, 86, 117
Reed, Tom, 85
Reedy, George E., 30
Rehnquist, William, 202
Reid, John C., 138
Republican National Convention, the (1972), 132
Republican National Committee, 132
Republicans, National, 69
Republicans, radical, and loss of power, 137
Reuss, Henry S., 164
Rhode Island, 12
Ribicoff, Abraham, 84, 87
Rogers, Will, 21, 22, 80
Roosevelt, Eleanor, 118
Roosevelt, Franklin Delano, 22, 80–82, 121, 143–145, 255
 and Congress, 85
 on the Constitution, 231
 at the Democratic Convention in Chicago, 80
 and executive action, 161
 on the Presidency, 233–234
 and Presidential leadership, 256
 and the press, 81, 185
 and radio, 17
 style of, 80, 82
Roosevelt, Theodore, 19, 24, 143–145, 160
 on the Canal Zone, 160
 as a coiner of phrases, 20
 on executive power, 229, 230
 and national security, 160
 and the press, 17
 and the "Square Deal," 85
Roper, Daniel C., 81
Ross, Irwin, 124
Rossiter, Clinton, 11
Rosten, Leo, 81
Rovere, Richard H., 146–143
Russo-Japanese conflict, 20
 and the American fleet, 160

S

Saint Lawrence Seaway, 147
Saint Louis Post-Dispatch, 184
Salant, Richard, 187
Saxbe, William, 86
Scammon, Richard M., 121
Schorr, Daniel, 189
Schlesinger, Arthur M., 142
Schlesinger Jr., Arthur, 255–261
S.E.A.T.O. (Southeast Asia Treaty Organization), 151, 163, 164
Secrecy, and Congress, 89
 in a free society, 191–195
Secret Service, operating budget of the, 206
Security, internal, 180
Selling of the Pentagon, The, 189
 and Public Broadcasting System, 190
Senate Foreign Relations Committee hearings, 165
Senate Judiciary Subcommittee, on separation of powers, 194
Seniority, in Congress, 88
Sheed, Wilfrid, 111–116
Sheehan, Neil, 190
Sherman, Roger, 11, 169
Sherwood, Robert E., 80
Silverthorn Lumber Company v. *U.S.* (1920), 181
Six Crises, 152
Smith, Hedrick, 182–186
Snyder, Alvin, 135
Southeast Asia Treaty Organization, 151, 163, 164
South Korea, and Vietnam, 175
South Vietnam, 164
 and SEATO, 164
Sovereignty, popular, 64
Spending discretion of the President, 176
Stanton, Dr. Frank, 189
Stans, Maurice, 132
St. Clair Expedition, 191
Stennis, John, 84
Stewart, Potter, 201
Stevens, Thaddeus, 16
Stone, I. F., 187
Strategic Arms Limitations Treaty talks, 196
Submarine warfare, and W W I, 161
Sullivan, William H., 198
Sun Reporter, 113
Supreme Court, the, 76
 Civil War, during the, 77
 under Richard Nixon, 200
Surveillance, electronic, 179–181
Symington, Stuart, 196–199

T

Taft, Robert, 121, 149
Taft, William H., 19, 21, 143–145
 on executive power, 249
 on Theodore Roosevelt, 250
Taney, Roger B., 71
Taylor, Zachary, 143–145, 159
Thailand, 175
Thoreau, Henry, and poll tax, 159
Thornberry, Homer, 201
Tilden, Samuel J., 136, 137
 "elected" President, 138–140
Tobin, Richard L., 57
Tonkin, Gulf of,
 and House Resolution on, 164
 and Lyndon Johnson, 163
 and Senate vote, 164
Totenberg, Nina, 202
Truman, Harry S., 17, 86, 118, 143–145, 147, 168
 and the Korean War, 162
 on the Presidency, 235–237
 and Presidential power, 31
 and press conferences, 185
 and undeclared war, 172
 whistle-stop campaign of, 124–129
Tweed, William M., 138
Twentieth Century Fund, the, 188
Tyler, John, 143–145

U

U-2 Affair, 148
Underwood, Oscar W., 123
United States, the:
   global involvement of, 29
   power of, 76
United States v. *Curtiss-Wright Export Corp.*, 111

V

Van Buren, Martin, 70, 143–145
Vice President, selection of the, 3
   term of, 6
Vietnam, 157
   peace in, 83
   and Presidential power, 255
"Vietnamization," 184
Vietnam, South (see South Vietnam)
Vietnam War, and legality question, 172
   and Lyndon Johnson's expansion of, 166
Virginia, division of into West Virginia, 76
Virginia dynasty, 73
Virginia plan, the, 13

W

Wade, Ben, 16
Wade-Davis bill of 1864, 75
War and the Congress, 166
War in Laos, 196–199
War, undeclared:
   and John Adams, 172
   and Dwight Eisenhower, 172
   and Thomas Jefferson, 172
   and James K. Polk, 172
   and Harry Truman, 172
   and Woodrow Wilson, 172
Warren, Earl, 201, 202
Washington, George, 14, 19, 143–145, 158
   "King George" of America, 58
   and Presidential power, 57
   and Presidential style, 18
Waterhouse, Dr. Benjamin, 66
Webber, Harold, 188
Webster, Daniel, 69
Weinberger, Caspar W., 84
Welles, Orson, 82
West Virginia, creation of from Virginia, 76
Westmoreland, William, on Congress, 88
Whigs; Jackson, attitude toward, 71
White, Byron, 201
White, Harry Dexter, 184
White House, the:
   domestic staff of, 207
   health facilities, 207
   library, 207
   life in, 17
   and National Park Service, 206
   operating budget of, 206
White, William Allen, 80
Wiley, W. Bradford, 187
Wilkie, Wendell, 121
Wilkinson, Gen. James, 67
Wilson, Henry Hall, 88
Wilson, James, 11
Wilson, Woodrow, 121, 143–145, 255
   and Congress, 85
   legislative success, 62
   on the Presidency, 231–232
   and undeclared war, 172
Wirt, William, 119
World War I, and submarines, 161
World War II, and submarines, 161

Y

Yazoo claims, 62
Youngstown Sheet and Tube Company v. *Sawyers*, 193

Z

Ziegler, Ronald L., 134

JK
516
.K5

JK
516
.K5